FINEST KIND
A Celebration of a Florida Fishing Village

by
BEN GREEN

Finest Kind, A Celebration of a Florida Fishing Village
by Ben Green

October 1985 printed under
ISBN 0-86554-208-2 (softbound) and ISBN 0-86554-159-0 (casebound)

Published by Florida Historical Society Press (copyright 2007)

ISBN 10:   1-886104-27-1
ISBN 13:   978-1-886104-27-3

The Florida Historical Society Press
435 Brevard Avenue
Cocoa, FL 32922
phone: 1-321-690-1971
website: www.fhspress.org

P•R•E•S•S

Contents

New Preface v

Original Acknowledgments ix

Prologue, Down to the Seashore 1

Part I, Setting the Stage 9

    Chapter I, "Something to Put on the Tombstone" 11

    Chapter 2, "You Gonna Sleep All Day?" 17

Part II, A Way of Life 41

    Chapter 3, "A Place Called Hunter's Point" 43

    Chapter 4, "Son, Them Days Was Rough" 65

    Chapter 5, "You Can Tell It First from the Hands" 83

    Chapter 6, "The Tie That Binds" 93

    Chapter 7, "Cortez's Grand Ole Opry" 103

A Cortez Album 113

    Chapter 8, Court and Spark 129

    Chapter 9, Roughnecks, Drunks, and Drifters 137

    Chapter 10, "We Had Something to Do" 151

Part III, Struggles 169

    Chapter 11, "We Could Have Had It All if We'd Stuck Together" 171

    Chapter 12, "The Finest People on Earth" 187

Part IV, Facing the Future 195

    Chapter 13, "The First Thing a Yankee Learns to Say" 197

    Chapter 14, Prodigals Returned 211

    Chapter 15, The Next Generation 215

    Chapter 16, "The Smugglers Might Kill Me,
    But They Sure as Hell Can't Eat Me!" 221

    Chapter 17, Waiting on a Southwester 239

Epilogue, "Just Say You Read the Book" 257

Postscript 261

For Papa Tink . . .
the words he could never say.

And for Jenny, Bekah, Ryan, and Kristen . . .
so they won't forget.

"It looked like a rogues' gallery down at the dock." Old-time
fishermen recall the early days of fishing in Cortez (clockwise
from bottom): Marvin Carver, Gene Fulford, Man Adams and
Earl Guthrie (1981).

New Preface

Twenty-two years have passed since this book was first published. At that time, I struggled over whether to subtitle it a celebration or an epitaph, and although I eventually settled on the former, that was mostly bravado and wishful thinking. More realistically, I feared that I was writing an epitaph for the fishing village of Cortez, which has been home to my family for 120 years.

I felt a sense of urgency to record the history of this little place before it was gone. When I started working on the book, in 1981, condominiums and new housing developments were marching ever closer to Cortez, filling up the seven mile stretch of Cortez Road between Bradenton and the Gulf of Mexico. This was also the era of "square grouper," when some fishermen in Cortez, including a few of my cousins, were sneaking out under cover of night to smuggle bales of marijuana. Between the condos and the dope smuggling, I figured the village was not long for this world.

I was afraid that Cortez would be bulldozed and turned into a parking lot for new transplants from Michigan or Ohio, who would not even realize that a community had existed there before they came. The memories, stories, and collected histories of three generations of Cortez natives would be lost forever, buried like artifacts in a Timucuan kitchen mizzen.

This book, then, was my personal diatribe about growth in Florida, as seen through the eyes of this little village. In 1985, if I had been asked whether I thought Cortez would still exist in 2007, I would have responded, "Probably not."

I am happy to report that such a prediction would have been wrong. Cortez still exists, and in some ways is more secure than it was twenty years ago. The importance of this community has finally been recognized, and steps have been taken to protect it by the federal, state, and local governments.

In 1995, the village was listed on the National Register of Historic Places as a historic district. Shortly thereafter, Manatee County designated Cortez as a historic neighborhood, and a preservation board now must approve all applications for development. More recently, the county has provided additional zoning protection by naming Cortez as a historic overlay district. And the Waterfronts Florida Partnership, a statewide program designed to help revitalize traditional communities, has designated Cortez as a Waterfront Florida Community.

Twenty-two years ago, one of my greatest concerns was that so many Cortez residents felt powerless to even attempt to fight the outside forces that were threatening the survival of their community. Thankfully, that has changed.

One of the most important advocacy groups is the Cortez Village Historical Society (CVHS), which has become far more than the stereotypical "tea and crumpets" historical society. CVHS has spearheaded numerous battles to keep out recreational marinas and high rises, and to prevent construction of a new bridge to Anna Maria Island that would have blocked four entry roads into Cortez.

In 1991, the Florida Institute for Saltwater Heritage (FISH) was chartered as a 501(c)3 corporation, and has successfully raised thousands of dollars to purchase and preserve historic properties in the village. Included among those is a 95 acre tract of waterfront on Sarasota Bay, which FISH bought for $250,000; and the old Albion Inn (also known as the 1890 Burton's store), which was saved from demolition and is now being turned into a family life museum.

Such projects have been funded, primarily, by public and private grants. In 1999, for instance, Manatee County secured a $350,000 grant from the Florida Communities Trust to purchase the 1912 Cortez Schoolhouse, along with an adjoining parcel, which together form the Cortez Nature Preserve. Nearly $1 million has been raised to restore the schoolhouse, which re-opened in the fall of 2006 as a community center and meeting hall. The school also houses the Florida Maritime Museum, which will showcase local history and sponsor environmental education programs.

Manatee County has provided full-time staff to run the Maritime Museum, and for a boat-building project that is teaching volunteers how to build traditional sailing skiffs like the ones used in Cortez at the turn of the 20th century. As an offshoot of the boatbuilding program, Cortez hosted the Second Annual Gulf Coast Small Craft Festival in April 2007, which attracted traditional sailing craft from all over the eastern seaboard.

There have been other successes. The Cortez Fishing Festival, which attracts tens of thousands of visitors each February, recently celebrated its 25th anniversary. The CVHS has produced a series of books by local authors, including "Cortez, Then and Now," "Cortez Families," "What's Cooking in Cortez," and a video entitled "Commercial Fishing Through the Centuries." The Florida Endowment for the Humanities funded a "Community Portrait" project, and Florida Public Television produced a documentary called "Down A Lonesome Road."

So there have been many positive developments since *Finest Kind* appeared. I am proud of whatever small role the book played, through the power of the written word, in drawing outside attention to the village. Even more important, I believe the book gave native Cortesians a greater sense of their own identity: "Hey, someone wrote a book about us!"

If I could end this preface here, I would be a happy man. Despite these reassuring developments, however, all is not well in Cortez in 2007, and there are deep-seated problems that frighten me just as much as those that loomed in 1985.

At that time, I believed that the three biggest challenges Cortez faced were development, drugs, and threats to commercial fishing. Ironically, the three biggest challenges today are development, drugs, and threats to fishing. While some of the specifics have changed, the general threats remain the same. And unfortunately, today's perils may be even more insidious, and harder to combat.

The development pressures in 1985 came from the outside: the Sherman-like march of condominiums drawing ever closer on Cortez Road. But the biggest development pressures today come from *inside* the village itself. Soaring property taxes and homeowner's insurance are making it difficult for some Cortez residents to stay in their homes.

Cortez is not unique in this regard, as Florida is facing a statewide crisis over property taxes and homeowner's insurance. In the wake of the devastating 2004-2005 hurricane seasons, when eight named storms hit the state, thousands of Florida residents had their homeowner's insurance cancelled. Many Cortez residents were among them, and must now depend on Citizen's Property Insurance Corporation, the state-funded safety net which writes policies for 1.3 million residents who have been dropped by private insurers.

For those who can afford to pay their property taxes and insurance, there is a temptation to sell out anyway, as Florida's booming real estate market has driven up prices for waterfront property to unimaginable heights. Despite a recent softening in the market, some Cortez natives have chosen to get out while the getting is good. For example, one small cracker-style house with only 63 feet of waterfront, which had sold for $65,000 a few years ago, sold recently for nearly $800,000. The owner of the Cortez Trailer Park, which has been in existence for decades, recently was offered over $10 million to tear it down and put up a condo. Lots on the north side of Cortez Road, juxtaposed from Cortez proper, are selling for $500,000.

That kind of money puts tremendous pressure on working families to sell out, no matter how strong one's ties to the village. A number of Cortez residents, including some of my relatives, have made that decision. They've sold their homes and moved to town, into nondescript developments where they join the faceless throngs of Americans who don't know, or speak to, their neighbors. In Cortez they were part of a community of extended families and kinfolks going back generations. Some of them they liked, some they feuded with, others they ignored. But they knew them all. In their new stucco and concrete neighborhoods, they are just anonymous strangers.

The new owners of their old houses in Cortez are typically retired northerners, who may spend many thousands of dollars fixing up their new "vacation cottage," then visit several months a year and rent it out the rest. Although they may appreciate Cortez' "quaint charm" and temperate winters — they will never be part of the community.

So while Cortez may have succeeded in staving off the condos, for now, it has not been able to stop the exodus of natives being replaced by outsiders. Because of its protective zoning and the restrictions of the National Register, Cortez may remain a quaint, picturesque fishing village for years — only without any fishing families.

Indeed, what is driving away many of the native residents is not so much the lure of big bucks in the real estate market, but the death of commercial fishing as a way of life. Without a sustainable livelihood, there is little reason to stay.

There have been pressures on the commercial fishing industry in Florida for decades, many of which I wrote about in *Finest Kind*: dredge and fill operations, construction of seawalls and finger canals, the dumping of raw sewage and industrial pollutants in the bays, the destruction of thousands of acres of wetlands that feed the estuaries, local anti-netting regulations, and a protracted, ferocious war between the commercial and recreational fishing industries. The commercial fishermen brought some of the threats on themselves: the development of more efficient nets and boats, particularly the kicker boat, led to an explosion of part-time fishermen who invaded the bays on the weekends, particularly during the mullet roe season, catching more fish than had ever been possible before.

Ultimately, however, the most decisive issue proved to be the war between commercial and recreational fishermen. And to put it bluntly: the recreational fishermen won. In 1995, a constitutional amendment, the so-called "net ban," was passed by an overwhelming 72 percent of the Florida electorate.

The campaign that led to the passage of the net ban has been widely analyzed and critiqued, and I won't replicate that here, but suffice it to say that both sides attempted to disguise their own self-interests under the guise of "conservation," and both were guilty of hyperbole and false claims, although the recreational fishing coalition, which spent millions of dollars during a two year campaign, was the worst offender (in the most egregious example, the public was bombarded with heart-rending TV commercials showing dolphins and sea turtles caught in nets, although it is now widely accepted that those ads were faked or distorted). The saddest commentary on the net ban campaign was that there was little, if any, objective scientific data about the actual health of the mullet fishery. Ultimately, this was a campaign about resource allocation—"Who gets the fish?"—more than it was about conservation.

The net ban outlawed the use of gill or entangling nets, and limited net size to 500 square feet, using a one inch square mesh. Since its passage, there have been a series of lawsuits filed by commercial fishermen challenging its implementation—including the shape and size of legal nets—and the commercial fishermen have lost nearly every one. The courts have upheld the legality of the net ban and the sweeping powers of Florida Fish & Wildlife Commission (FWC) to define the rules governing Florida's fisheries. The challenges continue, however. Commercial fishermen have decried the fact that the one inch mesh nets they are required to use kill an inordinate number (as high as 98 percent of the total catch) of young fish that are too small to keep. And several state legislators have introduced bills to open up the FWC rule-making process to public scrutiny and review.

The impact of the net ban has been dramatic. According to the FWC's Research Institute, statewide commercial landings of fish have declined 67% since the net ban, from an average of 25 million pounds a year to 8.1 million; and the total number of fishing trips has declined 54%. In the case of mullet, total landings dropped from approximately 15.5 million pounds in 1994, worth an estimated $11.5 million; to 6.6 million pounds landed in 2006, worth an estimated $4.9 million.

In Cortez, the impact has been devastating. The number of mullet caught has dropped from 1.1 million pounds in 1994 (for all of Manatee County, although Cortez is by far the largest fishery) to 168,000 pounds in 2006.

Beyond the decline in the number of fish has been the decline in the number of fishermen. Some gave up trying to catch mullet with a cast net and switched to stone crabbing or bait shrimping. Some considered getting into clam farming, which the state was encouraging, but the waters in south Florida proved to be too warm, or polluted, for successful clamming. Many other Cortez fishermen gave up on fishing altogether, and sought jobs in other fields. Most of the local fish houses have closed, including Fulford Fish Company, which my grandfather started in the 1940s. There is only one viable fish house in Cortez today, A.P. Bell Fish Company, and it depends more on offshore grouper and shrimp boats than on local in-shore fishermen.

The net ban has inadvertently contributed to the third big threat facing Cortez today: drugs. In the 1980s, the drug problem in Cortez came from inside: local fishermen smuggling marijuana. But the drug problem in Cortez today comes primarily from outside: the offshore grouper boats tend to attract outsiders and transients to work on them, some of whom have substance abuse problems, and this has led to problems with crack cocaine and methamphetamine. Where Cortez had drug smugglers in the 1980s, now it has drug users. Abandoned or rundown houses have been turned into crack houses where the "druggies" hang out.

Fearing that the problem was getting out of hand, the community has held a series of meetings in recent months with law enforcement, and a crackdown has begun. Several arrests have been made, abandoned houses and lots have been cleared out, a neighborhood watch has been established, and community leaders hope that a corner has been turned.

We will see.

No matter how tenuous its future, however, the history of Cortez remains just as important as it was twenty-two years ago. Perhaps more so. It's a story about a magical little place with a cast of fascinating characters, wild adventures, humor, love, and an abiding faith in each other and their life on the water. I hope that this reissue of *Finest Kind,* for which I express my great appreciation to the Florida Historical Society, particularly Nick Wynne, will help to keep that story alive.

One final note: between the time I wrote this book and it first appeared in print, a half dozen of the main characters passed away. Now many more are gone, including most of the old-timers you will read about: Manly Bell, Marvin Carver, Goose Culbreath, Grey Fulford, Gene Fulford, Letha Garner, Doris "Toodle" Green, Woodrow Green, Charlie Guthrie, Bob and Ruth Knowlton, Julian and Bessie Taylor, among others. On a most personal level, my grandmother, Edith Fulford, and my father, Clyde Green, have both passed away.

After my father died, in 2001, a good friend who had lost both of her parents told me that she was surprised at "how present" her parents were still in her life. I found comfort in that in dealing with the loss of my father. I hope the reissue of this book will keep all of these wonderful folks present in our lives.

And despite so many being gone, there are many new arrivals who have appeared since 1985, including my two daughters, Emmy and Eliza. I hope the book will help them understand their father, and their extended family, a little better.

Ben Green, Tallahassee, Florida, April 2007

Original Acknowledgements

It's a cliché, of course, but this book couldn't have been written with-out the help of many people. I'd like to thank a few in particular: Ticie Watson of the Manatee County Historical Records Library; Carl King of the Manatee County Historical Society; Dorothy Dodd, a retired but still active librarian at the Florida State Library; Jennifer Miller, former editor of Southern *Exposure,* who provided valuable editorial assistance; and Ray Stanyard and Larry Coltharp, who answered dozens of questions about photography and provided technical assistance in the darkroom. Earl Morrogh took a special interest in the book and designed the dust jacket.

I would also like to thank the Florida AFL-CIO and the Florida Education Association/United for the use of photocopying and transcribing equipment.

Doris "Toodle" Green deserves special mention. Toodle was my Sunday school teacher many years ago in Cortez, and my biggest cheerleader throughout this project. She is the resident historian of Cortez and provided many of the historic photographs. Whenever I was in doubt about something, I turned to Toodle.

The members of my family have let me know that the book was important to them. Sometimes, it was a simple question, "How's the book coming?" Other times, it was by their tears or laughter when reading a particular passage, which let me know I was on the right track. Those tears and laughs kept me going.

I'd like to especially thank my good friend John Leach for the many hours we spent talking about "what we want to do when we grow up," which helped keep my priorities straight.

Finest Kind

Old Lynn Tupin has it on his tombstone,
with a granite mermaid on each side.
Come what may through eternity's ages,
for every question the same reply:
      "How're you feeling?"
      "How'd you do fishing?"
      "How's the tide runnin' across the bay?"

      "How'd you sleep last night?"
      "Is your boat running right?"
      "Did the old lady cook mullet today?"

The outsiders never see it;
only the khaki and the drawl,
sunburned necks in old straw hats,
scooter-poops with net or trawl.
But underneath the toughened visage,
close to heart and in the mind,
if you look with love and caring,
you'll see "the finest kind."

July 15, 1981

Down to the Seashore

ON MORNINGS LIKE THIS in Cortez, I want to believe that nothing has changed. I wake up hot and clammy as the sun burns through the middle bedroom of my grandma's house. Dressing quickly, I go to the bathroom and splash water on my face to wash away the cobweb feeling and, as always, that first strong smell of artesian water burns in my nostrils.

I walk out the screen door, down the narrow sidewalk, across the sandy road in front of the dock. The fish house is cool and breezy in the morning air; the men move stiffly to their work, lingering in the shade and talking for a few moments before facing the glare of the sun.

To me, slumped in an old chair on the front of the dock, Cortez looks the same. A young boy in cutoff shorts drags a box of crushed ice to his daddy's boat tied alongside the dock and shovels it into the narrow icebox behind the engine, ready for their first strike of mullet. The father checks the gas tank, motions to the boy to untie the stern line, and pushes the bow away from the dock. He presses the ignition button of the outboard motor; the engine catches and their kicker boat roars down the channel and across Sarasota Bay.

Minutes later, an old scooter-poop—a small open boat with an inboard engine—eases up to the dock, and a weathered fisherman opens his icebox and begins throwing his catch of mullet on the dock. My uncle Ralph "Pig" Fulford comes out of the office and, while joking easily with the old man, shovels the fish into a large metal vat. He'll ice the fish down, weigh them out—100 pounds to a box—and store them in the cooler.

All along the waterfront, the morning activity is beginning. Gillnetters in their small boats come and go—some returning from all-night trips to Sister Key or Palma Sola Bay, while others are just getting under way. Young bearded crewmembers on the Bell Fish Company's fleet of grouper boats straggle down to the boats with the day's first cold drink in hand and slowly return to the painting and engine work that must be done before their next trip to the Yucatan. Bait fishermen begin loading big boxes of ice into the holds of their open boats, using a hydraulic hoist on a sliding beam. Then they head out through Longboat Pass to the Gulf of Mexico where they'll spend the day purse-seining for Spanish sardines and thread herring. One by one, bait shrimpers drift down to the docks after a few hours of sleep. Gathering near their shrimp boxes to check the pumps, they speculate on where the shrimp can be caught tonight.

It has been much the same in Cortez for a hundred years. Some of the particulars have changed; today's kicker boats, monofilament nets, and deep-sea grouper boats are a far cry from the sailing skipjacks, limed cotton nets, and poling skiffs that were used at the turn of the century. But otherwise, the names, faces, and the mood on the docks are not much different from when Cortez was first settled in the 1880s.

That's what I'd like to believe anyway. The truth is that underneath the serenity something is powerfully out-of-sync in Cortez, Florida. There are forces at work inside and out of this little village that, if not controlled, will destroy this way of life completely. There are some who say it may already be too late. Others have given up. A few continue to fight.

Pure and simple, Cortez is fighting for its life. For a hundred years, the people of this small, unincorporated fishing village on the Gulf coast have lived a quiet life, earning a hard and honest living from the sea. But that way of life is threatened now by the twin plagues of the Florida coastline: high-rise condominiums and drug smugglers. This book is about the people of Cortez and their struggle to preserve a village that is one of the last of its kind in Florida.

Cortez is a community of about 500 people located on Sarasota Bay, seven miles west of the city of Bradenton in Manatee County. It was settled in the 1880s by North Carolina fishermen who came south seeking one thing: mullet. The tens of thousands of Northern retirees who have settled in the state in the last two decades have come seeking one thing as well: to spend their retirement years in the sun. At one point in time, these two motivations might have been compatible, but they aren't any longer.

This little village is on the brink of being destroyed in the next ten years unless the onslaught of condominiums, housing developments, and shopping malls is stopped or controlled. And it will die just as certainly, from within, if the cult of drug smugglers continues to eat away at the heart of the community. If the village dies, a great deal more perishes as well— a history and a way of life that are the closest thing this state has left to a native tradition, other than the Seminole Indians. In its place will be something far cheaper, shallower, and more mundane. A hundred years hence, no books will be written celebrating a culture built on shopping malls and condos.

This book is an attempt to capture the richness and joy of the people of Cortez and, also, with unashamed subjectivity, to raise the deep moral and political questions of whether this nation as a whole, and the state of Florida in particular, can afford to lose these few small communities that remain. In short, can a nation afford to destroy its traditions and its roots, and at what price?

I cannot be objective in this book—Cortez is home for my family in the deepest sense of the word. All of my mother's family, the Fulfords, are from there, and most of my father's family have lived there at one time or another. Growing up in Tallahassee, I spent every summer in Cortez, as well as every Thanksgiving, Christmas, and Easter.

Cortez is truly a community of kinfolks. Most people are related to each other by blood or marriage, if not both. Those who aren't related might as well be, since no one can keep track of their kinfolks anyway, except at family reunions, and only then with the help of nametags. Many a youngster in Cortez has called an old-timer "Uncle" or "Aunt" when they were not actually related. For the last ten years, I've told friends about my cousin Bubba Capo, one of the first Cortez fishermen busted for dope-smuggling, and only recently did I find out that we're not actually related.

The village claims about 20 extended families and, in the course of this book, the reader will meet them all: the Fulfords, Guthries, Taylors, Lewises, Adamses, Garners, Joneses, Culbreaths, Bells, McDonalds, Capos, Greens, Coarseys, Moras, Carvers, and Drymonds. There are others among them—the Hornes, Williamses, Browns, Fews, and Pringles—who no longer live there, but are still intimately connected to the village.

The lines between the various families fade very quickly. When I started this book, I asked my mother and my grandma to help me compile a Fulford family tree so I could keep track of who I was talking to and how I was related to them. It didn't do much good. Almost everybody in Cortez showed up at some point, and the same thing would be true for the Guthries, Taylors, or Bells. No matter, a family tree would be virtually useless without one other anthropological tool: a cross-reference list of nicknames. Almost everyone in Cortez has a nickname, and sometimes two or three. One cousin is known as Tommy Fulford to some people, Blue Fulford to others, and Sonny Fulford to still others. I've heard him called all three names by the same person in the same conversation. There are people in Cortez whose real names I've never known, while my mother, perhaps, may not know their nicknames. It's like speaking a foreign language. But it wouldn't be Cortez without the nicknames: Goose, Forty, Gator, Tink, Cock Robin, Snooks, Pig, Snake, Jap, Doc, Toodle, Man, Baby Gilbert, Popeye, Trigger, Tater, Fido, Bunks, Mouldy, and Talkin' Charlie.

My parents moved from Tallahassee to Bradenton in 1974, so I still visited three or four times a year, but until I started this book, I hadn't actually spent any extended time in Cortez in ten years. In the summer of 1981, I went back for two months and walked around the village carrying a tote bag of camera equipment, a tape recorder, and a stack of blank cassettes. It took me a week to get beyond feeling like a tourist. I wanted to talk to everyone in the village and, although I didn't quite do that, I ended up with more than 400 pages of transcribed interviews and 25 rolls of exposed film.

This book's format is a mosaic of what I call "living histories." Each chapter begins with one or more of the people in Cortez, and the topic of that chapter unfolds through their memories, stories, and anecdotes. Through the eyes and voices of its inhabitants, I've tried to reconstruct the fullness of their culture and way of life.

In the process, I have had to discard every preconception that had prompted me to write this book in the first place. Reality has a way of doing that if given the chance. I found out that most of the images of myself and my family which I had carried around all my life were false, and that many perceptions which I had thought false were actually true.

For instance, four years ago I decided to learn to play old-time fiddle, feeling all the while like I was attempting to adopt a Southern music tradition that I wasn't really part of. But I learned from talking to relatives that my Grandpa Green and his brothers Henderson and Elverton had been fiddle players in their youth and that Goose Culbreath and other Cortez natives whom I've known all my life are as much a part of old-time music as the mountain fiddlers of North Carolina and Tennessee. The only thing that separated me from that heritage was one generation's worth of middle-class veneer, a big dose of AM radio and television sit-coms, and the undisputed linking of "dancing, drinking and the devil" in my Church of Christ upbringing. But the music has actually been around me all my life, and it still is.

Similarly, I have spent the last six years working as an organizer and writer for the labor movement and being inspired by the struggles of coalminers and textile workers in other parts of the South. During these years, I had often thought how sad it was that Cortez fishermen were so indoctrinated against unions; it seemed like a natural progression for them to identify their association, the Organized Fishermen of Florida, as a fullfledged union, rather than continue to be isolated from the other working people who are their natural allies.

I discovered later, from a passing reference by an older cousin, that Cortez has had union battles that have been just as fierce and heroic as those of workers anywhere in the country. I found out that relatives whom I'd perceived solely as fishermen or shrimpers had traveled up and down the Florida coast in Model T trucks organizing for the Seafarers' International Union in the 1930s, had stood on soap boxes before hostile audiences in Ft. Myers Beach to speak out fearlessly for the United Packinghouse Workers in the 1950s, and had gathered around small fires along the Cortez shoreline on winter mornings to revive their spirits during strikes. There is more romantic labor history in my own family, if I ever needed that for inspiration, than I could find in any labor-history text.

But not everything I learned in working on this book was enjoyable or fulfilling. I learned some things that I wish I hadn't and other things that I still don't know what to do with. I became a collection point for ancient indiscretions and rowdy adventures that would curl the hair of surviving relatives. At times like these, the lofty ideals of journalistic integrity came into sharp relief against the image of my grandma being on the rampage at me for the next five years; in some cases I'm not sure which side prevailed.

All in all, I learned more about myself than I did about Cortez or my family. I had to push myself to do something that I'd been afraid to do before: to talk at length and in depth with my family and kinfolks. That should be the most natural thing in the world, but it scared me every time I walked over to see someone and knocked on their door.

When I talked with strangers, I might have worried about what they thought of me at the time, but with kinfolks I worried about what they'd thought of me all my life. In my mind I was eight years old again and dripping wet from falling overboard from my grandpa's boat, 18 years old sitting in church with long hair and a scraggly beard, and now 33 years old, wondering, "What do they think of how I've turned out?" I'm happy to say that they thought that I turned out just fine—at least from what I could tell.

I learned, too, that even if you don't water such roots regularly they still live. All it took was saying, "I'm Tink Fulford's grandson," or "I'm Clyde and Mary Frances's boy," and cousins I hadn't seen in ten years, or people I'd never met at all, would open their souls and pour them out. I like to think that I'm a pretty good listener and a skilled interviewer, but in listening to the tapes it's obvious that something much deeper than interviewing skills was at work. Call it blood, spirit, or heritage, all I know is that I was a recipient of information that went way beyond me as an individual to encompass the lives of all those who have gone before. That is a weighty gift that I hope to have handled well in the pages that follow.

What began as a celebration of my family's heritage in Cortez—a "white man's 'Roots'," as one friend described it—now seems likely to end up as an epitaph for the place that has bred and nurtured those roots. I struggled for weeks to define the book as one or the other: celebration or epitaph. But in the end I realized that the book is and must be both. Cortez is the joy and the sadness, each one in abundance, and this book must be that, too. There is the celebration of what has been; there is the grief for what has been lost; and, then, there is the fight to keep the rest.

The people of Cortez let me know in a thousand ways that I was part of the family, part of the bloodline of proud men and women who have worked hard to earn a living and a life from the sea. That pride will come through, I hope, between the sorrow and uncertainty about Cortez's fate. My cousin Grey Fulford put it best when he told me: "Son, when Jesus went looking for disciples, you know where he went first, don't you? He didn't go up to Washington and ask the politicians. He went down to the seashore and found him some fishermen."

If he came back looking today, I bet he'd go there again.

PART I

Setting the Stage

"Some folks fished to live; Tink Fulford lived to fish." Mark Green, *age three, helps* Grandpa Tink *unload the catch (1959).*

Chapter 1

"Something to Put
On the Tombstone"

THE COMMON JOKE THAT "nobody is from Florida" raises an important question, Where did the native Floridians go? The answer in most
cases is: nowhere. They are still there—in the building-trades unions, in
the black neighborhoods, behind the check-out counter at the "7-11," or
on the outskirts of Florida's sprawling metropolises, with a johnboat parked
on a trailer at the side of the house. They can be found, too, entire villages
of them in fact, in the few small communities like Cortez.

By now, there have been millions of words written about Florida's
population explosion during the past 15 years, and the resulting strain on
water resources, coastal land use, wildlife, and the general quality of life.
The issue has been popularized on CBS News' "60 Minutes," by a headline article in *Sports Illustrated* entitled "There's Trouble in Paradise," and
by dozens of other articles and newscasts. Too, there have been numerous
reports on drug smuggling operations along the Florida coastline. Smuggling has become, according to some estimates, the leading industry in the
state.

But hidden from view in most of those reports is the plight of the native Floridian and the small native communities that have too often been
trampled in the rush. Major environmental campaigns have been launched
around the rallying cries of "Save the brown pelican" or "Save our bays,"
but nary a cry has been raised to "Save the native Floridian." The closest
thing to it is a bumper sticker put out by the Organized Fishermen of Florida which reads: "Save an endangered species: commercial fishermen."

My intent is that this book will be a voice for a few of those people—
the 500 or more who live in Cortez. The stories of others across the state

should be recorded as well, before they are gone forever. I hope this will be a start.

What is happening to Cortez is not unique by any means. A dozen or more small communities in Florida have already been overrun, as have probably hundreds of others across the South. Indeed, it seems to be the special curse of Southerners to have to witness the destruction of their hometowns by forces outside of their control. The specific threats to Cortez may be in the form of "Mr. Bull Dozer, Mr. Dredge Boat, and Mr. Drag Line," as my cousin Blue Fulford described the onrush of high-rise condominiums and housing developments that are overwhelming the Florida coastline, but there is a deeper explanation behind the threat to Cortez.

Inevitably, explanations in the South seem to go back to the Civil War, and that's where one must look, once again, to understand the fate of Cortez. Taking a brief historical excursion now may make what follows more understandable.

Simply stated, in the 20 years preceding the Civil War, while Southern slaveowners and Northern industrialists jockeyed for political power, the psychological groundwork was laid for the destruction of Cortez and other Southern communities. During those years, both sides used the press and the pulpit to ridicule the other. Working-class Southerners were washed along in the tide of ridicule aimed at Southern aristocrats, who made up only 20 percent of the population at the most. Poor white Southerners were portrayed in Northern newspapers, sermons, and textbooks as ignorant, slow-witted hillbillies and rednecks. This ridicule helped obscure the fact that Southern whites were sorely burdened by an economic system that forced them to compete with slave labor.

Once the war broke out, those cumulative decades of ridicule made it easier for the slaveowners to convince Southern whites that a war to preserve an obsolete slave society was actually a fight to "defend the homeland." It worked. Tens of thousands of white workers marched off to the slaveowners' war and died in their "gallant lost cause." Had they won, they would have insured themselves a future of impoverishment that was nearly as great as that of the black slaves. It was the ultimate trick.

By the end of the war, the Southern economy was in shambles, with General W. T. Sherman's march to the sea the most infamous example of the North's "scorched earth policy," which almost totally destroyed the South's rail lines, factories, industrial centers, and several major cities. The interests of Northern capitalists might have dictated destroying Southern industry in order to eliminate future competition, but only years of psychological conditioning against Southerners could have given rise to the charred vengeance with which Northern troops desecrated the South.

The meager postwar beginnings of political and social equality for poor whites and blacks that were achieved during Reconstruction (such as the establishment of free public schools) were quickly reversed by the Great Compromise of 1876. It solved the disputed presidential election by giving the presidency to Rutherford B. Hayes, the Republican candidate, over Democrat Samuel Tilden, who received the larger popular vote, in exchange for the Republicans' promise to remove Northern troops from the South. But the actual heart of the deal, according to historian C. Vann Woodward, was to return political and social control of the South to the old slaveowners in exchange for giving economic control to Northern capitalists.

The old plantation owners regained the ballot box and the front seat in the railroad car through the use of the poll tax and the black codes, while Northern "titans of industry"—or robber barons—such as J. P. Morgan, Jay Gould, and Cornelius Vanderbilt, took the coal, timber, textiles, and rails. The only thing left for working people, both black and white, was sharecropping on rented land, "moving to the mill" to work for low wages in textile or lumber mills, or, in the case of Cortez's ancestors, eking out a living from the sea.

Most attempts through the years by black and white workers to get any more than that have been crushed by violence or by waving the bloody shirt of race hatred. However, there is an important, but little-known, history of blacks and whites uniting together in the Knights of Labor in the 1890s, in the Industrial Workers of World in the 1910s, and in various CIO unions and the Southern Tenant Farmers' Union during the 1930s.

It's not farfetched to see, 100 years after the Great Compromise, the pending demise of Cortez as a direct offshoot of that corrupt backroom deal and the social forces that sprang to life in its wake. Some modern historians have gone so far as to describe the postwar South as a colony of the North, with the economic resources controlled by Northern interests. Those scholars would certainly not be surprised to see native communities like Cortez being trampled on and eradicated, to serve, in this case, as warm-weather havens for Northern tourists and retirees.

I'd wager too that if a legion of white-suited, mint-julep-sipping "Colonels" from the 1880s arose from their graves and returned to stroll the halls of the Florida Capitol in Tallahassee or any county courthouse south of Orlando, they would embrace the members of the Florida legislature and the county commissioners as their own.

Of course, these politicians would rear back in horror at the thought of old Redeemer graybeards slobbering bourbon down the front of their Pierre Cardin suits and tracking horse manure across the deep-pile carpets of their outer offices. They'd shout hosannahs to heaven about the "progressive change in the 'New South,' " and with righteous indignation disavow any connection with "these drunken bigots." They'd probably even call the cops.

But take away the blow-dried haircuts and the public relations stunts that show their "understanding of the working people" and Florida's political leaders and the rotting "Colonels" are one and the same. In fact, the modern Southern politician may be worse. The "Redeemers" sold the South's birthright to Northern entrepreneurs in exchange for political control, and then returned to the big house to oversee the "respectable wealth" generated by their sharecroppers and tenant farmers. But the current crop of developer-politicians who control Florida, and their yes-men cousins in other Southern states, want a bigger piece of the action. They want to make sure that when Florida finally runs out of drinking water, beachfront property, and unspoiled land and air, that they were the ones who made the killing on it, not some outsider who doesn't care. This is, after all, their home.

What the Redeemers had to barter with in 1876 were mineral rights and a wealth of natural resources. In 1984, what's left for the snake-oil salesmen to dicker over is year-long sunshine and just enough prime waterfront property to dredge out a series of finger canals and build one more look-alike housing development—or even better, a high-rise condominium. "Retirement coffins" stacked to the sky mean quicker turnaround time on profits and less land to buy.

Cortez's problem is that it sits squarely in the path of the real estate profiteers in their modern-day march to the sea. Where General Sherman cut a swath of torched cotton fields and twisted railroad ties from Atlanta to the Atlantic, his modern-day offspring have wreaked equal havoc with bulldozer and dragline.

Cortez is the ground-zero point for their next assault. What made it a perfect harbor for my great-grandfather Capt. Billy Fulford, his brothers Nate and Sanders, Capt. Jim Guthrie and Charlie Jones when they moved there in the late 1880s from North Carolina, now brings drool to the lips of Manatee County's development junkies, who lie awake at night craving the next hit.

This is the last point of land between Bradenton and the Gulf of Mexico that has not been pumped in, carved up, and sold off to Northern retirees looking for paradise in their last years. It is one of the few remaining examples of native culture on the Suncoast where one would feel silly asking the question, "Are you from Florida?"

If the threat from developers wasn't enough to jeopardize the future of Cortez, then the threat from the smugglers would be. Since the early 1970s, Cortez has fallen victim in a big way to marijuana smuggling. It is common knowledge that a number of Cortez fishermen have been engaged in the dope trafficking business, slipping out under cover of night and bringing ashore tons of marijuana from Colombia. Some have gotten into the dope business on a short-term basis, made a quick bundle, and then gotten out. Others have stayed in it and made a killing. Still others have been killed by it. Three Cortez fishermen are currently serving time in federal prison for smuggling; many more have been implicated.

In years past, Cortez had the reputation as "one of the largest fishing villages on the west coast." Today it carries the same reputation for smuggling. Signs of the smuggling are everywhere. Big money is floating around the community—going into huge, elaborately equipped fishing boats, fleets of Lincoln Continentals and souped-up vans, and cedar facelifts on old white-frame houses. There are 35-year-old fishermen who have suddenly "retired," content to live off the $100 bills buried in sealed PVC pipes in their backyards.

Yet more than the money, the smuggling has brought a new and foreign element to Cortez: fear. For the first time in its history, the people are afraid of each other. The honest people are afraid of the smugglers, and the smugglers are afraid of everybody.

But even with the condos on its doorstep and the smugglers firmly entrenched, it may not be too late for Cortez. That was my hope when I started this book. I wanted to give the village "a shot at trying to preserve itself," as I told a friend. However, when I went down to Cortez to begin the book, I found only one person who was optimistic about the future of the community: a planner in the Manatee County Planning Department, who told me confidently that "Cortez will be there for years to come." But for him, "being there" means a road sign on the highway and a couple of fish houses on the shore. That may be, but unless these influences are thwarted, Cortez as a community, a feeling, and a legacy of kinfolks and bloodlines will have disappeared long before.

I realized early on that just writing a book wouldn't make a difference in saving the community, so I began telling friends that "at least it would record what Cortez was like before it's gone." I would like to think that there's a big dose of my own hopelessness in that view, and that our notorious "Southern despair" is keeping me from seeing that what happened to Kissimmee, Venice, Homosassa Springs, Osprey, Naples, and New Port Richey doesn't have to happen to Cortez.

Maybe so. But one thing is clear: the despair that has been ground into Southern working people over the past 100 years, as they've seen their lives manipulated by distant despots and local swindlers, is operating full-throttle in Cortez. "The people just won't seem to fight," said Wyman Coarsey, the Cortez postmaster, describing the residents' passivity in recent rezoning battles to keep out the high-rises. And the same county planner who told me that Cortez will be around for years to come also said: "We wanted to help them keep the community the way it is, but they wouldn't believe us. But then, why should they trust us? I can understand them not having much faith in the planning department or the county commission."

If the people stay locked in their helplessness against the forces crushing in around them, then Cortez will be recorded as one more in a long line of victims to the god of profits. If they rise up and take their future in their own hands, they face a protracted struggle that will consume them and their children for years to come.

That choice won't be made in this book. Only the local people can make that choice. Only the local people can make that fight. But if they choose to fight, and win, this book will stand as a proud celebration of a thriving community. If they lose, the book will be just as proud and respectful, but in the end, like Blue Fulford said, it will be "something to put on the tombstone."

Chapter 2

"You Gonna Sleep All Day?"

YAAWL . . . GET UP, GET OUT OF BED, time to go fishing . . . you
gonna sleep all day?"

That is how it has to start. That is how it always started—rough,
leathery fingers reaching out in the dark at four o'clock in the morning
and pinching me, hard and crab-like, on the upper arms and chest. And
the voice: growling, rumbling, snorting. The pinches and the growls were
a perfect match, practiced and honed over the years to do their job quickly
and efficiently. The pinches started slowly and got faster with each growl,
sending me twisting away from one and leaving myself open for the next,
until the growl that said it all: "You gonna sleep all day?"

No sir, you could bet your life against that one. Nobody was ever gonna
sleep all day when Tink Fulford was around. No one who ever felt those
pinches or heard those growls has forgotten them, although Grandpa has
been dead 19 years now. In that one gruff sentence, orchestrated by strong
fingers that had shucked thousands of mullet out of gillnets and endured
many a catfish fin and stingray barb, he said more about his life, about
Cortez, and about who I am than other people could have said in a lifetime. I could probably fill up a couple of hundred pages and not find more
eloquent words to describe what Papa Tink (as we called him until our
embarrassment made us change to "Grandpa") taught me about life and
about what's important.

He taught me two things: that you can find meaning, dignity, and
maybe even beauty in working hard every day of your life, and that you
can find all of that in commercial fishing, at least in fishing the way he
did it, which was the right way.

Walton "Tink" Fulford was a man of few words and many growls and snorts. The few words he did use were spit out two or three at a time, sand-wiched between an "arrwh" or a "yaawl" at the beginning and a snort or a sniff at the end. It was always the same pattern, the only variation being that a flying wad of tobacco juice might erupt at any time—at the front of the sentence, at the back, or on your foot if you weren't watching.

I've heard many imitations of Tink Fulford's "arrwhs" and "yaawls" in Cortez, but nobody can do it quite the way he could. It was a warning sig-nal that a garbled message was coming across the airwaves, and as soon as you decoded it, you'd either find yourself overboard and carrying the end of the net ashore, or dripping copper paint in your hair while painting the bottom of a skiff, or shoveling cow manure and old mullet carcasses into his coconut trees for fertilizer. In other words, you were going to be work-ing.

Talking wasn't something that came natural to him and trying to un-derstand him when he did say something was an art form in itself. "Tink had the worst habit of anybody I ever saw of talking to you with his back to you," said Wyman Coarsey, who fished with him in the 1940s. "He'd get off there in a skiff and start hollering: 'Arrh rawh rawh rawh,' and you'd yell back, 'What'd you say, Tink?' He'd go 'nawh rawh rawh rarwh the boat.' I tell you, sometimes he'd get us all fighting mad."

His "you gonna sleep all day" speech was the wordiest he got. In fact, to him it must have seemed like blabbering on all night. Those were the most words he ever said to me at one stretch, and I figure some of them were thrown in as a grudging compromise to my being unconscious when he started. Otherwise, he would have never needed to say "get up and go fishing." If Tink Fulford was awake, he was going fishing. If he woke me up at four in the morning, then I was going fishing. And if he wasn't fish-ing he was doing the absolute minimum number of things he had to do before going again. That category included everything else: eating, sleep-ing, mending net, pulling nets off the spreads and into the boat, and, cer-tainly least important of all, talking. Like my uncle Pig said, "Other men fished to live, but Daddy lived to fish."

And that's what he did for 62 years, until the doctors opened him up in 1965 to remove an intestinal obstruction, and then rolled him over and noticed the black moles on his back that turned out to be malignant mel-anoma. He worked hard and he fished hard, and there wasn't much time or inclination for talking along the way. But his life said the words for him, which is why this book has to begin with him, and why everyone in Cortez still feels the shadow of his life on theirs, 19 years after his death.

He was a different sort of person from the start. Born in 1903 to William "Capt. Billy" and Sallie Fulford, he was the seventh of nine children: Dora, Clyde, Clayton, Bessie, Willie, Thomas, Tink, Grace, and Sally. Aunt Sally, called Sissie, is the only one still living.

Capt. Billy was one of the original settlers of Cortez; he moved from Carteret County, North Carolina, in the 1880s with his brothers Nate and Sanders, Capt. Jim Guthrie, and Charlie Jones. The "Capt." on the front of his name was as much a part of him as the Fulford. He wasn't Billy Fulford or William Fulford, he was Capt. Billy. Being the son of Capt. Billy meant something in Cortez, and to young Tink Fulford, it must have meant something extra special. Capt. Billy was considered the best fisherman in the village, and Tink was to follow in his footsteps.

W. H. "Man" Adams, the eldest son of Dora Fulford and Willis Adams, was four years younger than Grandpa. He recalled what Grandpa was like growing up: "I never did see Uncle Tink get out there playing like kids do, playing ball and such. He'd be down there in a boat somewheres messing around. He didn't stay in school but till the third or fourth grade, and anytime he wasn't in school he was out fishing. Granddaddy had a big crew and whenever he'd get nets that was getting too old he'd save them and give them to Tink, and we'd take them old nets and shove over to Tidy's Island or Coon's Key in a skiff and go 'root-bumping'—run them nets out around those little islands—and when the tide went out the fish had to gill. Oh, Uncle Tink was always in a boat."

By the time he was 18, in 1921, he had his own boat and crew. At a Church of Christ meeting that same year, he met Edith Wilson, a thin, red-haired 15-year-old whose family had a ten-acre farm out in the sawgrass east of Bradenton in a little community called New Pearce. To hear her tell the story of that encounter, her first impression of Tink wasn't exactly a knockout: "Well, we usually went to church in Oneco, right near our farm, but every now and then we'd come down to Cortez for a church meeting. So one time we come down and Grandpa (Capt. Billy) invited us to stay for dinner. I think I must have sat next to Tink . . . I guess it was him sitting there, but he didn't say nothing."

He still wasn't talking, but after dinner Tink did what young men have always done, and still do, to impress a young woman: he took Edith for a boatride. "We went to the beach and went swimming, and then Tink took me and Otto, this boy I was seeing, out in the boat and carried us boat-riding in the Gulf," said Edith.

The next thing she knew, this big bony guy was pulling up at her door unannounced a week later in a taxi. "He didn't ask me for a date or nothing," she said, "he just come up out there. We was all fixing to go to town when Tink come up in a taxi, so Papa told me and my brother Frank to take him to New Pearce and show him around. Then we fixed a place for him to sleep and he spent the night at our house. Otto didn't like that 'cause he thought Tink liked me . . . and I don't know, I guess I liked him, too. So directly, we just started going together."

Tink would arrive in a taxi, and Edith would drive the family's Model T to Bradenton, where they'd go to the show and to the ice cream parlor. They split up several times in the next three years, but finally, in 1924, after Tink ran away to the east coast when his parents tried to send him to school in Tampa, they were married. Edith had four children in the next six years: my mother Mary Frances in 1925, Ralph (Pig) in 1928, Belinda in 1929, and Irene in 1931. She waited nine years before having Anna Dean in 1940, Wayne in 1943, and Gary in 1949. Somehow, without much talking or expressing much emotion, Tink Fulford had a powerful loving influence on his children. He wouldn't have made high marks by today's parenting manuals, but he got the job done.

He never talked about the pressures in his life, but they obviously gnawed at him, driving him to work tirelessly in the hot sun, riding up and down the beaches looking for fish. "Daddy was real proud of being Capt. Billy's son, and he was the darling of Grandma Sallie," said Momma. "They depended on him, too. He was their youngest son, but then Clyde died in 1918, Clayton died in 1919, Uncle Tommy died fairly young, and Uncle Willie had his alcohol problems. So Daddy was the one they looked to. And he supported them from 1928 on, after Grandpa had to have his leg amputated and couldn't fish any more. All of that put a strain on him, and he drove himself so hard because he wanted to be able to provide for his family the way Grandpa had. Grandma and Grandpa had nice furniture in their house and even had a piano, and Grandma was used to having nice dresses and hired help. But all we had in our living room when I was growing up were two old rocking chairs, a little table, and a radio. We had a table and some spindle-backed chairs in the dining room, and that was it. Things were real hard for Daddy during the Depression, too. We lost ten acres of land out in Myakka because we couldn't pay the taxes on them, and Daddy had to mortgage the house to Charlie Guthrie, and finally, his fish house folded when the banks closed."

Because of this pressure, he couldn't stand to see anyone not working; it didn't matter who they were or, in some cases, what they were. "Daddy came walking down to the dock one day and there was an old cat laying there asleep on the front of the dock," said Wayne. "He walked by and booted that old thing up in the air and said, 'Yaawl, get up and do something!' He couldn't even stand to see an old cat not working."

He was as hard on the family as he was on anyone else. As soon as the boys were old enough, meaning almost as soon as they could walk, he had them down at the dock shoveling fish or pulling nets. No respecter of gender when it came to work, he saw to it that the girls put in their long hours at the dock as well, in addition to the household chores that Grandma assigned them.

"All the other kids couldn't wait to get out of school every day and come home," said Wayne, "but I didn't care if I ever got home, because I knew there'd be a shovel and a hoe and a rake leaning up against the side of the house waiting for me, with a file there to sharpen them. I'd creep by the house and peek down at the dock, and if there weren't fish piled up down there I knew I was gonna spend the afternoon hoeing in the trees."

Working in the trees might have been the worst job of all. Grandpa had two big empty lots next to the house where he grew coconut and palm trees to sell to nurseries. He'd dump a truck load of coconuts in one pile and a truck load of cow manure in another, and then he'd get us kids out there in the heat of the day to plant those trees. We'd hoe, then dig a hole about 18 inches deep, rake the manure into it for fertilizer, drop in the coconut, fill the hole half full with water and get down on our hands and knees and pack the mud around the nut. It was hot, slimy, tedious work, with that sandy soil so hot from the sun that it'd burn our bare feet. The gnats and mosquitoes buzzed around us so fiercely that we'd end up with mud caked in our hair from trying to swat them away. But the work didn't end with the planting. Once the small buds showed, Grandpa kept us out there hoeing, weeding, or doing his favorite job of all—digging in mullet carcasses for fertilizer.

"Oh, them trees of his!" said M. C. "Mac" McCarter, one of the first black men to work in Cortez; he worked at the Fulford Fish Company from 1956 to 1969. "I bet I dug a hundred scow-loads of fish into them coconut trees and palm trees. I'd dug so many mullet into those trees that I'd stick my shovel in the dirt and all I'd hit was fish. Couldn't hardly find the dirt for all the fish. They hadn't even rotted from the last time, but Mr. Tink said he wanted them trees fertilized, so I did it."

No youngsters were safe sitting around on the dock if Grandpa came by; he'd put them to work doing something, whether it needed doing or not. Generation after generation of Cortez youngsters learned that the hard way, and they all adopted the same strategy: running away. "When I was small enough, I'd crawl in the kitchen cabinets to hide," said Wayne. "I'd stay quiet in there until he left the house. But when I got too big for that, I'd run out the back door when I heard him coming. Or if I was sitting down at the dock and heard the front door slam up at the house, I'd know he was coming, so I'd sneak around the side of the dock and go next door to Gayboy's fish house [Star Fish Company]. I'd go over there and get me a big cold drink and be sitting there laughing to myself, 'Yeah, I outsmarted that old man this time.' About that time I'd hear a big 'sniff' right behind me, and I'd just wait for the lightning to strike me dead. He'd snuck right up behind me."

By the time I was coming along, our escape plans were practiced like an air-raid drill. There were five of us boys within two years of each other: my first cousin Rusty Fulford (Pig's son), my uncle Gary, my second cousins Jimmy Guthrie and Larry Fulford, and me. We were on Grandpa's fishing crew all summer and when we weren't fishing, we were hiding from him. It was guerilla warfare—when he went to the house, we went to the dock; when he went to the dock, we went to the store.

The only safe time was when he was asleep, which was three or four hours a day at the most. We'd come in from fishing around ten o'clock in the morning, and Grandpa would stay around the dock long enough to see that the fish were unloaded. Afterwards, he'd head to the house to eat breakfast and try to sleep.

That's when we'd make our break. The five of us would have spent the night snoring our brains out in the cabin of the *Anna Dean*, Grandpa's 33-foot launch, except for the minimum amount of time that he could roust us out of bed to make a strike. Then we'd help clear the net, scarf down a peanut butter sandwich or a couple of slices of white bread with syrup, and hightail it back to the bunks. By ten in the morning we were raring to go.

If we could avoid Grandpa from the time he left the dock until he went to sleep, then we were free to tear around all morning, roaming from one dock to the other, spraying each other with shaken-up cold drinks, jumping overboard at high tide, or trying to catch pelicans with a piece of mullet tied on the end of a length of fishing twine. If we weren't down at the docks, we were stalking doves and sparrows with our bows and arrows, or engaging in our favorite pastime of all: hanging out at Mittie Parent's corner store or Hoot Gibson's grocery, guzzling RC Colas and chocolate Yoo Hoo's and ruining our dinner with ice cream sandwiches and honey buns.

That might not sound like much, but it sure beat working in the trees, mowing yards, hauling away rotten palm fronds that the wind had blown down, scrubbing barnacles off the bottom of boats, bailing out skiffs, or any of the thousand other jobs that Grandpa might assign us.

We had a pretty good system going for awhile. We'd hear his heavy footsteps on the walkway that led from the dock to the house and with a frantic whisper—"Here he comes!"—we'd trample each other in our rush to squeeze through the back door, bolt across the back yard, and down the dirt road.

But he caught on to that one pretty quickly, and our whole system collapsed when my brother Mark, who was five years younger than me, got big enough to follow our tracks. He became Grandpa's messenger boy and straw boss. We would be camped out on the front steps of Mrs. Parent's store, settling in for our second round of RC's and leafing through the back issues of *True Detective* that she kept on top of the cold-drink cooler. Suddenly, cutting across the empty lot, here'd come this skinny little seven-year-old in cutoffs and a wrinkled t-shirt, with a big round head covered with freckles, and rings of sunburn around his neck and arms where the shirt ended. As soon as he saw us, he'd start calling out in a tinny, squeaky voice that could carry across a half-mile of open water: "Graaanpa wants y'all to finish painting the big scow."

"Oh, for crap sakes!" we'd scream in unison—it was our strongest expression at the time. We'd stomp around and mimic his "Graaanpa," but the subpoena had been served. The only natural thing to do then was run from Mark, too. That must have been great for the psyche of a seven-year-old—to see his older brother, cousins, and uncle go tearing out of the store, slamming the screen door so hard that the little girl on the Sunbeam Bread sign rattled for five seconds afterwards, and streaking down the road whenever he came around.

Years later, we all expressed regret for having run away from Grandpa, hiding out at the store, and hitting the bunks as soon as the *Anna Dean* left the dock. "I wish now I'd spent more time up there on the bow with him and less time in the bunk," said Pig, expressing my sentiments exactly.

If he worked the family hard, he worked himself even harder. "He punished himself, by golly," said Man Adams. "Why, when he died he wasn't but 62 years old but he looked like he was 80. Fishing was his living and he followed it day and night. That's all he thought about was fishing. Why, I've known him to stay up for a week. One time he said, 'I'm gonna stay up a week and not go to bed.' And he stayed awake, just to do it, and went fishing day and night. Just to show you how he'd do, one time we was over across the bay, around Mullet Key, and we had run a stop—put out the nets and everybody had laid down and went to bed. Well, instead of him laying down, I seen him pull up an old skiff and get into it and start poling off. I'm a light sleeper and after awhile I heard the skiff bumping against the old *Ralph*, the boat he had before the *Anna Dean*. I raised up out of the cabin and got out and he says, 'Lots of mullet over there around Tarpon Key.' I said, 'Tarpon Key! That's about 10 miles! Tink, you been to Tarpon Key?' and he says, 'Yeah, I shoved all the way around Tarpon Key.' Well that was more than 20 miles he poled—10 over and 10 back. That's the way he was. Then he got in there and slept for about an hour and it was time to go to work. He murdered himself around like that."

There were plenty of other good fishermen in Cortez and plenty of hard workers, but no one drove himself as hard as Tink Fulford did. And by the end of World War II, he had acquired more gear than anyone else—more boats, nets, and skiffs—so he was also able to go at it in a bigger way.

The only time he let up was on Sundays. His mother and father went to church regularly and so did Grandma, but he stopped going in the 1930s and didn't go back until just before he died. "Tink didn't ever go fishing on Sundays," said Woodrow Green, my second cousin who ran the Fulford Fish Company in the 1940s, "but he'd roam them whole bays on Saturday night, just going around looking, and trying to find where he was gonna go on Sunday night."

"His job on Sunday mornings, after he busted up going to church, was to put on a white shirt and his good hat and go down to the dock, sit there on the head of the dock and get him a knife and start whittling," said Gene Fulford, his first cousin. "I'd always be down there at eight o'clock to see what he was gonna do. All of us would be down there, talking and whittling, and every now and then Tink would say something, but mostly he was a big listener. Somebody'd heard about some fish over at so and so. Tink, he'd be listening, see. He'd sit around and sniff and sniff, whittling on an old stick, and he'd be figuring out right then how to catch them same fish that fellah was talking about. It used to tickle me, them boys talking 'I'm gonna catch so and so,' and, if something didn't happen, Tink would be catching them same fish at midnight on Sunday night. He didn't mend no net or nothing on Sunday, but when twelve o'clock in the night come, that's when he went to work."

If there were fish around, Grandpa would be after them, and it didn't matter who'd spotted them first. Man Adams laughed about one such incident: "Back in the '20s, Uncle Tommy Fulford's store was the gathering-up place, see, and he'd stay open till eleven or twelve o'clock at night sometimes, as long as there was customers. After supper all the men'd get out there and all they'd talk about was fishing. That's all they knew. They'd tell about how many sets they'd made that day or how they'd struck a good bunch of them somewheres. Uncle Tink'd be down there and he wouldn't say nothing—just be sitting out there in the dark. And they might be saying there was fish up there on Seven Pines. Well, Tink'd be saying to himself, 'The tides gonna be high about two o'clock in the morning,' and first thing you know, he's got a crew and he's up there on Seven Pines at two o'clock waiting.

"He even did that to his daddy one time. I'll never forget it," he added. "Tink said to Granddaddy, 'Where was you fishing today, Poppa?' He says, 'Up on the reef, there's quite a few fish.' First thing you know, we got off and we was up there on the reef and made a strike and caught 3,500 pounds. 'Bout the time we got the fish in the boat we heard the old *Hustler* a comin'—that was Granddaddy's boat—and he come up to the edge of the reef and stopped, and he says, 'Is that you Tink?' 'Yes sir,' he said. We'd caught his fish! And Granddaddy cranked up and went on and made a pretty good set himself. But I've laughed about that a lot of times, how Uncle Tink asked his own daddy where they were and then went out and caught his fish!"

Some called it conniving, others called it compulsion or determination, but whatever the case, Tink Fulford couldn't let anything stand in his way of catching fish. That drive was what made him such a good fisherman—the will to keep going when others had quit. Wyman Coarsey told a story to illustrate the point: "One time after World War II we was over in Muddy Bottom, across Tampa Bay. We went over there with a stop-net rig, but when we got there, there was already other crews there, so we couldn't put in a stop. Well, we sat over there all night, all of us mad and disappointed 'cause we thought we was gonna make a dime.

"Well, the next morning Tink Fulford got up on that bow and drank his coffee and spit tobacco juice all around where it'd blow back in our eyes. That was the way he'd keep us awake, see . . . I've wiped more to-bacco juice out of my eyes! Finally, he got up and he walked back and un-tied a skiff and got in it and started poling away from the launch. He got off there about a hundred yards and got to hollering: 'Narw rarwh rarwh rarwh,' with his back to us like he always did, and we was hollering back, 'What you saying, Tink?' We was all still mad, see, and Grey Fulford was the only one that had the nerve to talk back at him, and Grey started yell-ing: 'Well why don't you tell us what you want! Stand out there and hol-ler!' So finally we understood what he wanted. He wanted us to get a couple of them boats with some shallow nets on them, and we went out there and he told us what to do with them. We pulled them nets out and run them around a basin, that's what he called it, but it wasn't a thing in the world but a pothole. We took in that pothole and we started dragging them nets—tightening those nets up. We started getting that compass drawed in a little bit and pretty soon the fish started a-boiling. It was low tide, mind you, and the fish had all settled in that hole.

"We commenced to seeing fish and mud and fish and mud. We caught 7,600 pounds of redfish and sheephead! We had 'em, boy! We had the prettiest catch of redfish I ever saw. We caught redfish so big that you couldn't reach your fingers between their eyeballs. We had to go ashore on Rattlesnake Key and cut mangrove roots and make billyclubs out of them, and we'd tighten that net up, roll it up till we got the fish up out of the water, and then beat them in the head, grab them by the eyeballs, and toss them in the boat. We had more fish than we could handle and we had to go get Curt Johns to come and mate with us, and we filled Curt's launch to the gunnels. Well, we was still mad, but actually we all felt like asses 'cause Tink had shown us something. We'd done give up, but not Tink Fulford, he didn't give up."

He worked hard both because of the pressures on him and because he loved fishing, but he might have worked that much anyway simply be-cause poor circulation in his legs kept him from sleeping. It's a Fulford family trait—Capt. Billy had open sores on his legs for years that never healed up, and every night Grandma Sallie wrapped them with long rolls

of bandages. Eventually, in 1928, Capt. Billy had to have his leg amputated.

The pain in Grandpa's legs kept him from sleeping, and standing up
all night in a boat, wet from the waist down, compounded the problem.
"A lot of people don't believe it, but Tink worked so hard 'cause his legs
hurt him so bad," said Gene Fulford. "They'd get to hurting him and he'd
say, 'Well, just as well get up.' And we was going fishing. His old feet used
to turn right black they'd hurt him so bad. The doctor finally cut out one
of them big veins in his leg and that helped him some, but I know how he
suffered 'cause I've got those varicose veins, too. Mine don't hurt so much
like his did, but they turn numb in the winter like I was paralyzed. One
time Tink said to me, 'Gene, you got your waders on?' and I said, 'Yeah.'
'Well, take her overboard,' he said. I jumped overboard with the net and
I didn't have my waders on. My feet was so durned cold anyway that I didn't
even know it."

Grandpa's inability to sleep more than a couple of hours at a time is
the inspiration for a lot of the stories still told about him. "Me and Blue
Fulford fished with him for a long time, and sometimes he really made me
mad," said Buck Jones, another Cortez fisherman. "Once he wanted a 100-
mash bluefish net [the number of meshes, called mashes in Cortez, determined the depth of a net], and instead of buying a 100-mash net, he bought
two 50-mash nets just to make us sew them together. It wasn't cheaper
that way, he just wanted to keep us busy. He was so restless and he wanted
to keep everybody else the same way.

"Another time we went out there with a brand new 140-mash bluefish
net, which was too deep, but we run it overboard anyway, out there between Egmont Key and Passage Key, and it got all snagged up," said Buck.
"So we come back in and Tink says, 'Yaawl, cut 40 mashes off that net.'
So me and Blue sat out there all day and cut 40 mashes off and sewed the
lead line back on. We went back out that night and come back in, and
Tink says, 'Yaawl, sew them 40 mashes back on.' So we had to sew the
whole 40 mashes back on. Went out the next night and come back, and
Tink says, 'Yaawl, cut them 40 mashes off again.' We cut that 40 mashes
off again and told him, 'That's it! If you want that 40 mashes on again,
you're gonna have to do it yourself.'

"He just couldn't ever sleep," Buck added. "We'd go out there and put
in a stop, and instead of him anchoring the *Anna Dean* offshore a-ways so
we could sleep, he'd anchor right on top of the breaker bar and we'd lay

there and it would beat and pound the hell out of us all night. He'd stay awake anyway, poling around and looking at the nets, but he wanted to make sure that nobody else got any sleep either.

"But one time I finally got him back. We was out there around Egmont Key looking for bluefish and we saw a whole bunch of fish. Tink says, 'What in the hell is all that?' I said, 'I don't know, but if you shine your spotlight down there and see a bunch of pink eyes, we'll know its bonefish.' So he shined the light down there and pink eyes was everywhere. Tink says, 'Yaawl, run her overboard. Maybe there's some bluefish in there.' We run her overboard and filled her smack up with them big old skinny bonefish—I mean full of that trash. We just roped the net in the boat and me and Blue went to clearing the net. Tink come on through the pass and anchored inside there. Well, we knew what he was gonna do. He was gonna go in there and go to sleep while we was clearing the net. So every time I pulled one of them big old bonefish out of the net, I threw it just as hard as I could against the cabin door—crack!! Just as hard as I could! I did that about 10 times and old Tink came out of there a'cussin' and started her up and headed home."

If his bad circulation hadn't kept him awake, his coffee surely would have. Today, doctors rail against the bad effects of caffeine, especially for people with circulation problems. But even if his doctors had told him to give it up, I know Grandpa would have kept on drinking the stuff. It wasn't the volume of coffee that he guzzled that made it so important to him, it was the potency. "What was commonly known as 'Tink Fulford coffee' had to have a blue slick on top of it," said Wyman Coarsey. "It was so strong that it looked like an oil spill, with a blue skim floating around on top. And he wouldn't drink it any other way."

Almost every grown man in Cortez spent some time fishing with Grandpa and credit him with teaching them most of what they know about fishing. But of all those who fished with him, there were a select few who had the odious job of making his coffee. They were like the vestal virgins—the keepers of the sacred flame—but instead of wearing white robes, they were recognized by the ashen, sickly look that still comes over them when they remember the smell of that stuff.

It ruined me for life. To this day, I almost get sick from one whiff of coffee. Others may be able to conjure images of "the aromatic smell of fresh coffee brewing on the stove" to justify their daily habits, but all I can summon are the memories of mushroom clouds of Maxwell House coffee rising from the spout of the *Anna Dean*'s battered aluminum coffee pot, which had a terminal case of what my cousin Rusty called the creeping crud. Seagulls flying through the clouds of stench emanating from that old pot were killed instantly. Seriously. They'd hit that first wave of stink and do a nosedive like they'd been shot. And I'll bet that wherever that old coffee pot is—probably buried under tons of garbage at the county land-fill or covered with barnacles at the bottom of Sarasota Bay—that to this day radioactive ions are springing off that thing and causing birth defects and cancers from here to Japan.

How bad was it, truthfully? Buck Jones, one of the honored fraternity of coffee-makers, described it: "I'd get those one-pound bags of Maxwell House and start the water boiling in that big old pot just about the time we left the dock. I know I'd dump half a pound, sometimes three-quarters of a pound of coffee in it and boil it up. He wanted it so black and strong that I couldn't stand to drink the mess, and when I'd try to cut back on it sometimes, he'd always complain, 'What's the matter, you run outta coffee?' Finally, I just started bringing my own pot and making my own."

It wasn't just its industrial-strength potency that made it so bad, it was also the way he liked to drink it—right out of the spout. "I've seen him sit up there on that bow and drink that stuff right out of the pot, and he'd get the grounds all in his mouth and just spit them out in the water," said Buck.

If you could handle how strong it was and then had the willpower to drink it straight out of the pot, grounds and all, there was one more hurdle to cross to become a true initiate—reheating his coffee. Commercial fishing requires that you spend long stretches of time just riding and looking for fish, followed by periodic frenzies when you spot a school and strike them. Once the net is pulled back in and the fish are cleared and iced down, the riding begins again, leaving plenty of time for coffee drinking.

That's what the grown men did; us young boys headed straight for the bunks whenever we could. But being the youngest, it fell to me during the last couple of summers before Grandpa died to do the one job that had to be done before going back to sleep—reheating his coffee. I'd stumble around trying to light the propane stove and then watch while the coffee perked and bubbled like ancient primordial soup. Then I had to carry the steaming pot through the cabin and up to the bow without scalding myself or my snoring cohorts; all the while the boat was lurching and rolling in the waves.

Three or four times a night I warmed that same pot of coffee with those same old muddy grounds, or what was left of them that Grandpa hadn't already chewed up and spit out. By morning, when I reheated the pot for the last time, those grounds looked like the old wads of chewing tobacco that Grandpa spit out on the ground—all clumped together and oozing in their own juice. They smelled even worse.

There was one final element that made it worse, and he did that—gladly. He drank that warmed-again swill when it was hot and gurgling, and he drank it too when it was as cold and slimy as 90-weight transmission oil. "He sent me to the boat many a time, wading to the skiff to get his old quart jar of coffee that he kept under the bow," said Wyman Coarsey. "It had an old rusty screw lid on it, and he'd screw that lid off and it'd be plum cold and cankered all over the top. And he'd drink it off. Cold coffee, jet black, right out of the jar. And, you know, something gets to stinking when it's in an old jar like that, but that's the way he drank it."

Coffee was mostly what he drank, but it wasn't the only thing, and in the course of my summer in Cortez, a number of stories turned up about Grandpa sneaking off every now and then to partake of stronger medicine. Sneaking off was exactly what he'd do, too, because the religious beliefs of Capt. Billy, Grandma Sallie, and Edith left no room for alcoholic beverages. "You'd better not be messing around with no such of a thing" was Grandma's judgment then, and it still is. In the face of an attitude that "anyone who ever sniffed a cork is an alcoholic," Grandpa did his drinking on the sly.

"Sometimes he'd arrange for somebody to bring him a bottle, and he'd hide it down at the dock until he could drink it," said Grey Fulford. "Other times he'd come over to see me 'cause he knew I kept a bottle. He'd walk in and the next thing I knew half my bottle'd be gone. Tink'd be wiping his face and saying, 'I don't see how you drink that junk—it'd rot my guts out.' But half my bottle'd be gone."

With the sentiment so strong against drinking of any kind, it's hard to know how much he actually drank and how much of a drinking problem he had, if he had one at all. "I really believe that when Daddy died, he didn't think I knew that he drank," said Momma. "But it was a sad thing for Ralph, because he was the one who had to go over to a bar or someone's house and bring Daddy back home when he was drunk."

It's the one place where the pressure showed. The silent, hard-driving exterior would crack open for a few hours, long enough for him to go to a bar somewhere and down a few beers, maybe even tear up the place a little bit, then pay for the damages, pick up his hat and head home, and be out fishing the next day.

"During World War II, Tink was making so much money he had to spend some of it, and he'd slip off once in a while and spend a few dollars in a beer joint," said Gene Fulford. "He'd enjoy it, but Edith could smell the beer on him when he got home and she'd say, 'Where you been, you old stinker?' But one night, I never will forget it, he wanted to take me to Tampa 'cause I was in the Coast Guard [but couldn't because] I had to be back at work at eight o'clock in the morning. So we went up to Bradenton to this all-night place and we ordered some beer and oysters. The waitress come back with his order and there was only three little old oysters on the plate. He looked at 'em and called her back over and said, 'Is that all the oysters you get with an order?' She said, 'That's all.' So he just turned the table and the whole works right over and said, 'Come back when you get some more oysters.' Couple days later he went back and paid for it."

There's another story about him going into a place that had a big mirror behind the bar. After asking the bartender how much the mirror cost and counting out the exact amount in cash, he picked up a beer bottle and took the mirror out with one throw. But regardless of the reasons, he was just as sly about his drinking expeditions as he was about catching somebody else's fish. He would have his fun, but he wouldn't talk about it, and he would make sure that there were no loose ends that would come back to haunt him.

"Tink was one of the slickest persons that ever lived," said Wyman Coarsey. "He was so cautious. One time that struck me as extra funny was when him and Albert Few had been off somewheres having a couple of drinks, which was dead against the law with Edith, you know. They were coming home in the wee hours of the night and Albert had a brand new car, and he run that thing off the road and ran slap dab over another car. Tore 'em all to hell, his car and the other one. Well, as soon as the dust cleared, Tink was gone! Wasn't nobody in that car but the driver. After the law had come and questioned everybody and everything had settled down, well about that time up walked this big tall fellow, chewing tobacco, and he says, 'Albert, you have a wreck?' It was Tink, see, and it was a smart move 'cause instead of two of them being charged with drunk, he just hit the woods and come back later asking what had happened. I understand that he helped Albert pay for the whole thing.

"Another time, back about 1946 or '47," added Wyman, "I had a Model A Ford that I had cut the body off of and built a flatbed on the back and made into a truck. I could haul five or six boxes of fish on it. So one day Tink comes up to me and says, 'Hunkie'—that was my nickname—'Hunkie, how about let's go get some manure for my coconut trees.' Actually, his words was 'I want to put some shit on my nuts.' So we crawled in that Model A truck and we headed out to Burnett's Dairy and the guy gave us all we wanted for free. We loaded up six or eight boxes and set them on my truck, but they were really too much for it and they were sticking off the back end. Coming home, we came to the junction of U.S. 41 and Cortez Road, what we called Parker's Corner. There was nothing there then but a stop sign and a narrow dirt road, with a Sinclair station on one corner and a juke joint called The Knick Knack Club on the other. Well, on this day there was a lot of traffic coming and going, and that old Model A only had a little old four-cylinder engine in her, sitting there going 'chooka chooka chooka.' I'm looking one way and looking the other and Tink had a mouthful of tobacco, and he says 'Aww, go ahead on, Hunkie.' So I went! Man, them cars was bearing down on us, and in that old Model A you didn't change your mind. Once you let out the clutch, you were going. Well, I got a little excited and gave it the gas, and off the back went three boxes, right in the middle of the highway, dumped over upside down. I pulled over to the side and commenced to stop, and Tink looked back and saw a bunch of people standing on all four corners looking, and he spit that tobacco juice out and said 'Go on, Hunkie, don't stop!' So we left three hundred-pound boxes of cow manure right in the middle of U.S. 41. Old Tink would have killed me if I'd stopped and he'd had to go back."

Clearly, Grandpa drove himself hard, and the drinking was one way that he tried to relax. But that was incidental compared to the main thing he did to relax: eating ice cream. If there was one true passion in his life, besides fishing, it was ice cream. "Ice cream was Daddy's favorite food," said Momma. "When I was growing up, we'd make ice cream every Saturday night with Uncle Bill Ireland, even in the winter. And we'd never make a trip to town without stopping at the ice cream parlor on the way home. On Saturday afternoons, the ice cream man started coming to Cortez, and he'd back his truck into the loading pit at the dock and Daddy would go down and buy ice cream for all the kids."

In the 1950s and 1960s, when I was spending summers in Cortez, Grandpa would lie down on the living room couch, plop a half gallon of vanilla ice cream on the floor next to him, and eat away at it with a fork. I never understood the fork, but if you were lucky enough to be around when Grandpa got a craving, you could grab your own fork and help him stab away. It was all you could eat, too, despite Grandma's protests—"Tink, don't you let them kids eat all that mess of ice cream."

He was a big man who loved to eat, and Grandma loved to cook; it might have been where they were the most compatible. Dinners were a social occasion at the Fulford house; they were one of the ways that Grandpa showed his hospitality to other people. "He never met a stranger or a bum who he didn't bring up to the house for dinner," said Momma. "Everybody who came down to the dock got invited up for dinner, and we were always bringing home people from church. Daddy really enjoyed that role—being able to do that for others."

Cortez fishing families are money-poor, but they are food-rich. Even if they were eating mullet every night of the week, there was always plenty of it: big platters of fried fish that had been caught that morning, with fresh field peas or green beans, big bowls of grits, and pitchers of iced tea. And all of it was fresh, too.

So fresh, in fact, that they have a problem that few, if anybody else in the world, have: too-fresh fish. "When mullet's too fresh, it just don't taste right," said Pig. "You take a fish right out of the net and stick your knife in it and it'll shrivel up about one-third of its original size. And it shrinks up even more when you cook it. It tastes kind of tough, too, like the fish is still all tensed up from dying. I like my fish to sit for a couple of hours, till they're good and relaxed."

They really did eat fish every day of the week. "We'd eat fish during the week and then try to have a chicken or roast for Sunday dinner, except during the Depression, and then we ate it every night," said Momma. "But it'd be different every meal. One night Momma'd cook it with onions on top, the next night she'd fry it with grits, the next night I'd put ketchup on it, and the night after I'd squeeze lemon juice on it."

Mullet was the staple on Grandma's table, but at other times it was filled with fried or boiled shrimp, fried scallops that the women or youngsters had caught that afternoon in "The Kitchen" (a sandflat south of the Cortez fish houses), bluefish, snapper, snook, redfish, mackerel, or Florida's "cadillac of eating fish": pompano. For variety, Grandma would order big blocks of baloney from town, and cut off strips and fry them. Or she'd make a dish that Grandpa called slumgullion: canned corn beef, potatoes, onions, and tomatoes all cooked together. I never had it, but the name sure seems to fit.

The Fulford dinner menu was so routinized that it got Grandpa into trouble on one occasion. "Momma always cooked hot dogs on Saturday night, no matter what," said Anna Dean. "But one time she cooked hot dogs on Friday night instead, and Daddy got up from the table, went to bed, and got up the next morning and put his Sunday clothes on and went down to the dock. He came back a little while later and said, 'Edith, what day is it?' Momma said, 'It's Saturday, Tink.' Daddy just shook his head and said, 'Aww, you and them hot dogs!'"

Besides the regular fare, there were also special occasions when Grandpa'd get hold of a bushel bag of oysters from an old friend or fish dealer who would have stopped by the dock, and the family would have an oyster roast. "Every Christmas we'd go out in the woods near Ruskin and have an oyster roast. That was our Christmas dinner," said Momma. The boys would get a fire going good and dump the oysters in one of the wire mesh fish baskets from the dock, and set it on the fire until the oysters barely popped open. Grandpa would reach down and grab one, pry it open with his pocketknife, scoop the little booger out and plop it on a saltine cracker, shoot a couple of drops of Red Hot on it, and eat it whole. If he couldn't wait for them to cook, he'd slide a raw one down his craw, accompanied by a big slurping sound that grossed me out so bad that I wouldn't try raw oysters until I was 23.

There were other special occasions when the family would load up in the launch on Saturday afternoon with a big picnic lunch and go out boat-riding in the Gulf. Grandpa'd sit up on the bow with one foot on the steering wheel, letting the younger boys and girls take turns steering. When he found a nice spot to anchor he'd grab the kids one by one and toss them overboard, growling and laughing down deep with mischief and delight.

His favorite eating occasions, and maybe the favorite events in his whole life, were the Fulford family reunions that he organized the last three years of his life. It was the place where he could relish his role as the patriarch of the clan. He started gearing up for them two days early by sending us boys out in a pickup truck with Mac to cut buttonwood—the "wood of choice" for smoking mullet. We'd stomp around in the swamps along the bay, dragging back enough twisted, craggy buttonwood to make a truck load. When we got home, he'd put us to work splitting and cleaning several hundred pounds of mullet.

Every smokehouse in the village was used, and on the morning of the big event, we'd stack racks of salt-and-peppered mullet three-high in the smokers, and let them cook for four or five hours. There's a thin line between smoked mullet that tastes fresh and juicy and smoked mullet that tastes like dried rope; very seldom have I found anything but the latter in restaurants. I guess family reunions have spoiled me.

The last two reunions were held in a big open shed next to the dock that was used for hanging nets, building skiffs, or storing odds and ends of junk. We would clean it out, rake it, and set up folding tables and chairs in rows. The shed has a long worktable down one side, and that's where the food went: the smoked mullet at one end, followed by chicken, ham, fresh peas and beans from summer gardens, potato salad, green salads, cole slaw, homemade rolls and biscuits, iced tea, lemonade, and at the far end, all sorts of cakes, pies, and cookies.

Inside the fish house, boiling in big metal pots over a propane cooker, was the other cracker delicacy: swamp cabbage. I never liked cooked cabbage much to begin with and I cared even less for swamps, so the idea of eating a steaming bowl of pale green "hearts of palm," as they're called in fancy Miami restaurants, was too much for me. I found out five years ago what I had been missing. I would have discovered swamp cabbage a lot earlier, and who knows what else, if Grandpa hadn't died. See, there wasn't any swamp cabbage served at Fulford family reunions after he died, because there weren't any reunions after he died. He was the driving force behind them, and when he died, they did too.

It wasn't until 1979, 14 years after his death, that the next reunion was held. That's when I tried the swamp cabbage and liked it. That's when Pig stood up in front of the 80 or so family members and read a list of all the relatives who had died and the babies who had been born since the last reunion, and then said the blessing for the meal. Tink Fulford's shadow was over us all. Momma put a nametag on my young niece Bekah that read: "Bekah Reibling. Tink's great-granddaughter."

More than family reunions were affected by his death. "Tink was the hub of this community," said Wyman Coarsey, "and since he died, it's been like a wheel with no hub. He was the one who really built Cortez up. He hired crews, he bought boats and nets and put people to work, and maybe he'd get a little dabble back every once in a while. Brother, he'd give them rigs that cost 15 or 20 thousand dollars and trust them to go ahead and work it and make it pay for itself. I learned a lot about work from Tink Fulford. When you start out with nothing, and Tink Fulford started out with nothing, you've got to just keep a-pecking and a-pecking and you think, 'Lord, I better not spend any of it 'cause I just don't know how long I'm gonna be able to get it.' It just hasn't been the same here since he died."

His death shook everyone with its suddenness. Yet it didn't happen overnight; he didn't keel over one day and was gone. But the cancer took him from what he loved most very quickly. This tower of strength, this man who pushed himself and everyone around him with hard work and constant fishing, was reduced in a matter of weeks to sitting helplessly on the front of the dock.

It started in May 1965 when the doctors discovered the intestinal obstruction. After the operation, Dr. W. D. Sugg noticed three black moles on Grandpa's back and removed them. But it was too late. The melanoma had already spread and was out of control. He came back home from the hospital and started feeling better, began to regain some weight, and started walking down to the dock to sniff around. But he wasn't the same. He knew it; I knew it as a 14-year-old; and everyone else knew it. He was vulnerable in a way that he had never been before, and the fear in the back of his eyes was obvious.

Wayne captained the *Anna Dean* that summer in his place, with Gary, Rusty, Jimmy, J. G. "Jake" Culbreath, and myself in the crew. It was a joke. I think I made a total of $15 the whole summer, and we were spending that much a week just drinking Mountain Dews and eating Almond Joys. When we'd come home from another failed mission to Mullet Key or John's Pass, Grandpa would be there at the dock, silent as always, but passive now, sitting in the shadows without the growls and snorts of his former strength. The cryptic rumbles that in the past had sent us scurrying off to work were gone. There was no longer any need to run from him.

A little of his fishing magic remained. Pig and Gene had been taking out Grandpa's new boat, *The Bluefish*, accompanied by Mac, my brother Mark, who was nine, and my cousin Randy Porterfield, age six, who was down from Montgomery for the summer. They had had little success, if any. During the last week of June, they went out the first four nights and caught only 200 pounds of bluefish all told. But on Thursday night Grandpa got to feeling better and decided to go with them. They caught a boatload—2,300 pounds of big blues. He went again the next night and they caught another 230 pounds. He never went again.

Early in July he had a seizure while sitting on the couch in the living room. He was waiting to go to town for a doctor's appointment, holding his hat in his hand, when Grandma saw him suddenly start chopping the air with his hat and clawing at his arm with his other hand. By the time she could stop him, he had scratched himself until he bled. The cancer was in his brain.

They put him in the hospital. The next day, Oliver Porterfield, Randy's father, drove down from Montgomery with his friend Emit Aikens, stopping in Tallahassee to pick up Momma. During those days in the hospital, the final transformation in Tink Fulford took place: he began to talk. Momma said that one night she and Oliver sat up all night with him and he never stopped talking. "He talked to me more that night than he ever did in his whole life," she said. "I think he was afraid he'd die if he went to sleep. He talked about everything—about fishing trips he had made, about things he had done in his life, about coming back to the church."

Although he was released from the hospital and came home, he never recovered from the seizure. In August, he said he wanted to go to North Carolina, so Grandma, Anna Dean, and Gary drove him to the mountains. The second night there he got sick and began vomiting. They drove home as quickly as possible to get him into bed. "He never was able to get out and go anymore after that. He just got weaker and weaker all the time," said Grandma.

He did get back down to the dock a couple of times, and even bought some new pompano net, but he never got to use it. "Just a couple of days before he had to go back to the hospital, boy, he made a boo-boo," Gene remembered. "He was down at the dock on a Sunday, thinking it was Saturday. The tide never had been any lower, and the old *Anna Dean* was aground with her old wheel sitting up in the air. He got out there and started her up and I shoved over in a skiff and said, 'What you gonna do, Tink?' He said, 'I'm gonna make us a channel so we can go bluefishing tonight.' I said, 'Tink, did you know today's Sunday?' 'It ain't no such of a thing,' he said. 'Today's Saturday.' 'No, Tink,' I said. 'Today's Sunday. Edith's in church.' Boy oh boy, he came out of there then!

"Well, he didn't know what he was doing," Gene added. "He bought more new net just before he died than he ever owned in his life. He bought a bunch of new pompano net and he had him a thousand corks for it. Well,

I had a thousand corks, too, and he said he wanted to borry my corks because he said they were better than his. But they were the same bunch, you know. But I said, 'OK, Tink, we'll change corks.' Pig tried to tell him, 'Daddy, you don't need a thousand corks for no more net than you've got. It won't take but 400.' I come down there and he had that whole string of corks trying to put them on, and I said, 'Tink, you got enough corks for four nets.' He said, 'Well I still want some more. I don't want it to sink.' I said, 'No, it ain't a-gonna sink.' He didn't know what he was doing, just sitting down there putting them corks on. But he was a good old boy, that's for sure."

The end came quickly after that, and thankfully, not too painfully. "He got sick on Sunday morning," said Grandma, "so Bessie and I stayed with him while the others went to church, and then that night Toodle stayed with him so's I could go to church. When I come home from church he was in a coma and he was burning up with fever, so we called the doctor. The doctor came out and sat down with me on the couch and said, 'Well, I believe this is it. You might as well make up your mind to it.' He couldn't give him anything to bring that fever down, you know, 'cause he couldn't swallow anything. He got worse that night and the doctor said we ought to take him to the hospital. So me and Anna Dean rode with him in the ambulance. About 45 minutes after we got there the nurse came in where we were, off in another room, and told us we could come in and see him. I come in there and stroked him across the head and said, 'Honey,' and he opened his eyes. He come out of that coma in that length of time, and then he'd just go back and forth in it all night. We took turns sitting up with him until he died." Nine days later, on 26 September 1965, he was gone. He was 62 years old.

They called Momma that morning in Tallahassee to break the news. She told my older sister Cathy and me, so we could make arrangements to miss school, but she waited until that afternoon to tell Carol and Mark, my younger sister and brother. We drove down that evening from Tallahassee.

The funeral was one of the most startling events in my life. I had no idea until then how many people knew Tink Fulford, how many people loved him, and how many people sorrowed at his death. "Oh, if you only knew how many people up and down this coast and the east coast knew Uncle Tink, and that's what they called him, 'Uncle Tink,' " said Gene.

"Everybody in Manatee County knew Uncle Tink, either from coming down here to buy fish or from fishing with him a little while."

The funeral director said it was one of the largest funerals he'd ever seen. All I could tell from where I was sitting in the family's chamber was that the chapel of the funeral parlor was full. It wasn't until we left to drive to the cemetery that the shock hit me of how many people were actually there. We followed the hearse around the corner of Manatee Avenue and headed north on U.S. 41 across the Manatee River Bridge, toward the Skyway Memorial Gardens. As we came to the top of the bridge I looked back, and cars were stretched out behind us in single file for a mile, it seemed, and others were still turning the corner on Manatee Avenue.

I was stunned. I knew that he was important to me, although at that time I couldn't have explained why. But what I couldn't understand, looking back at that line of cars glinting in the sun, was how my Grandpa could have been so important to that many people when he didn't talk, didn't tell people that he loved them, couldn't stand to see anybody not working, and wouldn't pat you on the back when you did.

I know now why they came. Tink Fulford couldn't say it, but he did it. He couldn't explain life, but he lived it. He pushed it, he stayed after it, he fought it, and he set a model for everyone around him that hard work might not bring riches, but it would bring more hard work, and more work after that, and still more, and that that was all right. If it wasn't an easy life, at least it was a full one. To every person who ever looked deep inside, saw their own fear and thought of giving up, his life said to keep trying. To those who thought of quitting, Tink Fulford's life said to go ahead on.

And he knew how to help people in his own way, without words. "If anybody around here got sick or needed money, he was the first one to help," said Grandma. "He'd put up a piece of paper down at the dock and write down how much he was gonna give, and then the others would write down their names and put how much they were giving. A lot of people thought a lot of him."

"He was the best-hearted man in the village, and he got ripped off a-plenty, too," said Wyman Coarsey. "He wouldn't say anything about it, but if you didn't pay him back or proved to be not worthy, why he'd just spit tobacco juice down in front of you and walk away. When he died, if he'd had all the money that he'd lost through goodness, he'd been in much better shape."

To show their appreciation, the people of Cortez took up a collection after he died and bought a marble headstone engraved with the words, "To Tink, from his friends."

Looking back now, I think he was trapped in his silence as much as we were. I carry the hollow pain, as do all who knew him, of never knowing the deep thoughts behind the silence. I never knew what he really thought of life, of loving—of me, for that matter. Was Tink Fulford happy when he died? Was his life fulfilled? I don't know. I only know that he worked hard, that he loved me enough to teach me that, and in the end, I loved him more for that than any words could say.

I know too that death must fit him worse than anyone who's ever lived. An eternity spent with other "souls at rest," stretched out peacefully with nothing to do, must be driving him crazy. Wherever he is, I'm betting that Tink Fulford isn't laying around doing nothing, and that even now he is prowling the outer reaches, pinching the slumbering ones with his steel-like grip and rumbling at them through the ages, "Yaawl, get up and do something. You gonna sleep all day?"

PART II

A Way of Life

"Unh, unh, unh, don't touch that dial! This is the Country Cracker Jubilee!" The Culbreath family played for WDHL in 1949 and on St. Petersburg's "Million Dollar Pier" (1949).

Chapter 3

"A Place
Called Hunter's Point"

I walked down the pathway along the shore,
and there she was, the wind blowing
through her silver hair.
Her eyes sparkling, she would say
"Hi dearie, isn't it a nice day?"
She would stand by her flower garden
and talk for awhile,
and it seems she always had that big smile
for the fishermen that walked by
and the children at play,
and it seemed that it always made my day.
But now her eyes are tired,
not as bright as that day.
You see, Miss Lela Taylor is 93 today.

28th of January 1981
Maida Culbreath

OH, WE HAD IT NICE, DEAR," said Miss Lela Taylor, sitting spryly, half-perched on a dining room chair, with her back to the bay. The waterfront stretched out behind her through jalousie windows that lined the wall of her second-floor kitchen.

From here, since 1925, Miss Lela has had the best view in Cortez: fish houses cranking with noise and bustle, boats of every description tied to their posts, sagging netspreads and old wooden camps built over the water, connected by a spiderweb system of walkways, and beyond—the whole sweep of Sarasota Bay.

Miss Lela sees it no longer. At age 93, cataracts have clouded her eyes and stolen her view. But her eyes still dart and prance, alive and brimming, and the memories remain. She is a small woman, bent somewhat by age, and her thin arms and animated hands show the years of hard work that she has done. She speaks with the rounded syllables of the North Carolina coastal plain, in a brogue that has not changed much since her forebears got off the boat from England, from Devon or Cornwall, some 300 years ago.

"Right, right, right, I've always loved it here on the water," she said. "It was kind of hard sometimes to figure where our next dollar was coming from . . . but it come!" She paused, thought for a moment, and then: "I'm still here!" She smiled, and the love and strength of this woman burned straight to my heart, straight to the bone.

Lela Garner Taylor is Cortez's oldest resident. There are several others who were born there before she arrived in 1911, but she is older by six years than anyone else in the village. She has seen it all: the changes, the joys, the sorrows. She has lived it all. And she remembers:

"I was born in Carteret County, North Carolina, on the 28th of January, in 1888, between Cherry Point and Camp Lejeune. We lived right on Bogue Sound. Oh, it was wonderful there. My daddy was a farmer and he'd go fishing, too, at night and late in the day. And my mother, she knew how to handle a sailboat as good as any of them. We'd go hook-and-lining. Oh, the boats were beautiful, beautiful, beautiful . . . North Carolina is one beautiful state. Across the sound they had churches and homes on the banks. Oh, it was beautiful, just beautiful."

In 1906, Miss Lela married Neriah Taylor, a widower. In 1907, at age 19, she had her first child. Uncle Neriah, as he was called, made his living with a big sailboat, a sharpie, which he used to tow logs to the sawmills in the towns along Bogue Sound—New Bern, Morehead City, and Beaufort. But Uncle Neriah had the itch—the Florida itch—and in 1911 they made the long journey south to Cortez. "My husband had been down here before and he liked it and wanted to come back," said Miss Lela. "So in July of 1911 we come on the sharpie to Morehead, me and him and our

first two children, and then we got on the train to New Bern and stayed
the night. That's where I saw my first automobile. We come on to Tampa
on the train and then boarded the steamer. It stopped in St. Petersburg,
then come on to Bradenton, and we got a taxi to come out here. I thought
we'd never make it. Once we got settled here I liked it, but that first year
I was still so homesick for North Carolina that I cried all Christmas day."

Despite the homesickness, they stayed. So did dozens of other Carteret County natives, all living within a 40-mile stretch of coastline, who
would make the same trek within the next 50 years. Why did they come,
those early ones? I haven't found an exact answer, but I've found a likely
one.

They came for the fish—mullet, to be exact, but redfish, trout, mackerel, bluefish, and pompano, too. And they came with the hope that the
mullet and the sweat of their brow would bring a better life. It was a promise that was hard to resist.

Sometime in the early 1880s, my great-grandfather Capt. Billy Fulford
and two of his brothers, Nate and Sanders, packed up their dreams and
left the Fulford homeplace on Bogue Sound, nestled between the tiny
communities of Straits and Gloucester. Fulfords had fished and farmed
there since 1700. Capt. Billy was no more than 18 when they left. Charlie
Jones and Jim Guthrie made their decision to leave about the same time;
I don't know if their decisions were independent of the Fulfords.

The fear and uncertainty and the gleam of excitement that must have
fueled that move is for the hand of fiction to unfold: How much did they
know about their destination? How had they heard about the fishing in
Florida? Was it the challenge of youth that made them leave, a feeling of
being hemmed-in by family and the status quo? Or was it more practical,
that the murderous hurricane, which struck the Carolina coast in 1879,
had devastated the fishing industry to such an extent that they were willing to gamble on the faraway swamps of Florida? Whichever it was, or a
combination of all of them, they followed the same trail, by rail and
steamer, that Miss Lela was to take more than two decades later.

The Fulford brothers came first to Cedar Key, which was a bustling
fishing community at the time. The fishing skills they had acquired from
generations in North Carolina helped them find work. According to the
1885 Florida state census, they were living in Cedar Key and working as
coasters. They began to put down some roots and stayed long enough for
Sanders to marry Lula Bozeman.

But something drove them on. With its own fishing fleet and a sizable population, Cedar Key might have been too similar to what they had left in Carteret County. If they were looking for a new frontier where they could carve out a reflection of their own skill and strength—an imprint of themselves—Cedar Key was not it.

So, about 1887, they moved south to Manatee County and began homesteading on Perico Island, a low, wooded point of land that juts out between Palma Sola Bay to the south and the mouth of the Manatee River to the north. In 1888, Grandpa Billy married Sallie Adams, and the young couple had their first child, Dora, the next year.

However, by 1889, the Fulfords had become dissatisfied with Perico Island as a harbor for their boats. Its flat western shoreline faced directly into the winds and waves coming off the Gulf and afforded little protection from the nor'wester gales. So they made what would be their final move to the next point of land south—a place called Hunter's Point.

Man Adams, the eldest son of Dora Fulford and Willis Adams, tells why: "There's a little point of land that runs out from Cortez and makes a natural slough, makes a nice little harbor. They located there and these sharpies from Cedar Key could come in and anchor and haul their fish back north to sell."

I don't know how long Hunter's Point had been established before they moved there, but clearly it had served for many years as a major fishery, supplying the Cuban markets. In 1879, a man named Silas Stearns was commissioned by the U.S. Fish Commission to do a survey of commercial fishing along the Gulf Coast. He traveled by boat up the west coast of Florida, stopping at each fishery and recording the activities in great detail. His records for Hunter's Point indicate that 28 fishermen were there when he arrived. "Many are natives of the Bahamas, and are called here, as also at Key West, 'conchs;' the rest are Americans."

Stearns went on to describe Hunter's Point: "The Hunter's Point fishery, one of the most important on the coast, is prosecuted with a special view to supplying the Cuban markets. . . . There are two seines in use . . . in October, November, December, and January. Mullet is the fish most largely taken. In 1879, 10,000 pounds were caught at a haul."

At the time of Stearns's visit, there were no permanent dwellings at Hunter's Point, only a large fish house for storing fish and two rooms built onto the fish house where the men slept. The crews spent only three or four months a year there and then returned to Key West or to the Bahamas.

The mullet and the roe were kench-cured—rubbed with salt and then dried in the sun—and shipped to Cuba to be sold. It wasn't until 1884 that Henry B. Plant built the first railroad between Tampa and Bradenton, thereby connecting Hunter's Point with the markets of Atlanta, Jacksonville, and cities further north. The railroad was the beginning of the end for both kench-curing and the dominance of the Cuban markets, since it was then possible to ship fresh fish on ice to U.S. markets. The advent of the railroad was a great incentive to American-born fishermen, such as my ancestors, to make permanent settlements on the coast, thereby displacing the seasonal fishermen.

The natural harbor at Hunter's Point that seemed like a perfect anchorage to Charlie Jones, Jim Guthrie, and the Fulford brothers is the same one that lies beneath Miss Lela's big kitchen windows. Today, real estate developers in Bradenton see a different image in their mind's eye: a natural harbor for a condominium community, with tennis courts, a covered parking lot, and a "picturesque," swept-clean marina for party boats and yachts. But I'm jumping ahead of myself; that part comes later.

The Carteret County natives bought strips of land along the shore from Otis Clark, who was the agent for the owner, Mary Gardiner. There is some uncertainty about those early purchases, and about how the village got the name Hunter's Point. According to Julian Taylor, 86, a Cortez native, the Gardiners had bought Hunter's Point from the state after a man named Hunter began homesteading the area but failed to "prove up" the homestead. Other old-timers think the area got its name from the deer, turkey, rabbits, fox, coons, and other wildlife that roamed the shores.

In any case, Cortez was born, although the little settlement wouldn't receive that name until 1896. The immigrants had found what they were looking for: Sarasota Bay, sheltered from the Gulf by Anna Maria Island and Longboat Key, provided miles and miles of fishing grounds that were teeming with mullet, redfish, trout, bluefish, snook, sheephead, and flounder. Just beyond Anna Maria with easy access through Longboat Pass lay the Gulf of Mexico, which had huge schools of mullet running along its beaches during roe season and, in the spring, a wealth of mackerel and kingfish.

It was all there within easy reach of young men and women with strong backs and a determination to work hard. The beautiful pristine environment must have looked like heaven, or something close to it, since at dusk the mosquitoes surely reminded them that it wasn't. But the fish were there in abundance, and, other than a few fishermen from Fogartyville up the Manatee River and a few other small villages scattered further south towards Punta Gorda and Charlotte Harbour, it was theirs for the taking.

Word quickly filtered back to North Carolina and launched a slow but steady caravan of kinfolks and neighbors to the Florida coast. Many of the new arrivals had been farmers in North Carolina, but most had had some experience fishing. Tired of trying to wring a living out of the sandy soil along Bogue Sound, they thought fishing in Florida would at least be more glamorous and exciting. "I was raised on our farm and that's where I done my work was on that farm," said Earl Guthrie, who made the trip to Cortez in 1921. "I decided I didn't want no part of farming and that's why I come to Florida."

Many of them were also motivated by the stories told by those who had already come, and, like all fishing stories, they were exaggerated with each retelling. "I thought everybody who come to Florida would get rich," said Manly Bell, whose older brother Aaron had come in 1912; Manly had followed in 1926. "There was an old man from St. Petersburg, old man Henry Hibbs, who'd made a fortune during the Florida Boom in the '20s, and he went to North Carolina and built a big old mansion about three-quarters of a mile from where I lived. He was always hiring boys to come to Florida and work in his fish house. But by the time I got down here, the bubble had busted."

As late as 1921, when Earl Guthrie came, it only cost $20.13 for a train ticket from Carteret County to Tampa, and it cost less than that to jump a boxcar. "Every one of them Guthrie boys up there, as soon as they was growed, they'd head for Florida," said Earl. "Somebody said that all the fish dealers had to do to get them down here was paint a picture of a swamp on the side of a boxcar and then run. That's how a lot of them come, by boxcar."

The young men quickly discovered that the stories about the good life in Florida weren't true. "I'd heard stories that it was a lot better down here, and that's why I come," said Earl. "But it weren't. Son, back in them times, there weren't no money. We existed. We didn't make a living. Shoot, if somebody went out fishing and made a hundred dollars, why, he thought he had all the money in the world."

But they kept coming anyway, many of them arriving for the fall roe season, beginning in September, and then returning to North Carolina in April. Slowly, as more stayed, the little village began to grow. The first settlers built homes along the water modeled after their houses in North Carolina: big, two-story, high-ceilinged, white-frame houses that faced the bay. The houses were big enough for the many children that were born, one almost every year, and for new arrivals from North Carolina who would move in with relatives until they could afford to build their own houses. The single-share fishermen rented a room in a family's home or, when times were rough, slept in old fish camps built out over the water.

At first, Hunter's Point's only link to the outside was by water. Runboats from Cedar Key brought in supplies and ice once a week and carried out the village's catch. But it was a tenuous link at best. The runboats were totally dependent on sails, and storms or calms at sea could delay their arrival for several days. To reach Bradenton, it was an all-day sail up the Manatee River or an even longer journey by horse and wagon over a winding rutted trail. Steamships had been operating in Tampa Bay and Sarasota Bay as early as the 1870s, connecting the settlements along the Manatee River with Tampa. But it wasn't until 1895, when the U.S. government dredged out Anna Maria Sound to open an inland waterway to Sarasota, that steamers began stopping at Hunter's Point.

The Mistletoe, a 100-foot steamer owned by the John Saverese Fish Company in Tampa, was the first steamer to make regular runs to Hunter's Point. It would leave Tampa one day and return the next, with stops at Sarasota and Hunter's Point for cargo and passengers. *The Mistletoe* sank in a 1911 hurricane, was rebuilt and renamed the *City of Sarasota*, and continued on the Sarasota-Tampa run until after World War I.

As the influx of people increased, Hunter's Point became more self-sufficient. The first store, owned by a family named Burton, was built on the shoreline near where The Albion Inn stands today. An icehouse was constructed; it held the ice brought in by schooner. Sometime before 1893, lumber was hauled by oxcart from Ellenton, 15 miles away, to build the first schoolhouse; it was a small A-frame building that is Earl Guthrie's home today. In 1912, the county built a new brick schoolhouse and generations of Cortez youngsters attended elementary school there until it was closed in 1961.

Mr. and Mrs. L. J. C. Bratton from Peoria, Illinois, moved to Hunter's Point in the early 1890s and became driving forces in the development of the village. Mrs. Bratton is given credit for donating land for the first church building in the village, which was constructed about the same time as the first schoolhouse. It was a community church, and the two congregations, the Church of Christ and the Church of God, alternated using it. One congregation would use the building on Sunday morning and the other would use it that night; then they'd switch the following week.

Mrs. Bratton is also credited with establishing the first post office in Hunter's Point. According to Julian Taylor, Mrs. Bratton wrote to Washington, D.C., in 1896 requesting a post office for the village. Before the service would open an office, the village had to be officially named, and evidently someone in Washington decided that it would be fitting to name the little community after Hernando Cortez, the "Great Conquistador" who conquered Mexico, even though he had never been anywhere near Hunter's Point. Ironically, another Spanish explorer, Hernando de Soto, allegedly made his first landing in the New World in 1539 at the entrance to the Manatee River, only ten miles from Hunter's Point. But, as there were already two other Desoto post offices in the state, one in Pinellas County and the other in Putnam County, some nameless postal official must have decided to spread the fame around.

In any case, now properly named and with its own post office, the little village continued to expand. Mrs. Bratton ran the post office, which was located in what Toodle Green calls the Cortez shopping center—a big fish house that Mr. Bratton built out over the water as a landing for the steamer. Bratton's dock, as it was called even after he sold it, eventually included a barbershop, a machine shop, a grocery and hardware store, a poolroom, and even a soda fountain. Fern Guthrie owned the barbershop, and Joe Guthrie owned the grocery store. There was one other store in Cortez, owned by M. H. Brown. While local people bought some food from the Cortez stores, they had to send to town for their larger purchases.

Cortez's first mailman was Uncle Henry Foreman, who left Bradenton every morning in a horse and wagon and wound his way to the community of Palma Sola and then across to Cortez on the old, bumpy Palma Sola Avenue. He brought the mail and also took orders from Cortez residents for supplies they wanted from town; he would bring those with the mail the next day. "Uncle Henry had a great memory and he never wrote down what people wanted, but he always got it right," said Toodle. "And he knew the birthday of every youngster in Cortez."

The Florida Gazetteer and Business Directory of 1911-1912, published by R. L. Polk and Company in Jacksonville, listed Cortez with a population of 100 and noted that there was a "daily stage to Bradenton, fare 75 cents."

The Brattons left Cortez about 1910 and were never heard from again, but before leaving they gave the little community its most famous landmark: The Albion Inn. The Brattons bought the Burtons' store, tore it down, and in its place constructed a two-story building out over the water. The original hotel had six-inch clapboard siding on its outside walls and only two or three bedrooms, but in 1901 the Brattons added another six rooms upstairs and a big living room downstairs. The inn was the centerpiece of the village for over 70 years. It had a rough-and-tumble history, surviving several boom-and-bust cycles, and continued to function as a hotel until 1974, when the U.S. Coast Guard purchased it and converted it into a Coast Guard station.

When the Brattons left town, they sold The Albion Inn to the Cheatem sisters from North Carolina, who then sold it to the Edney sisters several years later. When Joe Guthrie married Bessie Edney in 1912, they were given the hotel as a wedding present. The Guthries expanded the hotel to 24 bedrooms and, during the Florida Boom, business was fairly good. The dining room, which served family style, was open to the public, and yacht-owners tied their boats at the dock and ate at the hotel. The Ringlings, Sarasota's most famous residents, were occasional guests for dinner. Guthrie had several charter boats to take guests out fishing, and during the winter season, sportsmen and fishermen from around the country stayed at the hotel.

But when the boom went bust in the late 1920s, the hotel business just about died completely. It barely limped along during the 1930s and 1940s. Mr. and Mrs. Andrew Spolata, from Chicago, bought the inn from Joe in the late 1940s, but couldn't make a go of it, and in 1952 they sold it to August Antilla and his wife.

The Antillas began renovating and modernizing the hotel. They installed 14 bathrooms and placed ads in *The Saturday Review of Literature*, hoping to attract artists, writers, clergy, and university professors. As a result, The Albion Inn experienced a mini-revival during the 1950s.

For local people, the hotel was their major source of communication with the outside world. The hotel had the first telephone in town and, in later years, the first radio. Young girls went there to listen to popular music on the radio, practice the forbidden popular dances, and dream of Rudolph Valentino and other Hollywood stars. It was at the hotel that Cortez fishermen rubbed shoulders with Yankee businessmen and professors, heard discussions about politics and current events, and formed their opinions about the world.

Cortez's isolation decreased dramatically in 1908 when the Holmes Construction Company began building "the old shell road" to Bradenton. Julian Taylor, who was eight years old at the time, remembered the excitement. "The county contracted with Holmes Construction Company to build the road, and they come down here with about 25 mules and a crew of colored men to work them, and they rented Mrs. Bratton's big barn to keep the mules in. They started hauling shell from the old shell mound, and they made a little nine-foot road from here out about three miles to where 86th Street is today. Then they ran out of money, so it was just a grade from there on."

The shell road was finally paved in 1930, and since then has been called the hard road by many Cortez old-timers. Today, with traffic backed up bumper-to-bumper on Cortez Road, they still call it the hard road, but now the term describes what it's like trying to drive on it, not what it's made of.

Life was hard for the people of Cortez at the turn of the century. Drinking water was one of their major worries. "Rainwater was all the water we had here, and nothing but rainwater," said Toodle. "Grandma and Grandpa Fulford had a big rainwater tank, and the water would run from that tank into a wooden cistern. The cistern had a wooden cover, and the sides were built up so you could lower a bucket on a long rope. They kept it screened to keep the mosquitoes from getting in there and laying eggs, but we must have drank a million wiggletails [mosquito larvae] anyway. People went for years without ever cleaning them out. In a rainy season, the water would fill and overflow and keep it kind of fresh, but then in a drought the tank would be absolutely dry."

L. J. C. Bratton put down the first artesian well at The Albion Inn and, during droughts, he would let people come down and fill their buckets. But when the tanks ran dry, Cortez also depended on "the Halbert airlines" to supply water. Uncle Henry Halbert, an old mountaineer from Kentucky, made his living hauling water and firewood for Cortez families.

"I used to help Uncle Halbert in the mornings before school," said Man Adams. "He'd go out to a little sulfur-water spring in his horse and wagon and fill up 50-gallon barrels with water. He'd haul 100 gallons of water for a dollar—50 cents a barrel. I'd work with him a couple of hours before school, dipping water or cutting wood. He had a great big cross-cut saw, must have been eight-foot long, and he'd say, 'Boy, quit riding that saw!' I'd do anything to make a dime." Upon hearing that story, his sister Toodle added: "Yeah, Man would do anything to get out of school."

All of the cooking was done on wood stoves, until kerosene stoves gradually replaced them in the 1930s. They were also used for heating the houses in winter. "Most of the older houses had fireplaces, but they also had wood-burning heaters," said Toodle. "In our big old house, there was only one fireplace and that was in my Grandma's bedroom, of all places. We'd freeze to death in the upstairs bedrooms. Oh, it was cold! There was no heat whatsoever. Sometimes we'd heat up a brick and put it at the foot of the bed to keep our feet warm. Looking back, it seems like it was a lot colder then than it is now. I really think it was colder, because I know we would wear heavy clothes—flannel petticoats and that sort of thing, and you'd die now with all that on. And we weren't allowed to shed those heavy clothes until May. That was when winter was over and we could go swimming."

The rugged climate gave rise to another plague of Cortez life: skeeters. "Oh, the bugs!" said Miss Lela. "I tell you, if the mosquitoes were as bad now as they were then, I don't think anybody would stay here. We had screens on the windows, but sometimes the skeeters were so thick you couldn't see out the screens."

Lacking modern insect repellents to chase them away, the people relied on Bee Brand Insect Powder. Blue Fulford remembered: "At night, Aunt Lela would go around the house with big old clam shells and put Bee Brand Insect Powder in the shells and light it. The smoke would drive the mosquitoes away so you could get a little bit of sleep. If you didn't have that, you'd light an old rag to make some smoke and drive those little fellers away."

Diseases were a constant problem. Between drinking wiggletails in the rainwater and being bitten by the hordes of adult mosquitoes, malaria and impetigo were common occurrences. Ringworm and pinworms were part of everyone's childhood. There were major outbreaks of typhoid fever and tuberculosis in Cortez, as well as a major flu epidemic in 1918 that killed several people. "The flu epidemic just killed people like flies, because they didn't know anything to do for it," said Toodle. "If you got it, it was almost sure death."

The nearest hospital was the Gordon Keller Hospital in Tampa, which could only be reached by boat. The journey itself—in an open boat in bad weather—was credited with killing a number of people, including my great-uncle Clyde Fulford.

But despite the hardships, by 1920 things were looking up for Cortez. The general optimism that had infected the rest of the country at the end of World War I had begun to trickle down to Cortez. The local people had good reason to be optimistic. The introduction of gasoline engines had greatly increased the fishermen's mobility and thus increased their catches. An expanding national economy would certainly bring a better price for their fish. The Florida Boom was bringing more and more people to the beaches and, in 1920, a sure sign of progress appeared right outside their front doors: the county road department began work on a bridge to connect Cortez with Anna Maria Island. On every front, life was getting better and better.

All of the optimism ended on 23 October 1921. On that day, an unnamed and unannounced hurricane swept out of the southwest with 75-mile-per-hour winds and eight- to ten-foot seas, and completely destroyed the Cortez waterfront. What began as a slow rain on Saturday afternoon ended on Tuesday morning with the entire village flooded and much of it washed away. Gone were all of the fish houses, netspreads and fish camps, the Cortez "shopping center," the landing for the steamer, both grocery stores, the post office, the half-completed bridge to Anna Maria, and the front porch of The Albion Inn. Many of the fishing boats were sunk, most of the nets were lost or ruined. All that was left was an eerie maze of pilings and twisted stobs marking the spots where buildings had stood the day before.

The shoreline was in shambles and so was the rest of Cortez. Houses had been floated off their blocks and washed as much as 200 feet from their original locations. Ironically, one of the few structures still standing was the outhouse behind M. H. Brown's store, which was always tipped over by the youngsters on Halloween. Brown's store was flattened but the outhouse still stood.

Without a hurricane-tracking system to warn them of the storm's approach, the villagers were caught completely by surprise. As the winds and waves increased during the day, most of those living close to shore were forced to flee. They bundled up some belongings, loaded the women, children, and elders aboard skiffs, and the men pulled the boats down the flooded streets to the Cortez school. When the school was filled, they pulled the skiffs further down Cortez Road towards Bradenton. Townspeople had driven out to help and gave the villagers rides into town. Some of those who lived back from the shoreline stayed in their homes. My great-grandfather Capt. Billy Fulford climbed aboard his boat, *The Hustler*, set the anchor, and rode out the storm unharmed.

When the people returned to their homes Tuesday morning, the damage was appalling. My great-aunt Kate Pearson remembered the day. She was living with Elverton and Lizzie Green in a big house on the bay at the time. When the water reached the house, they went to the school, but it was already filled, so they had to go to town and spend the night in a hotel. She recalled their return to Cortez: "The next morning the sun was shining just as pretty as you please. When we got back to Cortez, it was a terrible mess. A big oak tree had fallen on our house, and we couldn't even get in until they cut it down. We had put the chickens in the house before we left, trying to save them, so you can imagine what the house looked like. The water had just gone everywhere. All of Cortez was strung out everywhere: clothes, cans of food, meat was washed all over the place, nets and ropes were scattered everywhere. It was terrible."

Henry Hibbs and John Saverese, outsiders who owned the only two fish houses in Cortez before the storm, packed up and left town. Local fishermen quickly took their places. "Judge" Millis opened the Star Fish Company, the first fish house operating after the storm; Jess Williams followed suit.

The tattered nets were pulled off pilings and mended; boats were repaired or rebuilt. As soon as they could afford it, families had their houses jacked up and set back on their blocks. Joe Guthrie moved the post office and his store into The Albion Inn, and M. H. Brown reopened his store in another building. Slowly, life returned to normal.

Since that day, the history of Cortez has been divided into two epochs: before the '21 storm and after it. On that day, the people of Cortez were reminded of the delicate balance of nature that must be maintained if one is to survive on the vulnerable shores of the Gulf. They have never forgotten it. Today, with the narrow barrier islands of Longboat Key and Anna Maria Island covered end-to-end with condominiums and resort hotels, their gleaming edifices taunting the winds to come again, the lesson of the

'21 storm has not been lost on Cortez. "If a storm like that hit the beach now, there weren't be nothing left," said Miss Lela. And there wouldn't.

There wasn't much left of Cortez on 24 October 1921, but the village rebuilt and grew steadily throughout the decade. The children of the pioneer settlers reached adulthood, married each other, and, in many cases, built houses on lots adjoining their parents. They began to give birth to the next generation. The slow influx from North Carolina continued, bringing new settlers throughout the 1920s and on into the 1930s.

The bridge to Anna Maria had to be started over, but it was eventually completed and opened with great fanfare in 1922. Wholesale fish dealers began replacing their old runboats with Model T trucks to haul Cortez's fish to the Tampa markets. By the late 1930s, trucks had replaced them altogether. Grocery stores in town began making weekly deliveries. Jess Williams bought the first Model T in Cortez and, as other families acquired them, the movies, music, and shopping of Bradenton became accessible.

Another milestone was achieved when Henry Norman, the Cortez mailman at one time, went to Chicago to be trained as an electrician. When he installed the wiring in Miss Lela and Uncle Neriah's new house on the shore in 1925, he was providing electricity to the village for the first time.

Other modern conveniences followed. Burns Taylor installed Cortez's first indoor toilet in his home. A bowling alley was built across the street from The Albion Inn. Several families bought hand-cranked victrolas, bringing the music of Tin Pan Alley to Cortez via 78 rpm records. But while the rest of the country was shimmying to the Charleston and drinking bathtub gin, Cortez youngsters were creating their own version of the Roaring Twenties back home. The rebellious spirit of the 1920s was pitted against the Prohibition Amendment, ratified in 1919, and the opposing social forces battered away at each other for a decade. If Cortez was any indication, and it probably was, Prohibition lost . . . and lost big.

"Shoot, every other house was making home brew," said Gene Fulford. "And the ones that wasn't, we used to tease them something awful. We used to have a lot of fun with one old lady, Mrs. Pringle, who was very religious and a leader in the Church of God. Us boys used to go up just for meanness and knock on her door and say, 'I hear you got some good moonshine.' She'd say, 'I'm gonna call the law if you don't get away!' But there was a bunch that did make home brew, and they was getting ten cents a bottle. They kept making it stronger and stronger, putting a little bit more yeast and a little bit more sugar, until it'd be so strong that it'd blow the cap off half the time if it wasn't good and cold. But, oh, it'd make you drunk if you drunk enough of it."

If the home-brewed beer wasn't strong enough, the moonshine certainly was, and Cortez had its share of stills out in the woods east of town. It also had its share of rumrunners who would sneak out at night, just like the drug smugglers do today, and bring in a load of contraband whiskey from Bimini. "Cortez had its rumrunners, and it went on for years," said Earl Guthrie. "It didn't go out at the end of Prohibition, by any means. See, that stuff from Bimini was better stuff than that old mountain dew. That moonshine was made out in the swamps in iron pots and it was run through old rusty iron pipes, but that stuff from Bimini was made like whiskey ought to be. There were boats that didn't do nothing else but run whiskey. And didn't nobody try to stop them either. There was one feller over on Longboat Key, he'd make a run to Bimini and then come in at night to avoid the Coast Guard cutters, tie his boat up at the dock, and go home to bed. His boat'd lay there all night and the next day till he took it on to St. Petersburg. That was headquarters for most of that stuff."

They could get their whiskey at home, but Cortez youngsters had to go elsewhere for their dancing. They would all pile into a Model T Ford and drive to the Lafayette Dance Hall in Sarasota or to The Pagoda, a dancehall on the beach that operated from the mid-twenties until it burned down in the mid-thirties.

However, the quality of life in Cortez has always hinged on the closeness of its people rather than on outside recreational activities, and informal socializing has always been Cortez's favorite pastime. "It used to be that at night, after supper, everyone went and visited other people," said Toodle. "That's what you did—visit. There wasn't anything else to do. Families would sit outside if the mosquitoes weren't eating them up and visit with the people walking up and down the street. And if anyone was sick, we'd go over to see what we could do to help them."

Nobody ever locked their doors in Cortez and, as Eva Capo described it, "it was like one big family." On weekends, families would walk across the Cortez Bridge to the beach, where for a dime they could rent a cubicle to change into their bathing suits. They'd have picnics on the beach, take long walks along the shore, or go fishing from the bridge.

There were also formal social events that brought the people even closer together. "We used to have what we called the 'community Christmas tree' every year, which was a great big Christmas party for the whole community," said Toodle. "We'd hold it in the community church or down at the schoolhouse. Everybody would come and each young girl would make a box supper and auction them off. You weren't supposed to let anyone know which box was yours, but of course if you wanted some boy to buy it, you'd let him know, 'that blue one up there is mine.' The boys would bid on them and whoever bought your box, you'd go eat supper with him. The last one I ever remember, I had fixed my box and I had somebody special that I wanted to buy it, but old man Aaron Bell outbid everybody for it, and I sat there and cried and cried. Poor old Aaron was bighearted and wanted to donate his part, you know, but he had no business buying a young girl's box supper."

There were big political rallies in Cortez, too. "Oh my, that was a great thing," said Toodle. "We'd have fish fries down at the school and all of the candidates would come down to get our vote. Aunt Molly Halbert, Uncle Halbert's wife, she was a great politician. In 1928, Herbert Hoover was running against Al Smith, who was a Catholic, and Aunt Molly thought that was terrible. Oh, I thought that poor old soul was going to lose her mind if Al Smith got the presidency. She thought that would be the last straw. So she put up a big sign in her front yard for Herbert Hoover, and the kids would go tear it down just to aggravate her."

Hoover won, of course, and the next year the country was plunged into the Great Depression. Cortez was swept down with the tide. The stock market crash on Wall Street didn't mean too much to the village, but when the mullet disappeared in 1929, hard times had arrived.

Although mullet were only bringing a cent a pound—a cent-and-a-half after the fishermen organized a local union and got it raised—the fishermen could still bring in some money. So when the mullet suddenly vanished, it was bad. Earl Guthrie described it: "It was so bad you could leave Cortez on the flood tide, go across Palma Sola Bay and right on across the mouth of the Manatee River, past Terra Cia and McGill's Bay, past Joe's Island, right on up to Bishop's Harbour, be there on the high water, turn around and come back the same way, go across to Anna Maria and down the Gulf side of Longboat Key and back to Cortez and never see the first mullet jump. Not the first one, day after day after day. Now, son, you can figure fish were scarce."

No one has ever explained what happened to the fish. "There was a lot of fools that done a lot of guessing, but it was just some silly mess like fools will do," said Earl. Some Cortez fishermen went other places to try their luck—south to Gasparilla or to the east coast of Florida—but it was no better there. Many of them had to quit fishing and find other work—any kind of work.

"Son, we got up and got a job," said Earl. "We didn't care how many hours or how much it paid, we'd just get out and get a job. If it paid a dollar, that was a dollar. People quit fishing and went everywhere and did everything. I went up to Palma Sola and got a job building the seawall, and when that was done I helped put in the waterworks." Others got jobs in town. Several Cortez men joined the Civilian Conservation Corps.

They struggled. They ate mullet twice a day. They traded fish for "taters and maters" with farmers in East Manatee. They helped each other. They never lost their fierce pride or their independent spirit. And they made it. Slowly, about 1938 or 1939, the mullet started picking up again, coming back in force in 1940.

That bleak period, from 1929 to 1939, is looked back on as one of the proudest times in the history of Cortez. Over and over again people told me, not boastfully but with quiet determination, that "Cortez was the only place in the whole country that didn't get a dollar of federal assistance during the Depression." They didn't make that claim themselves. Robert Ripley of *Ripley's Believe It Or Not* wrote it in his syndicated comic strip. While others starved and went homeless during those terrible years, Cortez people did have food in their bellies and a place to go home to. And of course, they had each other.

The Depression didn't really end in Cortez until Pearl Harbor, as was true everywhere else. After the Japanese attacked, 48 Cortez men joined the service. That total included just about every able-bodied man in the village who wasn't too old or didn't have a large family to support. Three of them, J. M. Campbell, Sonny Posey, and Warren Bell, were killed; several others were wounded.

With the local boys gone, a motley crew of outsiders drifted into Cortez to man the fishing boats. "These characters came in here that didn't know the first thing about fishing," said Toodle. "We used to say they were ordered out of the Sears and Roebuck catalog. One of them got a nickname, and it stayed with him: Brand New. He didn't know one end of the boat from the other."

During the war years, the mullet returned with a vengeance. More fish were caught in Cortez during the war than any other time, before or since. In 1945, the last year of the war, Florida produced a record 55 million pounds of mullet. By comparison, in 1977, the state produced only 21.6 million pounds.

When the war ended, the Cortez boys returned from the victory parades and went straight to the picketlines. The share fishermen had affiliated with the Seafarers International Union and, with the dealers selling record numbers of fish, the union demanded a higher price. The Cortez GIs joined the massive wave of strikes that swept the country at the end of the war and refused to work until they got their price. When they finally went back to work, they did it in a bigger way than ever before. Wartime profits had enabled the dealers to buy huge stopnetting outfits, and catches of 100,000 pounds in one strike were not uncommon. Stopnetting promised to revolutionize the fishing industry in Florida.

But two swift events killed that promise. In 1947, the first "Red Tide" epidemic hit the Gulf Coast of Florida. A microscopic organism, unexplained at the time, killed millions and millions of fish. In Cortez, they ran nets in front of the fish houses to keep out the dead, rotting fish. Then, in 1953, the Florida legislature outlawed stopnetting. "I was fishing with Tink Fulford then," said Wyman Coarsey, "and one day coming back across the bay I asked him, 'Tink, what's gonna happen to us when they outlaw stopnetting?' He said, 'Well, we're just gonna starve to death together, Hunkie.' I told him, 'Tink, I ain't gonna starve to death.' I went to Bradenton and got a job driving an oil truck, and I did it for 18 years. I had a bunch of kids coming every year, and I had to get with it."

Others quit fishing in 1953 when the Red Tide struck again and almost wiped out the Cortez fishing industry. "I quit fishing and got a job on a shrimp boat going to the Yucatan," said Blue Fulford. "But we got over there and got in a hurricane, and I got so seasick that I promised the good Lord that he wouldn't ever have to worry about me again if he'd just get me back home."

But as they had in earlier times, the people of Cortez survived. With stopnetting outlawed, the fishermen fell back on gillnetting and seining, although they would occasionally sneak out and put in a stop, despite the law.

The country had entered "the quiet '50s," and Cortez followed along. The villagers contributed their fair share to the postwar baby boom, with the numerous trips to Manatee Memorial Hospital signaling the end of the era of homebirths and midwives in Cortez. They flirted with the newfangled technological marvels that were dazzling the housewives of America: electric toasters, electric mixers, automatic washing machines and electric dryers, hair curlers, hair dryers, and vacuum machines. Women began driving into Bradenton to do their grocery shopping at big supermarkets instead of patronizing the local stores. On the political front, they watched impassively as Senator Joseph McCarthy battled his phantom "red tide of communism" in the state department and on the university campuses. Cortez had a more immediate red tide on its hands.

The new electronic media brought Cortez further into the mainstream of American life than the village had ever been before. The youngsters, who finished the eighth grade at the Cortez school and then rode the bus to town for junior and senior high, became increasingly influenced by national trends and fads. Boys started pegging their jeans, greasing back their hair in wavy ducktails, and spending long hours bent over the engine compartments of 1956 Chevys. Girls began applying thick layers of rouge, powder, and eye shadow to their faces, topping it off with one perfect beauty mark on the left cheek, and spending long hours bent over the family telephone, talking to boyfriends and girlfriends in town. On weekday nights, they addled their brains watching the adventures of Ozzie and Harriet, Beaver Cleaver, and Dobie Gillis on the boob tube. And on Friday and Saturday nights, they were hanging out at the A&W Root Beer Stand or the Burger Queen in town, sneaking into the Trail Drive-In Theatre with a trunk full of giggling stowaways, or drag racing on Cortez Road and 75th Street, with Elvis Presley crooning over the car radio.

Yet, despite outward signs that Cortez was becoming assimilated into middle-class America, it was still different. Cortez teenagers might dress like the kids from the suburban neighborhoods that were springing up around Bradenton, Cortez housewives might buy the same name-brand groceries as women from town, but below the surface they were vastly different.

They were different because Cortez was still a fishing village, and no external appearances could hide the fact that its families made their living doing sweaty, smelly, dirty, backbreaking work. Cortez kids were proud enough and tough enough to fight anyone who made fun of them, but still, they were set apart at school—in the social clubs, on the homecoming court, and at the junior-senior prom. In the community, Cortez adults were noticeably absent from the Rotary Club, the Junior Women's League, and the Chamber of Commerce.

By 1967, the differences had become more obvious. The first big wave of Northern immigrants and retirees began settling in Manatee County in the 1950s; with them came a fleet of dredge boats and bulldozers that would eventually push Cortez to the brink of destruction. The battle lines were drawn that year. Cortez Road, formerly a seven-mile stretch of mangrove swampland and scrub forest, had become littered with housing projects almost all the way to Cortez. The forests were gone and, more alarmingly, so were most of the mangroves. Developers dredged out networks of finger canals along the shoreline and built white, concrete-block houses along both sides of the canals. Small boat docks were built in front of each house for the family speedboat. Water skiing, sportfishing, and joyriding were right out the back door, through the canal, and out into the bay.

Such dredging directly effected the Cortez livelihood. Because mullet feed and spawn in shallow mangrove estuaries, they had no place to go but into the finger canals when the swamps were destroyed. Cortez fishermen had no choice but to follow. The people in the white concrete houses, who had decided to move south after reading real estate brochures about "a Florida paradise," had never pictured Cortez fishermen in old straw hats and ragged boats as part of it. So, after 100 years of battling the elements and the tides, Cortez discovered a new and unfamiliar enemy: anti-netting legislation.

In 1967, a coalition of developers and neighborhood associations proposed legislation to ban commercial fishing in Manatee County within 1,700 yards of any shoreline, which would have included almost the entire county. Similar bills were proposed elsewhere in the state. The people of Cortez were fighting a powerful enemy in an arena that they knew nothing about: big-time power politics. Out of desperation, they joined the Organized Fishermen of Florida and began speaking out at county commission meetings, reading environmental studies on the effects on the fish of pollution and dredging, and lobbying in the Florida legislature. They learned how to play the game, and they won some battles.

Despite the victories, the 1970s was a decade of slow retreat for Cortez. Manatee County had become one of the fastest growing areas in the country. Tourists continued to pour in and settle. Housing developments went up faster than ever, with perhaps a slightly more deft hand on the throttle of the dredge boats. High-rise condominiums, the ugly brother of the housing projects, got a toehold on Cortez Road and pressed ever closer to the village. The white sand beaches and stubby forests of Anna Maria Island and Longboat Key were obliterated by condos, tennis clubs, and shopping villas. With all this, too, came the smuggling—big-money financiers offering to pay local boys more money for one night of hauling dope than they could expect to make in years of fishing.

Sitting in her kitchen, Miss Lela looks back at the history of Cortez and wonders about the future. She still laughs recalling the pranks that were pulled on Halloween and the apple-bobbing at children's birthday parties. She still remembers the visits late at night to talk with sick ones and visit with relatives. And she worries about what all of these years and memories will mean if this village is no more, or if the future steals from it the specialness it once had.

"I miss that part of Cortez, like we used to have it," she said. "I won't never get used to it being so different. I won't. It's hard to tell what's going to happen, but I don't feel like it will be anything good. Not with so many people selling their houses and all the outsiders coming in. And that's just what they want us to do—leave. They've been trying for a long time to put up high-rises and all that. I wish that was one thing, if we could prevent it, that we would. I hope we can keep it like it is."

She turned and looked out the window, at the bay that she sees no more, and then, in a quiet, firm voice: "I'll keep trying as long as I'm alive."

Chapter 4

"Son,
Them Days Was Rough"

IT LOOKED LIKE A ROGUE'S gallery down at the dock. The old-time fishermen were out in force. There was Earl Guthrie, 81, pale after a week in the hospital following a heart attack; Man Adams, 77, wearing an old cap pushed back on his head and talking about the '21 storm; Gene Fulford, 67, hunkered down on a pile of net, squinting his face in his own familiar way; and Marvin Carver, 65, leaning in with his elbows on his knees.

They were talking low and steady about the past, sometimes one at a time, more often two or three at once. They moved easily from topic to topic, event to event, in a way that required none of the conventions of speech to guide their way. These four men, who have lived and worked with each other for more than 60 years, were storytelling—one of the greatest forms of Southern culture.

There are other old-timers who weren't there: Charlie Guthrie, their elder statesman, was laid up in the county hospital with a broken hip, and Woodrow Green, Manly Bell, Grey Fulford, OK Drymond, Hal and Goose Culbreath, Riley Lewis, and Bob Knowlton were among the missing. There had been many more.

These men sitting on the front of the Fulford Fish Company dock were the living links with a kind of fishing that is gone forever. It was a way of life that exacted a heavy toll in sweat and blood, and the marks of it show—skin cancers, bad feet, bum knees, circulatory problems, blown valves in the heart. They have paid their dues. Now they can slouch on the front of the dock and drift easily from story to story: about slot machines on the beach, moonshiners and legendary drunks, big hauls of fish, and the old days in North Carolina.

These are men who in earlier years poled miles and miles each day across every bayou and basin of Sarasota Bay, leaning on an eight-foot poling oar to shove themselves and their skiff across the water, and spent day after day in small, open boats out on the rough waters of the Gulf, either baking and burning in the glare of the sun or cramped together around an old seven-horsepower engine in the dead of winter, trying to share enough body heat to warm themselves against a nor'wester gale. These are men who worked 16-hour stretches in stopnetting operations, pulling miles of nets around mangrove islands, bowing their backs and straining their numbed shoulders against the weight of the bay on each pull, and cursing futilely as a thousand mosquitoes fought for their blood.

Earl Guthrie kicked it off: "I tell you son, there's a whole lot more to learn about fishing than people might have any idea. You have to make a study of fishing just like you do farming or anything else. In other words, you got to learn the bottom. You got to know when to fish, where you can strike and where you can't, where the fish feed and where they don't. You got to learn what kind of nets to use, you got to learn to take advantage of the tides—there's times if the tide was making right, I'd go to one place, and if the tide ain't right, you needn't be through there 'cause you ain't gonna catch nothing. It's something you got to constantly study if you're gonna make a success of it. Fishing ain't no easy life. Never let nobody tell you that, if they do, say 'Well, sir, you just weren't no fisherman.' "

Man Adams picked it up when Earl paused: "About the time I got out of school and started fishing, they had got motors in most of the fishing boats. But even after the motors come in, Granddaddy still had sails for auxiliary power. All they had was these seven-horsepower Myannis engines, and you take a little old engine like that and start towing four skiffs and that was slow going. So he'd put sails onto them when he got a fair wind, and they'd help him come on home. I remember one Sunday they were having a Church of Christ meeting down in Sarasota, and the whole family piled into Granddaddy's launch. He had her loaded! But he cranked up that seven-horsepower Myannis and put that sail onto her. They had a good northwest breeze, and she was laying right over there on her side and making good time going down there. They had sand bags so if she got to tilting over too far they'd throw those sand bags off one side to keep the lee side from going under. Yeah, they were just a'gettin' it that day."

Man was talking about the days in Cortez when wind and oar were the only power. It's hard to imagine it today, when giant diesels power the big launches and the flick of a starter switch on an outboard motor can send a kicker boat hurtling across the bay. But in the early days, they went by sail or by hand.

The sailing skiffs, called skipjacks, were 16 to 18 feet long, built with a rounded bottom called a dead rise. The same designs are still used today on the North Carolina coast. Julian Taylor, 86, who spent years as a marine mechanic in Cortez, was old enough to remember the sailboats. "Old man Sam Cobb on Anna Maria built a lot of those boats, and so did Mr. Walter Howland, Uncle Neriah Taylor, and an old man named Castenas. They built the front thwart out of a heavy piece of wood about two inches thick and a foot wide, going across her, and they had knees into her where she wouldn't give. That was part of her strength. Then they'd cut a hole about four inches wide, called the stopping, and down in the keel there was another recessed hole where the bottom of the mast set.

"In the middle of the boat, they had a case for the centerboard," he continued, "and they had a rudder on the back with hooks on it where a net wouldn't catch onto it. They made the sails out of canvas—ten-ounce duck they called it. They had sprit sails on them so they could take down the whole works real fast when they struck a bunch of fish. They had a long pole, the sprit, that held out the point of the sail. They'd pull out the clips that held the sprit, roll the sail up around the mast, take the mast and lay it down in the boat with the sprit alongside it. Then they'd pick up the rudder yoke, roll up the tiller lines, unhook the rudder and lay all that down, too. They'd grab their poling oar and run the net out. Buddy, them guys could handle it so quick, it didn't take long."

There would be four skipjacks in a crew, with one man in each boat. They would sail out to the fishing grounds together and then take down the sails and pole. "When they got out there and caught a load of fish and a calm came up, well, they had to pole her all the way home," said Julian.

The sailboat era came to an end just after 1900, when Capt. Nate Fulford installed a four-horsepower, water-cooled Barker engine in one of his skipjacks. "That old thing didn't have a muffler on it, and when he started it before daylight, it made the awfulest racket you ever heard," said Julian. "It would pop and snap and wake up everybody in Cortez. But after he got that engine, the others commenced to getting bigger motors all along."

At that time, they were mostly gillnetting or seining and, although the equipment has changed drastically, the same basic methods are used today. Man Adams explained the principle: "In the spring, the mullet are small, then they get a little bigger in the summer and when they get roe in the fall, they're even bigger. So you start out with a net that has a three-inch mash and then you have a three-and-a-half-inch mash in the summer, and right on up as the fish get bigger. In the fall, you use a four-and-an-eighth-inch mash when the big red roe mullet are running.

"If you've got four skiffs in a crew then they'll form-off, with one guy on the left and one on the right; the captain is offshore on the head and then you've got the inside guy. You let the fish come down and then all four skiffs run out their nets and just shut them up. Once you get the net around them, you start getting the compass drawed up, then you run your boats across the middle and beat on the side [of the skiff] with the poling oar to scare them into the net. Once they've gilled in the net, you pull it in and clear it out."

At certain times of the year, the mullet will school-up in the Gulf and run down the beach, and then the fishermen use a beach seine to catch them. A seine is about 500 yards long with a deep, V-shaped pocket in the middle. The net has small mashes that the fish can't swim through. When a school of mullet starts down the beach, the boat races to get in front of them, and a couple of men jump overboard and carry one end of the net ashore. The boat circles back around the fish, and the rest of the crew carries the other end of the net ashore. They pull both wings of the seine onto the beach, forcing the fish into the "bunt" of the pocket, then haul the pocket to shore and bail the fish out of it and into the boat.

Stopnetting was first developed in the 1920s although it wasn't widely used until the late 1940s. The fishermen surround a small island or close off a narrow cut of water with as much as 10,000 yards of net. Shallow nets are placed near the shore; deep nets are run offshore; and a bank net is run along the beach. The nets are placed at high tide, usually in the middle of the night and, when the tide starts going out the next morning, the fishermen begin working the nets down; the fish are forced out of shallow water and into the nets. A haul net, or seine, is used to bring them ashore.

Stopnetting has always been controversial, as Man explained: "When you put in a stop in the bay, you catch everything that's up there. You don't just catch the mullet—you catch trout and redfish and flounder and sheephead and all the catfish and pinfish. If there's any little mullet in there, well, naturally you're going to catch them and they'll be dead before you get them out. You can't help it. That's the bad thing about stopnetting. But people get the wrong idea—they think the fisherman's out there destroying all the fish, and that's just not so. That's your livelihood, and if you kill that little fish then you're not gonna have no big ones."

Stopnetting was so controversial that it led to a territorial war in Cortez between the stopnetters and the gillnetters when it was first introduced. "It was just like the cattlemen and the sheepherders out west," said Grey Fulford. The war between the two camps was the most violent episode in Cortez's history until the late 1970s, when drug smuggling brought murder to the village.

"It got pretty rough at times," said Woodrow Green. "There was never no one killed over it. Most everybody was handy with a gun, but they were never used. Now they tore up some nets, burnt some nets with acid, set some afire, and others was cut all up. My daddy was one of the stopnetters, and he had one of his seines tore up. They just taken a butcher knife and worked it over. I was pretty young, but I can remember sitting up with Poppa in his camp one night, guarding our gear with a shotgun."

The local row came to a head in 1928, when Joe Fulford's house was dynamited. He was a gillnetter, and the stopnetters were accused of setting it. Three young men were arrested but later released. "It tore up his bed and the wall in his bedroom pretty good," said Woodrow, "and there was a pretty good size hole in the floor. But he was up and about after that. I don't think it injured the old man where he had to go to the doctor or anything."

The battle raged on for a while longer until the stopnetters folded—some quit because of the intimidation and others because their nets were confiscated by the courts. But it never died out completely, making several strong comebacks in later years.

No description of the different types of fishing can ever accurately reflect the hardships of doing it. Not only was it physically demanding, fishing also exposed the men to the raw elements; their open boats, the only types used, offered them no protection from sun or storm. These boats had no cabins, no cookstoves, and no cover from rain nor heat. Nonetheless, Cortez fishermen did give their boats gallant names: Jess Williams had *The Jack* and *The Spray*; Capt. Billy Fulford had *The Fish Hawk* and *The Hus-*

tler; Julius Mora had *The Nightingale*; Capt. Nate Fulford had *The Frying Pan*; and Joe Guthrie had *The 79* and *The Ace*.

"There wasn't a cabin boat in Cortez," said Earl Guthrie. "We just sat out there and roasted." Roast was exactly what they did, and if all the skin cancers that have been taken off Cortez fishermen were laid end-to-end, they'd stretch all the way to Miami. The agony is obvious in some of the old photographs: a bunch of sodden, blistered men hunched up in the bow of their boat, coming home after a day of fishing, with the weariness burned into their eyes. Very likely, they had been wet and baked dry four times over during the day, and each time the salt spray was basted deeper in their skin, the wind and sun assisting in this curing process. "If that salt spray hit you in the face and you didn't get it off, it'd burn you bad," said Man.

Eventually their skin toughened and took on a deep brown hue, but even then Cortez fishermen hid from the sun behind long-sleeved khaki shirts and under big straw hats. Unlike Florida's frenzied sun worshipers, who stoke their tans for hours at a time as they stretch out like corpses on the beach, nobody in Cortez shows off their tan.

When it wasn't burning hot, it was often raining, or even worse, blowing a nor'wester. "Oh, it was bad out in them open boats," said Gene Fulford. "'Bout the time you'd lay down in the stern of the boat to go to sleep, it'd start pouring down rain. We didn't have no cabin, and all we had was foul-weather gear—old leaky oilers—and maybe an old piece of canvas to put over our heads. One time, your Grandma Edith decided to make us some oilers that wouldn't leak. She made some regular white-cloth overalls and painted them with some old mess to keep the water out. In wintertime, they'd stand up stiff and, in summertime, they'd slip around on you. They stopped the leaking alright, but every one of us broke out with a rash from them oilers."

Nor'westers were what they dreaded the most. "If you run across Tampa Bay and it happened to come out a nor'wester, you just stayed over there until it calmed back down, if it was one day or a week," said Earl. "We didn't have no big boats you could get back [home] in. Have to walk out there on the shoals and pick up black conchs and roast them and eat them. I done that more than one time when we didn't have nothing else to eat."

Even worse than their lack of protection in those open boats, they had no communication of any kind. Their only warning system of approaching storms, or even hurricanes, was what their eyes told them, and sometimes that wasn't enough. Earl Guthrie had a narrow escape in the '21 hurricane that proved it:

"Before I moved here from North Carolina, I had worked and saved just enough to get me a train ticket: $20.13. I got down here and a week later the '21 storm hit and wiped me out. I was out fishing with Les Guthrie and it started getting rough. We didn't have any idea there was a hurricane coming. So we were way down by Sarasota and one of Les's boats stopped—the engine quit—and he told me to get in there and get it started and come on through Midnight Pass and catch up with them. So directly I got her cranked up and come on through the pass, and I guess I was the last man to ever come through Midnight Pass 'cause the storm closed it up.

"So finally I got up with them and we all got in this little camp out in the bay that Les had built up on stilts. We stayed in that camp and it kept getting rougher and rougher. Les left us and said he was gonna try to take the boats to shore to protect them. It kept getting rougher, and finally I said, 'Boys, if we don't get out of this camp we're all gonna get drownded.' There was a boat tied up not too far from the camp, and I told them we better make a swim for that boat. They didn't want to do it, but finally I took off my clothes and jumped out the window and started swimming for it, and then the rest of them came, too. The engine wouldn't start 'cause the batteries were wet, so we just cut the anchor rope and let her drift. We didn't know where we'd come ashore, but we knew the wind would blow us to the mainland. So we cut her loose and we went through islands and over islands and everything else. We come ashore and drifted through the woods pretty near to the highway. It was all water.

"When she went aground, we jumped out and turned her over and tied her to a tree. And there ain't never been no more sandspurs in one place than there was there. Every one of us was barefoot, with no clothes on but our underwear. I just had on a pair of underwear and a little old blue cord shirt, and when we were trying to get through those woods, I busted the seat out of my shorts. One guy had an old sweater and I asked him for it, and I wrapped it around me for pants. We come ashore in Osprey, down below Sarasota, and I knew old Walt Taylor, who lived down there, and that's how I walked up to his house, with that old sweater wrapped around me. And I had the only nickel in that whole bunch. When we was sitting in that camp, I saw a nickel laying on the floor and I picked it up. I was cutting the fool and I said, 'Well, boys, I got a nickel and I'm going to put it nearest to my heart.' I put it in my shirt pocket and after all that wild ride coming ashore, it was still there."

Earl and the crew finally made it back to Bradenton, where a stranger paid for their meal and a hotel room. When they returned to Cortez the next day, everything he owned had been washed away. "I'd a whole lot rather have been back where I come from, I'll tell you that," said Earl. "I'd never seen as bad a storm as that. I was broke and I didn't know many people. If I'd had another $20.13, I'd a been gone, that's for sure. Right now! But we was the first boat out fishing after the storm, just as soon as it calmed down, and we caught a bunch of fish and I made $98."

Winter compounded the problems of the Cortez fishermen in their open boats. Northern tourists might lay on the beach right on through January and February, but out on the water, with the wind blowing through their clothes, Cortez fishermen know the true strength of Florida's winters.

"One night in November we had caught a bunch of fish down there to the Pass," said Man. "Then we went on down the beach and made another haul and had about 5,000 altogether. While we was bailing them, Uncle Tink told me to go back and get the launch. So I went back and got the old *Ralph*, and stopped her and I throwed the anchor off the bow. I was gonna walk back aft and shove her stern in and put a stern anchor out, but I hit a slimy spot on the railing where we had bailed that first bunch of fish, and my feet went out from under me and I went overboard out there in about ten-foot of water. My hat even floated off. And it was cold there in November, and me wet all over! We went on down looking for more fish, and we went all the way to Big Sarasota Pass. Finally we went ashore on Siesta Key and built us a fire until daylight. I thought I was gonna freeze to death. It was rough back then, I tell you. We'd just have to get out there and shake and take it."

The fishermen's constant companions, come rain or heat, were the skeeters, catfish, and stingrays. The bugs were terrible in Cortez, but they were even worse around the mangrove islands in the bay. Hubert Horne, my second cousin, grew up in Cortez and fished there until he left for Chicago in 1946 to attend air conditioning school. The skeeters were one of the primary contributors to his decision to leave, providing their own unique form of vocational counseling.

"The night I decided I didn't want to be a fisherman I was in Perico Bayou, putting in a stop with Tater Few," said Hubert. "I was rolling moss out of the net 'cause the tide was going out and all this grass was coming up there. The stingrays were in and out of my legs, and the mosquitoes were literally sapping me dry, and I said to myself, 'There's gotta be a better way.' Tater came out, tied the boat to the cork line right in front of me, and said, 'Get in the boat and go on back and get something to eat. I'll roll that moss till you get back.' So I worked my way down to the boat, slid up in it, and he went over the side and a stingray got him right in the foot. I threw him up in the boat and went back to the launch and said, 'I know damn well there's a better way. There's gotta be.' I've often said that if there was somebody I really hated I'd take them to Perico Island, strip them naked and make them spend the night. They'd be dead the next morning. The skeeters wouldn't leave nothing but the skin and bones."

There weren't as many stingrays as there were mosquitoes, but they were more deadly. "Lacking the proper medication, a stingray barb could lay up a fisherman for as long as two or three months," said Blue Fulford. "I've seen holes rot out in men's legs big enough to drop a 50-cent piece in."

But as bad as the stingrays and skeeters were, there has never been a more hateful creature on the face of the earth than an old slimy saltwater catfish. Sometimes a crew would strike what they thought was a school of bluefish, only to hear a chorus of low grunting sounds trailing across the water—they had a net full of catfish. Now you can't just shake a catfish out of a gillnet. They wrap themselves up in it so tight that the only way to get them out is to slip your fingers under their fins, push down hard on the railing of the boat, and break off the fins at their roots one-by-one. Then you can unwind the catfish and chuck it overboard. If you slipped, the catfish would drive a fin deep into the palm of your hand, injecting enough bacteria and scum to make you retch and vomit all day. A catfish wound had to be soaked in hot water with baking soda or bleach to draw out the poison.

As a youngster, it would sometimes take me ten minutes to get a big channel cat out of the net. I was scared to death of them to begin with and barely had the strength to break off the fins. In the late 1960s, when marine biologists discovered walking catfish coming ashore on the Florida coast, crawling inland for several miles on their fins, I had nightmares for weeks. I expected to wake up late one night and hear a legion of grunting, whiskered catfish surrounding my house, seeking revenge for their fallen comrades. I've heard that some people fry saltwater catfish and eat them, but I feel the same way Woodrow Green does: "I don't believe I could eat one; I just hate them too much."

The terrible working conditions of commercial fishing in those days had to be multiplied by the seemingly endless hours that were spent doing it. It was work that never stopped. "There weren't no typical day or no set time to go out or come in," said Earl. "If we was lucky enough to be home when night come, we'd go to bed. Sometime during the night, lessen it was storming, we got up and went fishing. We may get back the middle of the day, or we may get back the next night, or we may be back two days later. Fish was scarce and we didn't have nothing but small boats to haul them in. One guy'd come in with a couple thousand pounds, that was about all they'd hold, and another guy'd come in with a boat load, and yonder another guy with a load and, at the end of the day, it don't amount to nothing. One of these boats today could carry them boats and their loads, too."

One of the most familiar scenes in Cortez occurred at four or five o'-clock each morning, as the fishermen, dressed in khaki pants and old flannel shirts, trudged barefoot down the streets on their way to the docks. In one hand, they carried a jar of cold coffee and in the other their "bucket," an old three-pound lard can with their lunch—fried mullet, cold biscuits, and guava jelly. "I can remember as a little feller sitting on the porch in the evenings and watching them walk back down the road, going home with their bucket and an empty coffee jar, and maybe carrying a couple of fish to take home and fry to put in it tomorrow," said Blue.

Some of the hardest work awaited the fishermen when they got home. After the fish were unloaded, they had to pour a lime solution on their nets and then spread them on the netspreads to dry. The nets were made of cotton or linen, and if they weren't limed each day and thoroughly dried, bacterial action from the saltwater would destroy them almost overnight.

Man Adams described the liming process: "When I was a kid, they used to get unslacked rock lime in wooden barrels. I seen Granddaddy knock the head out of one of them barrels and pour water into it, and that lime would start foaming and slacking. He'd have two barrels of nice, fluffy lime when he got through. But this doggone lime we used later on, before we got nylon nets, was put up in 100-pound bags for making plaster. And it would get into the pores of your skin. You'd go home and wash with soap and water and dry your hands and they'd turn white—that lime was in the pores. Oh boy, I used to hate that! But, of course, you had to get in there and do it. When I was stopnetting with Uncle Tink, we'd fish Monday through Friday, put in a different stop every night in a different place. He'd have 18 deep nets and about 40 shallow nets—that's 1,800 yards of deep net and 4,000 yards of shallow net. Plus the haul net and the seine. And I've seen him get as much as three 100-pound bags of lime and put it in them nets, and that was every week. We'd have a scow with the shallow nets in it, and we'd put a skiff alongside and dump a bag of lime in it, and a couple of guys would get on the side of her and about put her under with water. When the lime had slacked, we'd pull them nets off that scow and into that skiff, with one guy throwing lime on 'em, and a couple other guys on the other side pulling them onto the netspreads to dry."

As much as they hated to do it, regular liming was the only way to preserve the nets. "We'd lime them nets every time we'd come in from fishing and spread them like they was the last net in the world—which they was," said Gene Fulford. "We had what they called these old 920 cotton nets, and I'm not lying, after you fished them about two years, they'd get so stiff from the lime that when you ran them overboard, the horse-shoe crabs would crawl right up it. I'm not a-lying, you just ask Earl." Earl agreed.

Mending net was another thankless but necessary task. Each day the fishermen spent several hours mending the holes that had been chewed by crabs, sharks, or bluefish the night before. "All that net had to be drug out and limed and dried and mended and then pulled back on the boat to go again," said Wyman Coarsey. "If these boys today had to get out there like we did all day on them spreads, sitting up there on the rail and the sun beating down on you, and mend those nets, they'd never do it."

A fisherman's worst nightmare was to run a net overboard and have a school of bluefish or redfish "eat it out of the lines"—chew it up so badly that the cork and lead lines came loose. "One time I was bluefishing with Uncle Tink and we caught 1,700 pounds of them big blues," recalled Man Adams. "We hauled up there and they like to eat it out of the lines. When we got home and pulled that net out, Rowland Culbreath came by and said, 'What in the devil happened to that net?' I told him somebody throwed battery acid on it, and that's just exactly what it looked like, by golly. We tried to mend it, but it never was no good again."

The development of nylon and polypropylene nets in the late 1950s and early 1960s, and monofilament in the mid-1960s, made liming obsolete, and thereby eliminated much of the drudgery from the life of the commercial fisherman.

A fisherman had to be strong and durable to be a success in Cortez, but he also had to be smart. Some of the strongest and smartest were the captains, men like Capt. Billy Fulford, Capt. Nate Fulford, Capt. Jim Guthrie, Jess Williams, Charlie Guthrie—the earliest captains in Cortez. In later years, Millard Brown, Tink Fulford, Charlie Lewis, Julius Mora, Burns Taylor, John Fulford, Guy Fulford, Ray Guthrie, Kurt Johns, and Joe Capo captained the boats.

Most of the fishing stories in Cortez are about these captains. One who is still talked about is Jess Williams. He built a fish house in Cortez right after the '21 storm and owned the first Model T in the village. Jess Williams was a sport. He would dress up on Saturday night with a hard collar and a tie, put on a big hat, and make the rounds of the juke joints in Bradenton and Sarasota. He caught his share of fish, and he did it despite having a rotten seine most of the time.

"I fished with him for about ten years," said Hal Culbreath, "and he caught a lot of fish. We'd catch fish every day—mostly trout and sheephead and bottom fish. First time I ever went fishing with him, we went over to Egmont Key and caught 7,000 pounds of great big old bull redfish. And we always knew just how many strikes we had to make every day. We'd make five strikes every day. That was enough for him and he'd come home. But he always did keep a rotten seine."

Man Adams explained why: "He'd take his wife fishing with him and the guys would get back there and relieve themselves on his seine and not say anything. They couldn't just let go with his wife there, you know, and that would rot that net in a hurry. Oh, his seine was always rotten. One time him and Burns Taylor was out there and they seen about 25,000 mullet. Jess Williams run his seine around them and somebody told Burns Taylor, 'Cap'n, if you want any of these fish, you better put your seine in back of him. When we haul up, that seine Jess Williams has got will melt like ice cream.' And it did, it melted just like an ice cream cone. They hauled up and didn't have anything in his net."

Man remembered another incident: "Uncle Tink didn't ever go fishing much on Sunday night because of his crew—there was Grey Fulford, Dewey Capo, Gator Mora and me, and he knew he couldn't go because we'd all be drunk. But one time he went without me. Later on, Guy Fulford came by the house and asked me to go with him. We went down to

Big Pass and the wind breezed up, and I looked offshore and the sea was breaking. I saw a school of mullet out there; I believe there was a hundred thousand pounds! I said, 'Guy, looky off yonder at that school of mullet off there.' By golly, he always kept a good seine, and about that time Jess Williams come up out there. Guy told Jess, 'I'm gonna go ahead of them fish and strike them.' Jess said, 'Go ahead.' So we took off and that durn Jess Williams run there behind them and struck them going away from him. We backed him up and took all them fish in, and his net was so rotten that you'd go to pull on it and pull it in two. I mean them mullet about beat it to pieces. We caught 19,000 in our net, but if he'd left them fish alone, we'd a caught a hundred thousand.

"Well, we got most of them bailed and a norther' come up, and we seen it was too rough to come home up the bay, so we went up to a little nightclub called The Blue Lantern and called Cortez and told them to send two trucks to carry them fish home. We loaded them trucks and then went back to the beach 'cause there was still about 4,000 pounds in the seine. Well, that doggone Jess Williams had headed straight to Cortez! He left his seine, his crew, and everything! We waited around for a while but he didn't show up, and it was cold—in December and blowing a norther! So we went and built a fire on the beach, and we all like to freeze to death. Bud Wilson just had on dungarees and a little old shirt, and old man Cliff Harris got so cold he couldn't even light a cigarette—somebody had to light it for him. We stayed there all night. Some of us would lay down by the fire and the others would go look for firewood. When morning came and Jess Williams hadn't showed up, we put them fish and his crew and his seine on Guy's boat and headed home. We got to Cortez and here come old man Jess Williams, dressed up, collar and tie and everything, and he says, 'Boys, when you spread my seine, will you lime it for me?' I thought that was the most nerve. It made me so mad 'cause on top of everything else, we had to lime his net! And it already rotten!"

The early captains in Cortez ruled with an iron hand. Millard Brown, one of the best fishermen in Cortez in the 1930s and 1940s, was one of the toughest in the old school. "I fished with Millard Brown after World War II, and he was kinda tough," said Woodrow Green. "He was one of the ones you always called Cap'n. That was before the war—after the war, you didn't have to call them Cap'n no more. That brought them down some. But that was a big deal there, buddy boy. They was Cap'n to everybody. I'm telling you how it was. Just to show you how Millard Brown was, Gil-

bert Mora and Manly Bell was fishing with him, and they come in one day
and Millard said, 'You boys go home and get some dry clothes and something to eat, and the last one back's gonna be left.' And he was! Gilbert
Mora was left! And he was walking in sight of them and they left him.
Now that's how the Cap'n was. He was just bound to leave one of them
unless they all come together at the same time."

Millard Brown was a strong-willed man who caught his share of fish.
"Millard Brown didn't care if he put his seine overboard for one mullet or
for a hundred thousand," said Hubert Horne, whose father Shorty fished
with Brown for many years. "It didn't make no difference to him. If he saw
one mullet jump, his crew would strike and catch that one mullet. He was
after the almighty dollar and he was a hard worker to get it. His crew probably made more money than anybody in Cortez, week after week, but they
worked for it. My dad would work for him awhile and then get so fed up
he'd quit, go work for somebody else and, when he wasn't making enough
money, he'd go back to work for Millard."

As Woodrow said, World War II brought the old captains down a
notch, and after that some of the old ways died out. "They tell a story about
Claude Fulford—that's Mouldy—and Charlie Guthrie," said Toodle
Green. "Charlie was one of the old captains and when he pulled his boat
up, you better stand at attention. Well, Mouldy was a young boy and it
was his luck that one day he was stretched out in one of those old fish boxes,
having his RC Cola and moon pie. When Charlie pulled up to the dock,
Mouldy didn't jump up to greet him. Well, that didn't go well with Charlie at all, and he said something to Mouldy. Mouldy said back to him, 'You
just wait till I finish my lunch. I'm having my moon pie and my RC Cola.'
Oh boy! Charlie didn't like that at all!"

Some of the most important, and least appreciated, people in the fishing industry are the workers in the fish houses. In the old days, life wasn't
any easier for the fish-house men than it was for the fishermen. Before ice
became available in Cortez, fish-house crews split and salted the mullet,
rubbing Liverpool salt into the bodies of the fish. After being "kench-
cured," the fish were packed in barrels and shipped to Havana or Tampa.
But when sailing schooners began delivering ice to Cortez at the turn of
the century, the work of the fish-house men became a race against time
to pack and ice the fish before they spoiled. Trying to keep enough crushed
ice on hand was a major headache. Prior to World War II, fish-house crews
used big pitchforks to chop 300-pound cakes of ice by hand. After the war,

most fish houses installed electric ice crushers, which relieved some of the strain, and, by the mid-1960s, giant ice-making machines were supplying crushed ice in abundance.

Wyman Coarsey described a typical packing operation in the 1940s: "I worked for the Fulford Fish Company and the Bell Fish Company after the war. I remember one time when we had 300,000 pounds of fish on the dock in three days. We worked night and day for three straight days. At the end of that, we just laid down on the gutting tables—just lay there and died. We were dead on our feet! That dock was always lined with mullet. We'd have a stop-net crew come in with 60 or 70,000, and before we could get them finished, there'd be another crew waiting to unload. We'd have two scows the full length of the dock, full of fish, and they'd be piled so high that we'd have to put boards along the edge of the dock to keep them from sliding back overboard when we shoveled them out.

"Back then, we had to go down to the old icehouse to get ice. We'd take the truck down there, drag them 300-pound cakes of ice out of there, with the floor solid ice, bring them out and scoot them in the truck. We'd bring 15 or 20 cakes of ice in a load, slide them off the truck down a chute, lay them flat on the dock, chop them into chunks, grab your tongs and throw them up into that grinder and beat yourself all night long trying to get enough ice to stay ahead. At the Bell Fish Company, we didn't even have a grinder, so every bit of ice had to be chopped by hand. You'd get one of them wide pitchforks and stand right straddle those cakes and shave it on a little bit of a slant. You'd hit one side and then the other, and walk it back, shaving that block right on down. Get one done and they'd shoot you another one. I have actually shaved hundreds and hundreds of blocks of ice by hand. Oh, it's so different today from what it was back then, you can't imagine."

Once the fish were weighed out, 100 pounds to a box, and iced down, the boxes were stacked head-high in the cooler. Throughout the day, wholesale fish dealers would back their semi-trucks into the loading pit at the dock and load up. By the end of World War II, Cortez's fish were being trucked as far north as New York.

As Earl Guthrie said, "Fishing ain't no easy life," but there is another side to the fisherman's life besides the bugs, the backbreaking work, and the harshness of the elements. For thousands of years, fishermen in every culture in the world have shared a deep communion with nature. It is a special and unique treasure that almost no other occupation can claim.

Out in his boat, with an offshore breeze blowing the mosquitoes away and the morning air still cool and fresh, the Cortez fisherman is one of the freest people on earth. Some of nature's most spectacular sights are the normal backdrop for his daily labors: white sand beaches framed by the brilliant blue of the horizon; billowy cumulus clouds rearing up to heaven; and at night, the Milky Way stretching towards distant galaxies, looming ice-cold and crystalline across the sky. There are few people who have seen such wonders and remained untouched by them.

Such a beautiful natural setting compensates for much of the misery of the work. The Cortez fisherman has never known the windowless walls of the textile mill or the cubicle cages of the skyscraper, and he couldn't bear them if he had. Riding the crest of the Gulf's waves, he is answerable only to himself. The measure of his worth is in what he can wrest from the sea each day with his own skill and brawn; he need not look elsewhere for answers.

A camaraderie develops among fishermen during those long hours on the bow that I have never seen among any other workers. I have never laughed as long and hard as I have in the cabin of the *Anna Dean*, rolling back and forth in the bunk and holding my stomach with both hands trying to keep the laughter from hurting so bad, while Rusty and Gary reenacted some incredible misadventure.

Funny things happen out fishing that have no equivalent, and they happen all the time. Some happen spontaneously. Someone falls overboard, tumbling backwards off the stern when a wave rolls the boat unexpectedly, his legs splaying out spastically as he cartwheels into the freezing waters. (It never seems to be as funny in the heat of summer.) Someone leaps for the dock a little too soon, trying to be the first one off the boat, bounces off the edge of the dock and falls straight into the muck and mire of low tide. Someone tries to slide a box of ice aboard the boat, slips on a puddle of water, and goes sailing headfirst across the boat and into the water on the other side, scattering pelicans in his wake.

Other things happen by design. Someone gets thrown overboard. Often. In hilarious positions. Screaming ridiculous threats. Carrying his tormentors with him if he's quick enough. Things like that happen to someone all the time . . . to someone like me.

Cortez fishermen are quite simply the funniest people I've ever met. It's not surprising, really—they've had years of practice. Earl Guthrie still cracks up remembering funny incidents that happened 60 years ago: "Back in the '20s, me and Walter Taylor and Charlie Lewis was fishing together. When it gets real hot, them old mullet'll go up in them bushes, up in them roots, and a lot of times you'd get a good strike—just run the net close along the shore and let the tide go out and catch 'em. We was going along there one day and Walter got to standing up along the railing of the boat. Directly Charlie come to some old turtle grass, or seaweed, and it was banked up against the woods pretty far. Charlie just kinda come offshore of it, with Walter standing up on that rail, and I was setting down behind him and I figured out a picture just like I wanted it. Directly I reached up real easy and caught my hand right on the cheek of his tail, and I shoved him just as hard as I could shove him. He went down yelling 'unghh, unghh' and hit that water and he scootered right on up pretty near to the roots, and when he stood up that old grass was a-hanging on him and he looked like some old sea monster. Boy! I'll never forget how he looked!"

Now, sitting on the front of the dock, the old-timers carry both the scars and the laughter of a lifetime of fishing. They know that the life they have lived has been replaced by synthetic nets and 40-mile-per-hour boats, and they don't begrudge the changes. But they know, too, the deep pride and confidence of men who have waged war against the elements and survived.

When they see the easier life of today's fishermen, they question whether the younger ones could do what they did. "Shoot, a lot of these fishermen today can't hardly go down to the Pass and back," said Gene Fulford. "They hire everything done. They hire somebody to build their boat. They hire somebody to hang their nets. They wouldn't know how to mend a crowsfoot in a net if they had to. I'll tell you, there just aren't very many real fishermen left."

It was getting close to dinnertime and the stories were winding down. About that time, Buck Jones, a fisherman who was recovering from a liver disease, poled up to the dock in a skiff. Just for fun, he had shoved out to an old fish camp in front of the dock and run a gillnet around the pilings, trying to catch a couple of mullet. As he was tying up the skiff, he and Gene had a conversation that told much about the past and the present in Cortez.

"Buck, that's the quietest running motor I believe I've seen in many a day."

"Yeah, it's quiet, ain't it, Gene?"

"Better'n them diesels, that's for sure."

"Don't burn much oil, either. Needs oil 'bout once a week."

"Buck, how many of these fishermen today do you think would make a living if they had to do it like that, the way we had to?"

"There wouldn't be very many, Gene."

And Earl Guthrie, who had started it off earlier in the morning, put in the final word: "We don't know when it will happen, and you and I'll probably never live to see it, but the Bible says that one day the fishermen will be driven from the sea. . . . That we know."

It was time to go eat.

Chapter 5

"You Can Tell It
First From the Hands"

YOU CAN TELL IT FIRST from the hands. You won't find hands like
these in *Cosmopolitan* or *Ladies Home Journal.* You won't find women like
these in there either.

Cortez women are working women, and it shows in their hands. Years
of saltwater, dishwater, and scalloping have left them rough and cracked,
with a permanent puffiness around the joints and a patchwork of liver-
spots on the backs of the hands. Age and arthritis have combined to twist
and misshape the fingers. They are not a pretty sight.

Realizing that their hands don't match the standards of "womanly per-
fection" preached by the Madison Avenue glossies, they are, quite frankly,
a little embarrassed about it. When Doris "Toodle" Green saw the pho-
tograph I had taken of her, her first reaction was: "Oh my goodness, why'd
you have to have my old hands up there like that?"

Why indeed? After spending a few weeks in Cortez, I realized that it
would be all too easy to write a book about a Florida fishing village and
completely skip the women. This travesty would be easy because, by def-
inition, a fishing village centers around fishing, which is generally a male
industry. Old boats tethered to their posts, scenic vistas of netspreads in
the afternoon sun, hardy fishermen returning from a hard day's work—
that's what the visitor sees, that's what the occasional newspaper feature
story records, and, in fact, that's what most of the women in Cortez describe when they talk about the village.

Yet there is a rich and powerful history of what women in Cortez have
done to survive and to make a life for their families. One could miss all of
that by staring wistfully at the waterfront, but there's no way to miss it

when you notice the women's hands. There, in flesh and blood, is a clue to the reality of life for women in Cortez. For one thing, the more time the men spend fishing, the more the women are left to keep the home, raise children, do fill-in work at the fish houses, and provide continuity to the community. "I raised my kids," said Edith Fulford. "Tink gave me the money to buy their food and clothes and that was it. I raised them. I guess it was that way with most families."

Toodle, who is 68 now, is the resident historian of Cortez and has done more than anyone to preserve the history of the village. A member of the Manatee County Historical Society, she has collected numerous old photographs and had copies placed in the county archives, along with a series of taped interviews she conducted with Cortez old-timers.

Toodle spent her early years helping her mother Dora Fulford with the family's nine children, and then raised two of her own. "I'll tell you, there wasn't much romance in it. It was just real hard living," she recalled. "I have often thought of my poor, little old mother—she had these nine children and she raised us the hard, hard way. Nothing modern, no modern conveniences. I couldn't begin to hold up to do the work that she did. I remember many a night after she got supper fixed for all of us, she'd have to turn around and cook another whole meal to fix buckets for the boys to take fishing. Often, with eleven people to feed, there wasn't enough left over after supper to make a lunch for the next day, and the boys were going to be out all night and the next day, all wet and everything, and they had to have something to eat. I have seen her do that many a time—she'd say 'I've got to pack a bucket,' and go in there and cook another whole meal.

"Aunt Bessie Evans used to tell a story about fixing a bucket for Uncle John. She said that every day she'd fix Uncle John's bucket and she'd always put this little jar of guava jelly in it. She thought: 'Well, if they stay out longer, at least he'll be able to have some biscuits and guava jelly.' So every day she'd stick it in religiously and he'd bring it back every night. Finally one day he brought his bucket in—and no guava jelly. She said, 'So you finally ate the jelly!' He said, 'No, I got so tired of seeing that old jar of guava jelly, I threw it overboard.' "

Food preparation in the old days consumed a tremendous amount of time, and today's modern conveniences haven't significantly decreased it. Cooking was often the first thing and the last thing that a woman did each day. "On a typical day if your husband was going fishing, you'd have to get up real early and fix breakfast," said Toodle. "And I mean breakfast!

You didn't give them a bowl of cornflakes! They had big meals—eggs and grits and gravy and buttermilk biscuits. That was during the week, but then on Sunday morning at Grandpa's house, where we lived, he wanted round steak, too. And I still think about that; Grandma would have to get up real early and cook all of that for breakfast—of course she had us girls to help her—and then come back from church and fix a great big Sunday dinner. That was the big meal of the week and you always wanted to have something special."

All the cooking was done on wood stoves until the late 1920s when kerosene stoves replaced them. "The kerosene stoves had four burners and a portable tin oven that sat on top, and, if you wanted to bake, you'd set the little oven over one or two burners," said Toodle. "If you had a deluxe model, the oven was built right on the stove. There was a little reservoir tank that held a gallon of kerosene, and it had a little nozzle that let the kerosene drip down when you inverted it. A lot of women still kept their wood stoves long after they got kerosene ones, and they'd cook on them during the winter to help keep the house warm."

Once breakfast was finished and the men left, the women's work began in earnest. Children were awakened and fed, the older ones dressed for school and sent on their way. Then the women set about doing their major tasks, all the while looking after infants and toddlers—a full-time job in itself.

Laundry was one of the most grueling jobs. "We didn't get electricity out here until the mid-twenties, and many families didn't have washing machines until long after that," said Toodle. "So what we had to do was put clothes to soak overnight in a couple of big washtubs. That was to get out what we called the sweat water, which was the loose dirt. Then we'd ring them out by hand and put them in another tub of water and scrub them, and then put them in a great big iron washpot and boil them. Now imagine standing out there with a great big fire on a muggy day in the summer. We'd stir the clothes with a long stick and keep poking them around, with the soapy water boiling up. After you figured they had boiled enough, we'd dip them out and take them back and wash and rinse them again. Oh, clothes were not considered clean unless they were boiled!

"After boiling them, we'd scrub them again with Octagon Soap. That Octagon Soap was a lifesaver. You can still buy it today. It was the greatest thing. We'd even use it for medicine: you'd take that bar and scrape some of it off and mix it with sugar and make a paste, make it real soft like an ointment, and put it on boils and sores. We used it for laundry, for washing dishes, for bathing, and for anything else.

"So we'd scrub them that last time and, then in the last rinse, we'd dump in a liquid called blueing, and it would turn the water blue and was supposed to make your whites whiter. I'll never forget one woman here who made her living doing laundry for people, and every day when she'd get through she'd give her little girl a bath in this blueing water. Well all at once, nobody could figure out what was happening, this little girl's hair turned blue! That's the truth, I'm not making that up. She was a little towheaded thing and her hair turned just as blue as you could get. We laughed and laughed about her and her blue hair."

The laundry operation took several hours and, for families with babies, it had to be repeated several times a week. Otherwise, the family wash was done once a week. "If you had young babies then you had to wash diapers every day or every other day, because there was no such thing as disposable diapers," said Toodle. "But you usually did the family wash once a week, because people didn't change their clothes as often as they do now, unless they got wet. A lot of times, if the fishing clothes were just wet and weren't really fishy, they'd just be rinsed out and hung up to dry and worn again the next day. And we didn't have the facilities or the water to bathe like people do now, either. Oh, you'd wash up every day—keep your hands and face and ears clean. But as far as baths, there was your Saturday night bath and that was it. And we took that in the same big washtub we did the laundry in."

On the days when women weren't doing laundry, they were likely to be shelling peas from the family's garden or in the kitchen canning. It's a tradition that is still alive in Cortez, although canning has been replaced to a large extent by freezing. Today, women drive out to "u-pick-it" farms that surround Bradenton, where they can pick their own beans, peas, tomatoes, strawberries, or peaches at prices far below retail. They pack the vegetables in airtight plastic bags and store them in the freezer.

In the old days, women spent long hours preserving and canning all sorts of fruits and vegetables. "I've often said that my mother raised me on mullet and guavas, and even now I can't stand the smell of a plain guava," said Julian Taylor. "I'd just as soon smell a donkey as smell a guava. My mother would preserve and can them every way she could. The guavas used to grow wild everywhere in Cortez, but then the '21 storm wiped out most of them and the Mediterranean fruit fly killed the rest."

Sewing was another chore that consumed much of the woman's day. "Women sewed nearly all the clothes, even the underwear," said Toodle. "They made everything except the men's good Sunday suits. A lot of the sewing was done late at night. You'd get the kids to bed and put an old kerosene lamp next to the pedal sewing machine and do your work. I remember Mama was so sick that she'd have us kids sit there and turn the wheel on the machine for her 'cause she was too weak to do it. And back then people wore their clothes until they couldn't be patched anymore. You just put patches on top of patches. I'd bet you couldn't find a fisherman here today who would think of walking down the street with a patch on his pants, but I can remember when the poor old fishermen were nothing but patches. The whole seat would be worn out and you'd just cut it out and sew a new seat in it. Everybody did it, so nobody thought anything about it. But, now, if a button gets off, you just toss it out."

The women's daily routine was more complicated during the spring mackerel season when the men fished at night and slept during the day. Bessie Taylor described what it was like in 1920 when she married Julian: "We were married on a Tuesday and on the following Friday night Julian's mother died. So his sister and her husband moved into the house so she could take care of the younger children. Julian and I had a little two-room apartment upstairs in the house. During mackerel season, Julian would be asleep in one room, his dad was asleep in one room, and Bill Guthrie, my brother-in-law, was asleep in another room. And there I was, trying to do my work in one little kitchen without making any noise to wake up those three men."

Cortez women suffered from the same physical hardships that the men did—heat, mosquitoes, disease—but there was an additional one that took an especially heavy toll on the women: childbirth. Most families had a baby every year, or at least every other. "Oh, the childbearing was rough on the women and they aged so fast," said Toodle. "Of course, there was no such thing as having medical checkups with a doctor during your pregnancy. Some women might go to a doctor and make arrangements for him to be there when the baby was born, but a lot of them never had a doctor at all. They'd just have a midwife with them. Miss Lizzy Mann was probably the first midwife in Cortez, and I guess Aunt Nola Taylor delivered more babies than anybody. And the midwives didn't just come in and do the medical end of it. They took care of the family, too. They'd fix meals for everybody, keep house, and take care of the other children for probably $5 a week or $1 a day or something like that."

Most of the community's medical needs were also taken care of by the women. With the nearest hospital a long boat ride away in Tampa and only a few doctors in Bradenton, they handled all but the most serious illnesses. "I can still remember my Grandma Sallie wrapping Grandpa's feet with these long bandages every night," said Toodle. "He had these terrible open sores on his feet for years, from bad circulation, and she would cut long strips of cloth for bandages and wrap his legs every night."

In the old days, home remedies were used to combat ills: herbs, poultices, and homemade concoctions. Some of them still linger. Edith Fulford still prescribes Watkins' Salve for almost any ailment, whether the afflicted one has asked for her advice or not. "I remember one Sunday evening after church, just a couple of years ago," said Toodle. "We were all standing in front of the church talking about one of our members who had just had a heart attack and was in the hospital. And just to tease Edith, Junie Guthrie said, 'Well, if they'd put some Watkins' Salve on him, he'd be just fine, right Edith?' and boy, we all laughed over that one."

Life was hard for married women in Cortez, but it was even harder for widows, divorcees, and single women. In the Church of Christ, there is only one scriptural reason for divorce: adultery. Marriage is considered to be a sacred institution and divorce is "the quickest route to hell." Consequently, divorces were few and far between. "It really had to be an extreme case to get divorced," said Toodle. "Once you were married, well, you just didn't leave. You stuck it out. And gracious, moving in and living together, without being married, well you just didn't do it! There were a few cases of people shacking up together, but it wasn't accepted. I'm sure men and women were just like they are today—they had their outside affairs, but it was a slip-around deal."

Because of the heavy stigma against divorce, women more often simply quit their husbands because of drinking, gambling, or physical mistreatment. My great-aunt Kate Pearson and her first husband split up shortly after moving to Cortez from Arcadia in 1917. Aunt Kate supported herself and her young daughter Mary by helping families after a new baby was born. When the midwife left, Aunt Kate would move in with the family and do the cooking and keep house until the wife could manage. It was a hard go.

"Aunt Kate told me a story about how it was Mary's birthday, and Kate wanted so bad to have a birthday party for her," said Toodle. "She said, 'I didn't even have the ingredients to make a cake. But I had some syrup, so I decided I could boil the syrup and let the kids pull taffy candy.' All the little kids from Cortez came to the party and they were playing and everything, and just when Kate got it to the point where the kids could pull the taffy candy, somebody knocked the whole works over on the ground. Aunt Kate said she just cried and cried. But luckily, Paul Taylor came by and said, 'Don't cry. We can all walk down and see the new bridge they're building.' That was when they were building the bridge to the beach. But that poor old soul, that's how hard she had it. Yet she can still tell those stories and not be bitter."

Women without husbands had a difficult time trying to make a living. "See, that was before the days of welfare, and if you were left a widow with three or four children and you didn't have a family to help you through the hard times, well, you were just at the mercy of the world," said Toodle. "Like Grey and Gene Fulford's mother Mamie whose husband Clyde died in the 1918 flu epidemic. She was a hardworking woman and she worked all the time. She'd take in boarders and do laundry for people. And she had a hard time of it, raising those kids. But luckily they had Grandpa Fulford and he was a successful fisherman. He never had any money except what he made with his hands from week to week, but he looked after them and helped the family out. People were real good to each other here."

Unmarried women did all kinds of work to get by. My great-aunt Letha Leeper, the younger sister of Lela Taylor, moved to Cortez from North Carolina when she was 18 years old. "I did every sort of job I could find," she said. "I worked at a restaurant on the beach; I worked in a department store uptown; and I did laundry for people, using those old washtubs and scrub-boards."

In 1946, Anthony Rossi opened the Tropicana juice factory in Bradenton, which has grown to be the largest processor of orange juice in the world. Over the years, many Cortez women have worked on the Tropicana assembly line—cutting, sectioning, and squeezing the pulp to make orange juice and grapefruit juice.

In general, the men of Cortez fished and the women worked at home, but there were times when the women spent as much time on the water as the men did. That was particularly true during the scalloping season. Until pollution closed Sarasota Bay to scalloping in the 1970s, many women in Cortez went scalloping every day during the summer, for 30 years in some cases, and brought home sizable contributions to their family's income.

Armed with an old No. 2 washtub and a wooden scallop box—a square plywood box with a sheet of plate glass in the bottom so they could see scallops on the floor—the women would pole out to "The Kitchen" in old skiffs or little rowboats. They would wade through the waist-deep water, pushing their scallop box in front of them and dragging their washtub behind them. When they'd spot a scallop buried in the sand, they'd reach down, grab it, and flip it into the washtub. Hours later, after filling several washtubs, they would pole back to Cortez and sit hunched over the tub for hours more, prying open the shells, scooping out the scallops, and cleaning and packing them in quart jars. They'd sell the scallops to fish markets or to restaurants at the going price.

For many years, the price was 14 cents a quart, but Lela Taylor remembers when the price got so low it was hardly worth going: "How many millions of scallops I've opened in my life I couldn't tell you. I'll tell you one time we went—I think Nellie Mae Taylor and your Grandma Edith Fulford was with us that day—and we went down by Crane's Bayou and caught a world of scallops. Your Grandpa Tink had built a little scallop house out over the water for us to open them in, and we sat up there until four o'clock in the morning opening and cleaning them scallops. We got them all washed and packed. The man had promised to pay 14 cents a quart—that was what we was getting. But when I taken them over to Palmetto, the fellow said he'd only give us 7 cents a quart. I told him, 'No, I'll take them to the county hospital before I'll do it.' So we come back and went on over to Hawkers Market in Bradenton, and he said he'd only give us 7 cents a quart, too. I told him no. And you know what? We taken them scallops to the county hospital and give that big dishpan full of scallops to them. I'll never know how many pounds it were, but oh my goodness, we had a lot of them. Good gracious, if I had that big dishpan of scallops now, there's no telling how much I could get for them."

The women also worked at the fish houses during the year. "My older sister and the girls her age would make just as much money gutting mackerel as the boys would," said Toodle. "They'd go down there and work all night and maybe take a short nap waiting for the mackerel boats to come in. Nobody thought anything about it. They'd gut mackerel all night and then go to school in the morning."

Today, women are more involved in the fish-house work than ever before. In fact, during fall roe season, the Fulford Fish Company employs as many as a dozen Cortez women in its roe packing operation. Each day the women split thousands of pounds of mullet, remove the roe and gizzards, and pack them for freezing and eventual shipment to Taiwan and Japan.

There is one woman in Cortez, Maida Culbreath, who has done as much fishing as any man in the village. Until health problems slowed her down in recent years, Maida went fishing every day in her old scooter-poop as a commercial hook-and-liner. She and her husband Julian "Goose" Culbreath raised their three children on the income from the mullet that Goose caught in his gillnet and the trout that Maida caught with her poles. For years, she was a familiar sight anchored near Longboat Pass, wearing a big straw hat and sunglasses, pulling in as much as 100 pounds a day of speckled trout.

Although she still goes fishing periodically, Maida now spends most of her time carving fishing lures and floats, tending to a yard full of exotic house plants, and talking on the CB radio. "Grandma Station" is known all over Sarasota Bay and has helped numerous boaters by relaying weather alerts, making telephone calls to families in town, and offering a friendly voice over the waves, especially during storms.

The women of Cortez have done it all and continue to. They raise the children, keep house, cook, clean, and do all the other chores that have been traditionally labeled women's work. And they have carried their weight at the fish houses, too. It has been a hard existence, full of sorrows and tears, but not without its rewards and pleasures. Cortez women have built support systems that have enriched their lives. The church is one of the most important. Church services on Sunday morning and Sunday night and mid-week Bible study on Wednesday nights are important socially as well as religiously. It's a chance for women to visit with friends and relatives, to catch up on recent events in the village and to strengthen friendships and family ties. Community fish fries and the monthly meetings of the Ladies Auxiliary of the Cortez Volunteer Fire Department, which was formed in the late 1950s, have served the same purpose.

Primarily, though, the support network for Cortez women has depended on the informal one-to-one phone calls and personal visits. Like everything else in Cortez, that too is changing. As the outside world has moved closer and closer, bringing with it the tempting attractions of television, shopping malls, and nearby fast-food restaurants, the old ways have begun to crumble. Ironically, with each new "time-saving convenience" that is supposed to free the women from their drudgery, they seem to have less time for the old customs and social rituals than they had before.

"Just in my lifetime it seems like the closeness isn't there like it was before," said Toodle. "I might go for a year and not see some of my relatives. It's not that anyone deliberately means to be that way, it's just that our life-styles have changed so much that there doesn't seem to be time to visit. I've said it so many times, but it just seems so sad to think that we don't see many of our friends and relatives unless it's at a funeral."

Despite the changes, what remains for the women is a closeness based more on blood and heritage than on the number of visits per year. There is still a deeply shared sense of community in this little place—an awareness built on generations of memories among the women. Their relationships don't have the glamour of the high fashion set at the Bradenton Country Club or the sisterhood of feminists in a consciousness-raising group. It's an aged, unspoken connection—an echo of many other women who have lived before them in this place. It will last as long as Cortez exists as a community, and when the village is gone, that spirit will be too.

Chapter 6

"The Tie That Binds"

THE OLD SONG DRIFTED OUT the front door of the church and into the parking lot as I was hurrying to get out of my car and up the steps. Having arrived late, I creaked open the front door, walked softly down the aisle to where my grandma was sitting, and sat down in the pew beside her. Her voice cracked and squawked on some of the sharper bends in the song, but she plowed determinedly through three verses and the last chorus. "Draw me nearer, nearer, nearer blessed Lord, to the cross where Thou hast died. Draw me nearer, nearer, nearer blessed Lord, to Thy precious bleeding side."

There are two places in the world where Edith Fulford feels at home. One is in her easy chair in front of the TV set, where she sits from 10:00 A.M., when "Truth or Consequences" comes on, until well after midnight for the late-night installment of "The Jeffersons" or "Quincy." The other is in her pew at the Cortez Church of Christ, where she sits every Sunday morning, Sunday evening, and Wednesday night for mid-week Bible study.

These are the two constants in her life: watching the game shows and soap operas on TV and going to church. The family kids her constantly about watching so much TV, but nobody kids her about going to church. It is the single most important thing in her life. Period. To Grandma, if you're not going to church regularly then nothing else you're doing matters much. She may have her faults and foibles, but being a hypocrite about religion is not one of them

All of the standard cliches apply to Grandma and her understanding of religion and what it means to her. The church is a firm foundation, a bulwark against the world, the rock of ages, a shelter in the night, and all the others. "For Mama and many other women in Cortez," said my mother, "their faith that there was 'a great day coming' and the dream of 'how beautiful heaven must be,' as the old song goes, was what gave them the strength to stand for hours over steaming washboards or hot stoves, trying to help their families survive. With the men gone fishing most of the time, it was about all they had."

Religion has been one of the most important influences in Cortez, although no more than half the population has ever attended church regularly. But what the faithful lacked in numbers, they made up for in severity of their beliefs. Unquestionably, the church has been the single biggest influence in my family. In her own stubborn and determined way, Grandma left the imprint of her beliefs on all of her children and, as much as anyone, she has been the main stabilizing force for religion in Cortez. "You want to know who went to church regularly in Cortez?" she asked, repeating my question. "Me and my kids. That was the way I raised them and they all turned out that way."

Understanding the role of religion in Cortez is simplified because there are only two congregations in the village: the Church of Christ and the Church of God. I have 30 years of firsthand knowledge about the Church of Christ and none about the Church of God, but even with my ignorance, there are some obvious parallels between the two. The churches are like two sides of the same coin: molded by the same historical forces, similarly rooted in the working-class South, and yet, as different as any two churches could be. Those similarities and differences have offered a very distinct choice to the people of Cortez—if they wanted a choice.

The Church of Christ and the Church of God are both native-born churches that took root among working-class Southerners during the late 1800s. They grew slowly during the first decade of the twentieth century and flourished during the fundamentalist movement of the 1920s. Religious historians have generally identified the fundamentalist movement in the South as a reaction against the "new morality" of the 1920s. Southern Protestant clergymen looked on in horror at the rise of skirts, motion pictures, smoking, automobiles, and dancing, and promptly called for a return to the simplicity of New Testament Christianity.

But fundamentalism was also a result of disillusionment with the involvement of Southern churches in social and political issues, particularly World War I, which, instead of "making the world safe for democracy," had ushered in the licentious shucking and jiving of the Roaring Twenties. At its roots, fundamentalism meant a turning away from "the social gospel," as it was disdainfully referred to, and a return to "personal salvation" and evangelism.

This reasoning was really nothing new in the South. Southern Protestants had never been as involved in political issues as had their Northern counterparts. Northern churches such as the Quakers, Congregationalists, and Unitarians have an activist tradition that has no equivalent in the South. While Northern clergymen were playing leading roles in the abolitionist movement prior to the Civil War, the Baptist and Methodist circuit riders, who were evangelizing the South, kept their messages pointed closer to home: to the temptations of Satan, the promise of heaven's pearly gates, and the eternal fires of hell.

The first major break in that pattern occurred during the Civil War, when Southern churches abandoned their isolationist view of the world and threw their full weight behind the slave-owning aristocracy. The fight to defend slavery and states' rights became a holy crusade, and Southern pulpits rang with invectives about the scriptural basis of slavery and the sinful nature of those who would presume to abolish it.

By 1865, when Lee's bedraggled Army of Northern Virginia finally turned in their swords and muskets to Grant at Appomattox Courthouse, the Southern churches' holy crusade had suffered a fatal beating as well. They quickly retreated to their prewar isolationism, and it took the looming specter of demon rum 40 years later to bring them out again.

The rise of the temperance movement at the end of the nineteenth century was the cue for Southern churches to reenter the political arena. They had no trouble finding scripture and verse to condemn whiskey drinking, but their criticisms of other social injustices may have been influenced by more secular tracts.

During the 1880s and 1890s, the Farmers' Alliance, the Knights of Labor, and the Populist party gained significant political strength in the South. Although short-lived, they must have had some influence on Southern churches, because, as Kenneth K. Bailey documents in *Southern White Protestantism in the Twentieth Century*, Southern Baptists, Methodists, and Presbyterians had gone on record prior to World War I supporting the rights of employees to organize, condemning child labor, sweatshops, crowded tenements, and "heartless greed in corporate wealth and graft in politics."

This period of political activity reached its peak during World War I, another war that took on the trappings of a holy crusade. Although this one was won, the crusade was a bitter disappointment to the churchmen and their flocks. As the ensuing decade gave birth to flappers, flivvers, and Sigmund Freud, Southern churches went into shock. Ensconced in the poverty of a feudal, sharecropping society, Southern clergymen responded by turning away from the evils of the world and leading their faithful followers toward a view of the world based on a literal interpretation of New Testament Christianity.

They would emerge briefly from that sheltered view once more, at the end of the decade, to fight for prohibition and against the 1928 presidential candidacy of Al Smith—who was, of all things, a Catholic. But it wasn't until the civil rights battles of the 1960s that politics would begin to seriously compete with evangelism and personal salvation in the Southern churches. Both the Church of Christ and the Church of God went back to the Bible during the fundamentalist era to define their practices and beliefs, but what they found on that journey was very, very different.

The Church of Christ was officially formed in 1906 when a group of conservative members of the Disciples of Christ (or Christian Church) split and formed their own church. The Disciples of Christ had been established in the early 1800s as part of the restoration movement, and the *Handbook of Denominations* calls it "the most American" religious group in the country, having "been born on the nineteenth-century American frontier out of a deep concern for Christian unity."

The *Handbook* estimates that the Churches of Christ currently have about 17,000 independent congregations, with a total membership of about 2,500,000. It states that "They are located in 50 states, with greatest concentration in the South and West, have congregations in 75 foreign countries, and in the past 20 years have emerged as one of the top 10 non-Catholic bodies in North America."

The Church of Christ was, and in many ways still is, the leading champion of the fundamentalist tide that swept the South in the 1920s. Its guiding motto is "to speak where the Bible speaks and remain silent where the Bible is silent." According to the *Handbook*, "one of the outstanding features of the Churches of Christ lies in their acceptance of the Bible as a true and completely adequate revelation. This basic concept has resulted in such characteristic practices as weekly observation of the Lord's Supper, baptism by immersion, a cappella singing. . . . They claim to be nondenominational with no headquarters, no governing bodies, and no clergy."

The churches' literal interpretation of the Bible is best reflected in its insistence on a cappella singing. The New Testament describes the early Christians meeting together on the first day of the week to "sing and make melodies in their hearts." No mention is made of any instruments; thus, the Church of Christ allows none.

Such tenets have given the church a reputation as "the most fundamental of all fundamentalist groups." Most members would consider that a compliment. As a friend of mine said when I told him which church my family attended, "Oh, y'all are the ones who believe everybody else is going to hell—even the hard-shell Baptists." Although that attitude may not hold true any longer in some of the more liberal congregations, it would still ring true in most of the others. Most Church of Christ preachers might not come right out and say that everybody else is going to hell, but they would be hard-pressed to name any other group that isn't.

It's harder to trace the origins of the Church of God because at least 200 independent religious bodies in the U.S. bear that name. The first of these originated in the late 1800s in Tennessee and, despite minor differences, most of the groups share a common doctrine. Its major tenets, according to the *Handbook,* include: "justification by faith, sanctification, baptism of the Holy Spirit, speaking in tongues, being born again, fruitfulness in Christian living, and a strong interest in the premillennial second coming of Christ. . . . [The Churches of God are noted for] stressing pentecostal and holiness tenets; practicing divine healing and condemning the use of alcohol, tobacco, and jewelry . . . and accepting baptism, the Lord's Supper and footwashing as ordinances."

The Church of God's literal interpretation of the Bible led it down the path of "charismatic Christianity," as it is called today. But the Church of Christ scholar would claim that the Holiness "went wrong in interpreting the Scriptures too literally," if that's possible. For instance, they continue to speak in tongues and justify it by pointing to the incidents in the New Testament when the early Christians exhibited that gift. Not so in the Church of Christ, which claims, based on its interpretation of the same verses, that speaking in tongues was a gift that God gave to the apostles and early Christians, but later revoked when the New Testament was written ("when that which was more perfect was come").

It's an argument that the outsider might consider trivial, but that believers of each sect will debate indefinitely. Regardless of who's right, that single interpretation has led to incredible differences in the beliefs and practices of the two churches.

Services in the Church of Christ are staid and reserved, with little outward expression of feelings. Members sit stiffly in their pews, reverently singing the old hymns, and listening silently as the preacher drones away in the pulpit. The only emotion that's expressed occurs during the invitation hymn at the close of the sermon, when new converts come forward to be baptized or wayward members ask for the congregation's prayers for forgiveness of sins. The Church of God, or "Holy Rollers" as its members are sometimes called, is at the opposite end of the emotional spectrum. At times during the service, members allegedly "receive the Holy Spirit" and begin quaking and rolling in the aisles, transported away into the realm of other tongues and trance-like states.

Some sociologists claim that church affiliation is based more on social status than on theology or beliefs; in other words, people choose to attend a church where the other people dress like they do, live in similar neighborhoods, hold jobs of similar skill and income, and have achieved the same status in the community. As individuals progress up the social ladder, they choose congregations that reflect their new-found status.

If such is actually the case, sociologists would be in deep trouble in Cortez. There may be some slight class differences between members of the Church of Christ and the Church of God; one relative claimed, "We were all uneducated, but a lot of people in the Pentecostal group could hardly read or write." There are indications that members of the two congregations didn't socialize much with the other group. But these differences were minimal.

However, once the people took their Saturday-night baths, put on their good clothes, and walked in the door of their chosen congregation on Sunday, the differences could not have been more striking. In Cortez, the choice of which church to attend was simple: did you want to sit in your pew on Sunday morning or jump over it?

The choice was even more clear-cut because there was no middle ground—other than not going at all. There was no Methodist congregation, no Lutheran, no Presbyterian, certainly no Catholic church or Jewish temple. I think the two most important factors in making that choice were family influences—probably the overriding motivation—and the degree of emotion that a person wanted to express in religion and, to some extent, in life.

Hubert Horne's family struggled with that choice: "See, I went to both churches when I was growing up. We'd go to one church sometimes and to the other one at other times, depending on how my mama felt that year. My mother went to the Holiness church for awhile until it got on her nerves so bad she had to quit—all that shouting and screaming and carrying on. But I used to go there with my best friend Richard Roberts and his family 'cause they were Holy Rollers. Something definitely happens to those people, and I don't believe it's mass hypnotism 'cause you couldn't hypnotize a person and get them to do some of those things they do. Why, I've seen some of them old ladies, 70 years old, do flips over benches and talk in tongues you never heard before. I saw one old lady jump over a bench one time, and she was so old she could hardly walk. Richard and I was about to fall out the aisle in the back row, because they were all talking in tongues, when all of a sudden she does a back flip and lands on her feet, still talking. I'm not kidding. You'd have to see it to believe it."

For Grandma, the choice was always very clear. Her family, the Wilsons, had been Baptists before joining the Church of Christ, while the Fulfords were probably Methodists back in North Carolina. "Brother W. A. Cameron came to Oneco and baptized my daddy and momma when I was growing up," said Grandma. "Brother Cameron lived up in North Florida, in a little place called Istachatta, and a friend of mine told me that her daddy used to carry Brother Cameron all over that area in a horse and buggy to preach."

In late 1923, a year before Grandma got married and moved to Cortez, Brother H. C. Shoulders started a Church of Christ congregation in Cortez. Over the next few decades, preachers from the surrounding area took turns preaching in Cortez on Sundays, and an occasional out-of-town evangelist would come to town to hold revival meetings. The little church could not afford a regular preacher until the 1950s. "About 50 or 60 members was as many as we've ever had regular," said Grandma. "We'd have revival meetings and maybe a few would get baptized, but not many."

One of the most notable of these meetings was when the most famous preacher in the "brotherhood," a black man named Marshall Keeble, held a tent meeting in Bradenton in the late 1920s. Keeble, who reportedly baptized 25,000 people during his preaching career, attracted whites in droves. "People from Cortez piled into the backs of the fish trucks, with blankets to keep warm, and flooded into town to hear him," said Momma. "It was the only time I can remember whites and blacks ever associating in public, and, of course, even in this case, the whites all sat on one side of the tent and the blacks on the other."

The Church of God congregation was as small as the Church of Christ, if not smaller. In fact, the two congregations actually shared the same building until 1921. "Back about the turn of the century, Mrs. L. J. C. Bratton donated some land to build a community church on, and local people took up a collection to build it," said Toodle. "And both congregations used the building. One would hold services in the morning and the other one would meet in the afternoon, and then they'd switch the next week. When the '21 storm hit, it floated the church off its blocks and nobody had the money to have it jacked back up. So some of the women went to Bradenton, my mother was one of them, and raised enough money from the merchants to have the church put back on its blocks."

Shortly after that, the Church of God collected enough money to build its own building. Years later, about 1950, the Church of Christ purchased the old community church building at a state auction and used it until 1954, when it built its present building on the adjoining lot.

The other consistent truth about religion in Cortez, besides the small numbers of the faithful, is that the women have been far more active than the men. "This is the only place I've ever lived so I don't know if it's more true here than anywhere else," said Toodle, "but the men seem to think that religion is all right for the women and children, but the men don't need it. The women would go to church on Sunday mornings and the men would go to the docks and talk and whittle, or to the poolroom."

The men of Cortez may well be less religious, in general, than men in other small communities, but Goose Culbreath told me a story that makes me doubt it: "When my family lived up in Hamilton County before we moved to Cortez, my Papa used to carry Mama to church in the horse and wagon, but then he'd go out behind the church where there was a little sinkhole, and he'd sit out there so he could chew his tobacco. By the end of the services, there'd be more men out there around that sinkhole than there was inside the church. Papa said that one day his brother, my uncle John Culbreath, got brought up on charges before the church for chewing tobacco. He come over to talk to Papa about it. He said, 'Dick, they said they was gonna kick me outta the church for chewing tobacco.' My dad said, 'Well, did you admit that you chewed?' Uncle John said, 'Hell no, I told them I never chewed tobacco!' He waited a couple seconds and then said, 'Course they never said nothing about dipping snuff.' "

There have always been some men in Cortez who attended church regularly. Capt. Billy Fulford was one of them. He had been quite a drinker as a young man, but then he "got religion" and went to church faithfully until he died in 1939. "My earliest memories of Grandpa [Capt. Billy] are of him walking down the road to church with a wicker basket with the communion in it," said Toodle. "They didn't take turns preparing communion like we do today, and every Sunday morning Grandma would prepare the communion and Grandpa would put the grape juice and the unleavened bread in that basket and walk to church."

For many years, the Cortez Church of Christ used only one cup to serve communion—another literal interpretation of the Bible. Jesus told his disciples to "take this cup and drink it" on the first day of the week to commemorate his death, burial, and resurrection. He didn't say anything about cups; he said this cup. But after half a dozen church members contracted tuberculosis, literal interpretation gave way to modern hygiene. "It was a big heavy glass and everybody used it," said Toodle. "We never thought anything about it, and we didn't really know anything about germs. But I'm sure that's why so many of us got tuberculosis. Dodie Jones and his wife both died of TB, and then Hazel Guthrie died from it, and at the same time she was in the sanatorium, I developed it and had to go. Then Brother Raymond Guthrie got sick, and another man named Kite got it and died from it. And all of us were members of the church. Well, once we learned about germs and disease, we got individual communion cups, but there were some congregations that were so narrow-minded that they actually split up over whether to use only one cup."

For Grandma and the other faithful wives, the church has been the spiritual and social center of the community. It has functioned as the house of the Lord and the Elks Club all rolled into one—it was where you worshiped your God and also caught up on the latest news about friends and family. Lacking social clubs or recreational facilities, church activities, such as "Sunday dinner on the grounds," were the major social events in Cortez. For young people of dating age, there was, and still is, great pressure to date a good Christian boy or girl, as the case may be. There is even more pressure to marry a member of the church, or someone who has agreed to convert soon after.

Grandma and Grandpa followed that pattern—up to a point. They met at a church meeting, and Grandpa was baptized shortly before they got married. "I wanted him to do it but I didn't beg him to," said Grandma. "He had to make up his own mind what he was gonna do and how he was gonna live." But Grandpa stopped going to church several years later and didn't go back until just a few months before he died. "Maybe once in a while he'd go, but he never did go faithful like he ought to until just before he died," said Grandma.

Grandpa's refusal to attend church just made Grandma's faith that much stronger. While he went to the dock, Grandma kept right on going to church every Sunday morning, Sunday evening, and Wednesday evening. And she carried her children, her grandchildren, and anybody else within earshot. There are some in Cortez, particularly the men, who might show up for services on Sunday and be cussing and drinking the rest of the week, but not Edith Fulford. Her faith in God and her belief in regular church attendance, which sometimes seem like one and the same, are the clearest, deepest, and purest aspects of her being. I have no doubts that she will be sitting in her same pew, singing the same songs in her broken soprano voice until the day she dies. She wouldn't want it any other way, and neither would I.

Chapter 7

"Cortez's
Grand Ole Opry"

HAL CULBREATH TOLD THE STORY this way: "Not long ago, a fellah asked Grey Fulford, 'Grey, how come you don't tear down that old
Culbreath house there in your front yard? It's old and rotten and nothing
but an eyesore.' Grey said to him, 'You think I'm a damn fool? I ain't about
to tear down my Grand Ole Opry!'" At that, Hal threw back his head and
roared with laughter.

His younger brother Julian "Goose" Culbreath laughed just as long and
hard when I asked him about the incident, and said, "Yeah, we played a
lot of good music in that old house, and Grey was one of the boys that
came over all the time to listen. Back in them days we was as good as there
was. Good as some of them on the Opry."

I wouldn't doubt it. Music has been a vital part of life in Cortez, and
the Culbreaths have been the first family of music for over 60 years. "Shoot,
all them Culbreaths played music," said Earl Guthrie. "There was more
of them in that family that played than in the whole rest of Cortez put
together."

It's a family tradition that goes back over 100 years, long before the
Culbreaths moved into the old two-story house near the shore that now
sits empty and termite-ridden in Grey's front yard. And the tradition is
still alive and well, although the last few years have taken a terrible toll
on the family. Early in 1981, two of the Culbreath brothers, Bud and
Charlie, both in their 70s, died just a few months apart. Hal died in 1982.
Out of nine original Culbreath siblings, only Goose, 68, is still alive.

Goose has played fiddle and guitar in the same band for over 27 years.
The group was originally called "The Top Four" and is now known as "The

Beachcombers." And despite the recent deaths of Hal, Charlie, and Bud, the music has already been passed on to the next generation of Culbreaths. One of Goose's sons, Lloyd, grew up playing in rock and roll bands with the likes of Dickey Betts, lead guitarist for the old Allman Brothers Band, and still plays regularly with his own group. Lloyd's oldest son Lowell plays in a band with some high school friends, and the youngest boy Duane, age 7, is already sitting in on the drums with Goose's group. Hal's son Richard, a postal employee in Bradenton with two high school daughters of his own, can play a mean flat-top guitar.

The music that Goose plays for pay has changed some to reflect current styles, but the heart of his music is still rooted in the old-time traditions of his father Dick Culbreath. James Charles "Dick" Culbreath was a small, spry man who stood no more than five-foot-six. He died at age 86, and even as an old man he was known to cut loose buck dancing in the middle of a song, then jump up in the air and click his heels together three times before coming down. He was known in Cortez for two things: his fiddle and his carefree manner. "He always had a big grin on his face, no matter what," said Earl Guthrie.

He carried his grin and his fiddle with him wherever he went. In one of the old family photographs that Goose keeps in a round candy tin, the family is lined up in the front yard, leaning on their car, and Dick Culbreath is cradling his fiddle.

The music started early for him. He was born on a farm in Milledgeville, Georgia. His father and uncle played the fiddle, as did all of his brothers. He stayed in Georgia until about 1900, when he married a local girl named Ella Hurst; they packed their wagon and headed south to Florida. They settled in Hamilton County in the northeast part of the state and bought a 40-acre farm on the Withlacoochee River near Jasper.

Dick's fiddle might have been the first thing they unpacked. Just down the river, near the junction of the Withlacoochee and Suwannee rivers, was an old dance hall. "My daddy used to play for square dances at that old dance hall all the time," said Hal. "He'd travel all over the place to play for square dances—Hamilton County, Madison County, Suwannee County. They used to have a big fiddlers convention in Madison. People'd come from Alabama and Georgia in horse and wagon. My daddy used to win them all. He'd go to every one of the conventions he'd hear tell of. I don't think they won much money at those contests, mostly they won sacks of flour and sides of meat or ham as prizes. They went mostly for the pickin'."

The oldest Culbreath children were born in Hamilton County, but then the family had to start moving around to find work. Nine children were born during those rambling years: RV, the oldest daughter, followed by Shel, Vera, Roland ("Bud"), Hal, Edger ("Ted"), Charles, Clark, and Goose.

The family's journeys took them south from Hamilton County to Wauchula, then back up to Suwannee County, south again to a place between Wauchula and Arcadia where they worked in the orange groves, then to Avon Park, back to Wauchula, and finally, in 1920, they settled on Perico Island, just north of Cortez. They might be there yet if the 1921 hurricane hadn't come along. "We was living there on Perico Island and farming right out in front of the house," said Hal. "There was an old Indian shell mound out there, about an acre big, and that's where we had our tomatoes planted. Right in the shell mound. You could grow things in them shell mounds that you couldn't grow nowheres else 'cause the shell mound caught the moisture and held it. There were only about three other families living out there, and there wasn't no bridge of any kind to the mainland. We had to ford it in our horse and wagon.

"When that '21 storm came up, we didn't know nothing about it," he continued. "I tell you, I've never seen the Gulf any rougher than Palma Sola Bay was during that storm. Boy, that was rough weather. We boys got out on that front porch and the wind would lift that whole porch up off the blocks and then drop it back down. My brother Bud was up there leaning against the wind, letting it hold him up, and all of a sudden the wind let up and he went slap down on that porch, right on his face. That island is 800 acres big, and water covered the whole thing. But we stayed right in that house and rode it out.

"The next morning after the storm, all our tomato plants and everything was gone. We'd had tomatoes on those vines as big as my fist. Just the morning before the storm we had been over there staking them up with strips of bedsheets, but hell, the morning after there wasn't any sign of a vine. It took everything. We give up on trying to make it over there. The ground was so salty after that storm that it wouldn't have grew anything anyway."

Just a few days after the storm, two of the Culbreath boys got jobs crewing for a Cortez fisherman and within a month the family had moved to the village. The older boys got jobs fishing, and Dick Culbreath gave up a life of dirt farming to become a commercial "hook-and-liner," catching trout on the grassflats of Sarasota Bay.

The Culbreaths made a living in Cortez, but it was a meager one. With nine hungry mouths to feed, Dick and Ella fed their kids on fried mullet every night of the week just like many other families in Cortez. But they had their music and that helped. Life was hard Monday through Friday, struggling to bring home a paycheck to last through the week, but at least on Saturday and Sunday they had their music to fall back on. Old-time music might not have quieted the ache in their stomachs or warmed the chill in their bones on winter nights, but it came close.

Sunday morning was when they really cranked it up. "Every Sunday morning my dad would get out his fiddle and start playing and people would come from all over Cortez to listen," said Hal. "A lot of times boys would come out from Bradenton, too, and everywhere's else. My dad would play the fiddle and me and Goose would play fiddle or guitar, Charlie played an old player piano we had; and Ted and Clark blowed these little mouth harps. My mother could play the fiddle too, and she'd play old tunes like 'Walls of Jericho.' "

The Culbreath boys could play almost any kind of instrument. "Ted and Clark were real good on the harmonica," said Goose. "Course they wasn't as good as Charlie McCoy and that bunch there, but for them days they was real good. They'd play them old tunes like Deford Bailey did on WSM radio." Bailey was a black harmonica player and one of the early stars of the Grand Old Opry. The opry was a big influence on the Culbreaths, although they often had a hard time picking it up on the radio. Goose remembers: "We'd try to listen to the Grand Ole Opry on Saturday nights, but it'd come and go. 'Bout the time it got interesting, the damn radio would fade out."

"Me and Hal used to play the straws too—what they call fiddlesticks," Goose added. "Way back in the old days, there weren't many guitars around so they didn't have no rhythm guitar most of the time. So the only rhythm you had was from the straws. Hal'd play the fiddle and I'd tap these two thin straws on his top strings to keep the rhythm. Charlie had him a mandolin, too, and he'd play chords on that like a guitar. He didn't pick it like you do a fiddle, but Bud Jones, they called him Dodie Jones, he could play the hell out of a mandolin. He'd play all them old tunes my dad played. He'd come over to the house and they'd sit there and play for hours. Papa would play the lead for awhile and then Dodie Jones would play lead. Oh yeah, we use to have that old house a-breezin'."

The Culbreath boys were always experimenting, trying to develop trick methods of playing. "Sometimes Charlie would play chords on that old player piano with one hand and I'd play the melody with one hand," Goose recalled. "We could tear up them old tunes like 'Lazy Bones.' Then me and Charlie got where we could play two different tunes on the same guitar at the same time. He'd be a chordin' one tune and I'd be picking out another tune on the high strings at the same time."

The music was so good that it just about split Cortez right down the middle on Sunday mornings—with half the villagers going to church and other half shaking a leg to the old fiddle tunes at the Culbreaths. And shaking a leg was exactly what they were doing. The music goes by several names—hoe-down, old timey, traditional—but all of it was dance music. Hundreds of years of fiddle tunes—jigs, reels, hornpipes, and waltzes—were brought to the United States from Ireland, Scotland, and England, and have been kept alive in the mountains and deltas of the southland. The songs have been passed down by ear from generation to generation. A tune may have picked up a new name during its journey from County Sligo, Ireland, to Cortez, Florida, and it may have some new variations or bowing styles, but the melody remains basically the same.

Those tunes are what Dick Culbreath played all his life and then passed down to his sons—songs like "Sally Goodin," "Hen Cackle," "Old Joe Clark," "Soldiers Joy," "Leather Britches," "Little Brown Jug," "Fishers Hornpipe," "Billy in the Lowground," "Arkansas Traveler"—and a hundred more. There are other songs that came out of the great blues tradition of black Americans, including "Milk Cow Blues" and "Carroll County Blues"—which were picked up by white Southerners despite the barriers of Jim Crowism.

I never got to hear the Culbreaths play for a square dance during the summers I spent in Cortez. I was one of the ones in church. In fact, every Sunday morning I got up, put on my Sunday clothes, and walked the shell road to the Church of Christ. Chances are that Goose was just stirring after a late gig the night before. But I never knew it. It wasn't until I started learning to play the fiddle myself that I found out that Goose and his music had been around me all my life.

A strong, handsome man with thick curly gray hair, Goose Culbreath is one of the friendliest people I've ever met. He inherited his daddy's friendly manner as well as his musical talent. Two images of Goose stand out in my mind: seeing him walking home barefoot from the dock with his khaki work pants rolled up to his calves, and his great big toothy grin. The bare feet and the grin will always be entwined in my memories of him.

My father tells a story about going to a wedding reception for Blue Ful-ford's daughter, walking into the banquet room and looking at the band on stage. They were all dressed in tuxedos, but the bass player looked vaguely familiar. "I walked by the stage a couple of times and kept looking at this guy playing the bass guitar," said Daddy. "I kept looking and look-ing, trying to figure out where I had seen him before. I finally went up and asked, 'Goose, is that you?' He smiled real big and said, 'Hey, Clyde, how you doing?' I couldn't get over it. I'd never seen Goose when he wasn't barefoot and I didn't even recognize him."

Neither would a lot of others. Twenty years ago, all of the fishermen and children in Cortez went barefoot during the summer. The fishermen had the toughest, scaliest feet in the world. Times have changed but Goose is one of the few who has stuck to the old ways.

He is also one of the few people in Cortez who is known by one name: Goose. His wife Maida calls him by his given name, Julian, but to every-body else he is Goose. He's even listed that way in the Manatee County phone book. The nickname has been with him since he was a kid. "When I was real little, Major Hall had nicknamed me 'Punch,' 'cause I used to go down to Tommy Fulford's store and always get a Delaware Punch. That was the best cold drink they had. But I got the name Goose when I had just started school. Tink Fulford, your granddaddy, brought home a baby goose one time for Mary Frances, your momma, and they kept it on their front porch. I thought that was about the prettiest thing I'd ever seen, and I'd go over there every day after school to look at it. Shoot, I never studied in school anyway. That was all the school house I got, down there at the Cortez school. I just studied fishing. But I kept going over to look at that baby goose and finally Major Hall started calling me Goose. It just stuck with me."

So did the fiddle music that he heard at his daddy's knee from the time he was born. "I learned to play the fiddle on a bet," he said. "There was this boy living with us who was about my age. We made a bet on who could learn to play a tune on the fiddle first. For three or four days you never heard such sawboning in your life, but after about four days I could play one old tune and that boy was still just a-sawing. I've been playing ever since."

When Goose started learning to play, he held the fiddle down low in the crook of his elbow, a method used by many old-time fiddlers and now popularized by Cajun fiddler Doug Kershaw. But he soon switched to the normal position of holding the fiddle under his chin. He plays the same fiddle that his daddy bought him when he was 12 years old.

It wasn't until the summer of 1981 that I finally got to hear Goose play. I went over to his house on a steamy July night to ask him to play. He had just come back from fishing and told me he was "plum give out." But despite the fatigue, he spent the next two hours playing every fiddle tune I could think of and a dozen more I'd never heard. And he did it well, despite his protests that he was rusty and out of practice.

Goose has played professionally since he was in his teens, and his fiddling style reflects the influences of popular Nashville fiddlers like Tommy Jackson and Benny Martin. He plays in the fast, driving style popularized by Jackson, playing the melody on one string while the adjacent string is "double-stopped" to give a powerful drone effect. The modern influences make Goose's version of "Black Mountain Rag," "Down Yonder," and "Mockingbird" sound quite different from the more traditional versions his father taught him.

Goose showed me some trick fiddling that he's used over the years as show-stoppers at square dances. On one song, he began playing while holding the fiddle between his knees, then picked it up, stuck the bow between his knees and played the tune by moving the fiddle back and forth across the bow. He fiddled another tune in the regular manner for awhile, then undid the frog on the end of the bow that holds the hair in place, draped the hair across the strings, brought the bowstick underneath the fiddle, held both the bow and the end of the hair in one hand, and played it that way. He also used a bow with no hair on it at all, just rosin on the bow itself, and played the tune with the bare wood of the bow. "I seen old Red Herring do that once when he come to Bradenton with Cowboy Copas, and I figured if he could do it, I could do it, too," said Goose. "Boy oh boy, it'd bring the house down!"

Goose told me his brother Hal would be "tickled to death to play his fiddle for you," so I stopped by Hal's house the next afternoon. He was sitting in the living room, barefoot of course, watching daytime game shows on TV, a popular pastime for retired Cortez fishermen. Within an hour he had his fiddle out and was playing "Hen Cackle," the song "my daddy won all his fiddle contests with." When I asked him how his daddy taught him to play, he said, "He didn't teach us. We just picked it up. The little ones would start playing in with the rest of them. I still don't know one note from another. We just had it borned in us, I guess."

Hal fished regularly until 1955, when a spinal fusion operation forced him to stop. He got a job with the Miller Trailer Company in Bradenton and worked there for 16 years, until 1973, when he reached the mandatory retirement age. "They took up a collection when I retired and bought me a castnet that I didn't need—but no pension," he added wryly.

There is a tragic note to my encounter with Hal. I tape recorded that first session of his fiddle playing on a little hand-held portable cassette recorder, which was all I had with me. When I came down a few months later for Christmas, I brought a studio-quality recorder, intending to get his fiddling on tape. Instead, I spent most of Christmas vacation in bed with a cold and, about the time I started feeling better, Hal came down with a cold. I called him and said, "Don't worry about it, when I come back down for Easter I'll bring the recorder and we can play some then." Several weeks before Easter, Hal Culbreath died at age 74.

After the Culbreaths moved to Cortez in 1921, word of their musical talent spread quickly, and they became regular performers at square dances throughout the region. For many years, they were regulars at Todd's Place, a small bar just across the Cortez bridge on Anna Maria Island. Hal and Goose also played at the juke joints along U.S. 41, between Bradenton and Sarasota. "I used to play all the time down at The Village Barn in Sarasota," said Goose. "Sometimes I'd play the fiddle for 45 minutes at a time without stopping. One time they had four different rhythm guitar players—I just kept playing and they'd swap off when one got tired."

The Culbreaths even became mini-celebrities the summer of 1949 when they got their own radio show on WDHL in Bradenton (now WRTL), and even performed several gigs on WSUN, located on the "Million Dollar Pier" in St. Petersburg. "We never did make no money out of it, but we had a lot of fun," said Hal. Their summer show on WDHL was called "Country Cracker Jubilee." It started each week with Shorty Wilson, my great-uncle and their voluntary announcer, shouting into the microphone: "Unh unh unh, don't touch that dial! This is the Country Cracker Jubilee." Then Grandpa Culbreath and the boys would rip into a fiddle tune.

The Culbreaths were the main music makers in Cortez, but not the only ones by any means. The Drymond family moved to Cortez in the early 1920s after homesteading at Port Charlotte, Siesta Key, Sneads Island, and Terra Ceia. They moved into a huge abandoned "clubhouse" that had been used for many years by the Georgia-Florida Land Company to entertain important clients.

"Somebody told my daddy that we could move into the clubhouse and take care of it," said OK Drymond, who was 14 at the time. "It had 32 rooms, all of them furnished, and there were three other families living in it. There was a big old room that was as big as most houses, and that's where we'd have square dances. My daddy would play the fiddle and Goose's daddy would play the fiddle, and the rest of them Culbreath boys would play guitar and harmonica. I don't even remember how old I was when I learned how to call square dances, but I did it for years afterwards." Shortly after the Drymond family moved out of the clubhouse, it was set afire and burned down.

Other Cortez musicians included Hardy and Chub Taylor, two brothers whom Goose had taught. They formed a dance band in the early 1950s called "The Sunshine Boys" and toured small towns in the midwest, with Hardy on guitar and Chub on fiddle and pedal steel. The band broke up when Hardy was called back to active duty for the Korean War. Another fiddle player was Strat Coarsey, Wyman Coarsey's father.

Besides the old-time music tradition of the Culbreaths, there was a strong Spanish musical influence as well. This strain was brought to Cortez by Grandfather Joe Mora. He was born in the Canary Islands, lived in Cuba and then in Key West before settling in Manatee County before the turn of the century. He eventually settled in Cortez and worked primarily as a boat carpenter until his death in the 1930s. He had nine children, most of whom married and settled in Cortez; many of Grandpa Joe's grandchildren and great-grandchildren still live in the village.

Music was a big part of the Mora family's traditions. When the family gathered at Grandpa Joe's for special celebrations and feasts, he'd play the Spanish guitar. "Oh, they had the best times ever over at the Moras'," said Miss Lela Taylor. "We'd go over to the Moras' house and Spanish people would come from all around and play music and eat these big dinners. We'd be there all night playing music—someone beating a fiddle, guitar, bones, and just whatever."

The Culbreaths, Drymonds, and Moras have given Cortez a rich and varied tradition. These cultural roots stretch back as far as the people themselves and are an integral part of the heritage of this village, so the fight to preserve Cortez goes beyond just its physical presence—the houses, the people, the fish houses. It is a fight to preserve the unseen as well—the cultural lineage that turns those physical objects into a community—a home.

On the shoreline, the old Culbreath house stands as a link between the physical and the cultural realities of the community. It is not the most beautiful monument in the world. The tin roof is rusted through and leaking; the floors are sagging badly; the windows are broken; the walls are infested with termites. Inside are the scattered remains of the last residents to live there: mouldy mattresses, a warped and splintered dresser, a white embroidered doily now turned brown with age.

But the importance of this old ramshackle house lies in what it represents, and in that respect it has never been more important. It isn't unusual to find an old house still standing in a small community like Cortez. But the fact that it is standing because of its memories—of good times and good music—is remarkable. That kind of sensitivity to the past exists nowhere else in Manatee County and in very few places in the country. Grey Fulford "ain't about to tear down his Grand Old Opry," but you can be sure that if the battle for Cortez is lost, this old house will be the first thing to go.

A Cortez Album

"Some of the strongest and smartest were the captains, men like . . . Charlie Guthrie." Charlie was one of the last of the old-time captains (1981).

"I've always loved it here on the water." Lela Garner Taylor, age 93, arrived in Cortez from Carteret County, North Carolina, in 1911 (1981).

"There is a rich and powerful history of what women in Cortez have done to survive." Doris "Toodle" Green is the village's resident historian (1981).

"There's a whole lot more to learn about fishing than people might have any idea." Earl Guthrie, mending a castnet in his living room, knows his business (1981).

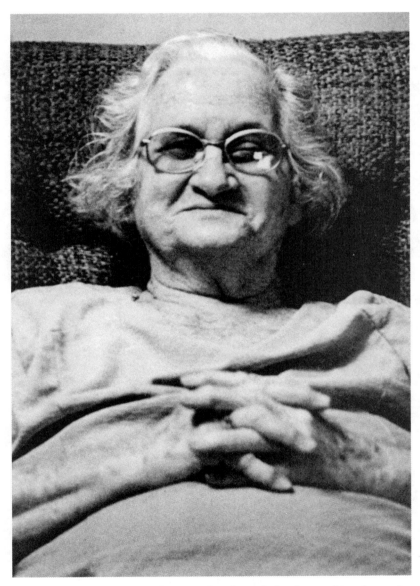

"To Grandma, if you're not going to church regularly, then nothing else you're doing matters much." Edith Fulford reared her family with religion and hard work (1981).

"Mac was my model of what it meant to be a man." Mac McCarter was one of the first black men to work in Cortez (1981).

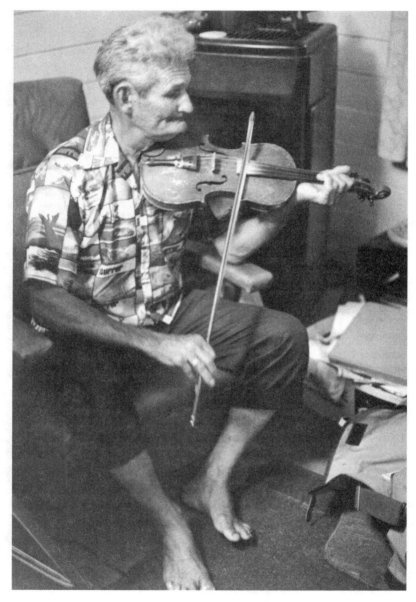

"The Culbreath boys could play almost any kind of instrument." Goose Cul-breath (his real name is Julian) learned to play the fiddle on a bet (1981).

"Being postmaster in my own hometown gives me a lot of pride." Wyman Coarsey is the leading advocate in Cortez opposing the development of high rises, shopping malls, and asphalt parking lots that dominate the rest of Florida's coastline (1981).

"You might say I'm just kind of a lone wolf." Julian Taylor grew up in Cortez and has seen drastic changes (1981).

"Somehow the two images—wildcat and philosopher—seemed compatible in this man." Grey Fulford's exploits as a young man have made him a legend in Cortez (1981).

"They're the hardest people in the world to organize." Woodrow Green was one of the original supporters of a fishermen's union (1981).

"It's a real important thing to have so much family here." Sylvia Bailey and her husband Tony want to make Cortez home for their three children, Brian, Troy, and the youngest, Jenné (pictured here, 1981).

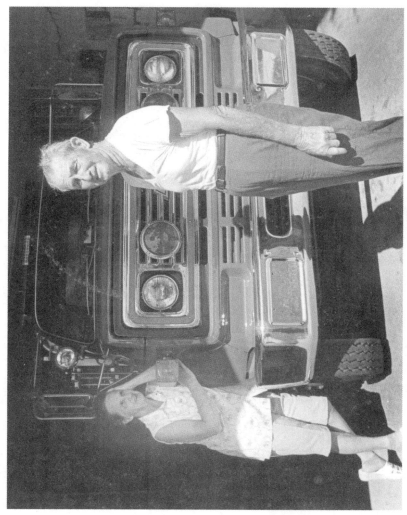

"Bob Knowlton knows more about putting out fires than anyone else in Cortez. . . . And he knows more about the history of fishermen's unions on the Gulf coast of Florida . . . than almost anyone else in the state." Bob and Ruth Knowlton command the Cortez Volunteer Fire Department (1981).

"By 1970, Sue Maddox's utopia was starting to go sour." Sue Maddox was the first person in Cortez to speak out publicly against drug smuggling. When she placed an antismuggling sign in her front yard in August 1980, it was torched that night. (Photo courtesy of the Bradenton Herald)

"This cluster of white frame houses and old fish houses was different. . . ." An aerial view shows the homes, fish houses, fish camps, and churches of Cortez, and the Cortez Bridge (1946; photo by H. R. Smith).

Chapter 8

Court and Spark

JULIAN AND BESSIE TAYLOR got married on the run. On the morning of 19 October 1920, Julian parked his old Model T on a side street behind Bessie's house and then waited while she walked down the street to the Cortez School, lied to the teacher, told her she was sick, and then hurried back and climbed into the front seat of Julian's car. The two young lovers slipped out of Cortez, scared and giggling.

They ditched the Ford in Bradenton for a rented Buick touring car, drove flat-out to Tampa, covering the 50 miles in a mere two hours and forty-five minutes, and at twelve o'clock sharp, with the noon whistle rattling the windows of the Hillsborough County Courthouse, they were pronounced husband and wife by Judge John C. White.

Sixty years later, a marriage that was begun in fear and trembling is still intact, and their memories of that day are as clear as they were then. "I was only 16 and I was afraid that my daddy and uncle were going to chase us," said Bessie, now 80. "Yeah, that's why we rented that Buick," added Julian, 86. "I didn't trust my old Ford and we wanted something that would go faster. I knew a taxi driver who had a brand new 1920 Buick, and we met him at the fairgrounds and he carried us on to Tampa."

By the time they returned home two days later, everyone in Cortez knew they had eloped. As soon as word leaked out, their friends started hatching plots to surprise them on their return. The two newlyweds figured as much, so after riding the train from Tampa to Bradenton, they stalled for time by eating dinner and taking in a silent movie at the old Wallace Theatre. "We wanted it to be after dark when we got home to Cortez," Bessie explained.

It didn't work. "When we come out of the theater there was a bunch from Cortez standing around Julian's car with tin cans and 'Just Married' signs, so Julian grabbed me by the arm and we headed down the street the other direction. We met one of Julian's buddies and gave him a dollar to go back and bring the car around, and then we jumped in and headed for Cortez. When we got to the Cortez schoolhouse, there was a whole gang of people waiting for us and they had the biggest pile of palmetto roots in the road that you've ever seen. But Julian had an extra set of headlights on his car and they was so bright that the people didn't think it was a Model T a-comin' so they started throwing the palmetto roots out of the road. By the time we got there, they'd cleared the road, so we drove right by, hollered 'Hi!' at them and come home."

So far so good, but Julian and Bessie were still worried that one wedding tradition would catch up with them: the chivaree. "People would gang up around the house and beat on tin pans until the couple came outside or invited them in and treated them," said Bessie. "Yeah, sometimes they'd get really rough. They'd take the guy outside and put him on a pole, tie his hands and feet around the pole and walk him up and down the street all night, bouncing him up and down," Julian added. "But we were lucky," said Bessie. "All they did to us was every once in a while somebody'd ring an old cow bell, and then during the night some of them pushed Julian's car way down the road."

Their good luck continued at the first confrontation with Bessie's parents. "When we got to her house, her dad was standing over against the fence," said Julian, "and I went over and shook his hand and said, 'Well, what you gonna say?' He said, 'Congratulations.' And I said, 'Yeah, that's all you can say now, ain't it?' Yeah, her folks were just as friendly as you please. Course there wasn't nothing they could do about it then." Then he and Bessie, still newlyweds at heart, roared with laughter.

The next morning Bessie had one more person to straighten things with: her teacher. "I saw the teacher walking down the road in front of my house, so I went to the gate and stopped her and apologized for telling her a story," said Bessie. "She said to me, 'Honey, you didn't tell me no story. You was the sickest little old girl I've ever seen in my whole life.' She said I had looked just as pale and white as a sheet, and she knew I was telling the truth."

Julian and Bessie's tale of young love on the run is hard to top, but it isn't that unusual for Cortez. More than a few marriage licenses have been filled out on-the-fly. In earlier times, the young lovers headed for the county line, like Julian and Bessie did. In later years, when Florida's age of consent was 18 and Georgia's was only 16, couples made the 250-mile drive to Nahunta, Georgia, where the justice of the peace would sign on the dotted line, no questions asked. Couples hurried through the marriage vows while glancing fearfully over their shoulder for the arrival of angry parents. But they never came. In a small village with only a few marriage-age men and women at any one time, parents were reconciled to the fact that young people were going to get married any way they could.

"Shoot, when I was coming up, there wasn't but four single girls in all of Cortez," said Gene Fulford. "You had to wait your turn to even get a date. One guy'd say, 'Well, I'm gonna see if I can get a date with so-and-so,' and the next week one of the others of us would try."

The pickings were lean and all too familiar. "Everyone had known each other all their lives, so we all just kind of switched around from one to another," said Toodle Green. "We were like every other red-blooded American boy and girl—we'd kind of eyeball somebody we liked. Things haven't changed all that much."

There has been plenty of romance in Cortez, even with the limitations. In fact, Cortez seems to have more than its share of couples who have stayed together for 30, 40, 50, or, in the case of Julian and Bessie, 60 years. It's clear that some of that staying power, perhaps the greater part, was a result of the stringent taboos of divorce. Between the weight of the church and the hand of the law, there wasn't much choice but to stay together and try to make a go of it. Even so, there is no question that love and companionship—which will sometimes do when the former is gone—have a high value in Cortez.

By today's standards, it's a wonder that any young people in Cortez ever got involved. There was almost no formal entertainment of any kind in the village, and very little money or transportation with which to partake of what was available in Bradenton. Lacking "things to do," Cortez young people were forced to make do with the simple things—like talking to each other—which may explain in part the long duration of the bonds that were formed.

"I moved to Cortez from North Carolina when I was 18, and it was a great place to be a young person," said Letha Leeper. "We'd get together, a whole group of us, and walk across the bridge to the beach and just sit and talk. There was a big pine tree on the way to the bridge and we'd sit under that tree for hours and just talk and talk. And sometimes us young girls would go down to The Albion Inn and play the radio and the record player and try to learn how to dance the new dances. I loved it here from the first day."

The beach and the water were the focal points of courtship. There were the walks to the beach, swimming and picnics at the beach, occasional races between fishing boats, and the greatest of all romantic ventures: boatriding. A boy and girl going boatriding—scooter-pooping as it was called—was romance at its highest. Alone in an open boat, especially if night was falling, the couple knew that friends were waiting breathlessly on the docks for a detailed account of what transpired. The suspense was almost unbearable.

If the younger set had the wheels and the money to venture outside of Cortez, there were two movie theaters in Bradenton at their disposal. "You could go to the show . . . and that was it," said Gene Fulford. "That's all there was to go to, and you really thought you had something if you had enough money to take a girl to the show."

"There were two picture shows in Bradenton and one in Palmetto," added his brother Grey, "so if you had a dollar on Saturday night you could go to all three, plus buy a bag of popcorn for a nickel."

For the religious ones in the crowd, going to the movies was all there was to do. Those who drank and danced had a few nightclubs to enjoy, but they were a far cry from the Copacabana. "In the thirties, they opened The Lafayette Dance Hall in Sarasota, and that was headquarters for dances for years," said Earl Guthrie. "A whole carload of us would drive up from Cortez. They sold a little bit of home brew, which was illegal, but they had to have a little sideline to make a few dollars." Besides The Lafayette, there were two clubs on Anna Maria: The Pagoda, a small dance hall with a five-piece orchestra, and another club called The Blue Moon.

If they wanted to dance, the Cortez crowd frequented either or all three, but for everyday drinking, hanging out and carrying on, their favorite spots were Jack Faltz's poolroom on 124th Street and Todd's Place, a little bar at the foot of the Cortez Bridge that spawned more excitement and romance than any other place around.

Life was spiced up during the winter months when Northern tourists arrived for the season. Most were older people, but some families came down to Anna Maria for the winter, and if there were school-age children, they would attend the Cortez school during their stay. This fresh influx of

Yankee manhood and womanhood generated more than a few winter romances. The other major period of excitement in the social life of Cortez occurred during World War II, when thousands of servicemen were stationed in Manatee County. Half a dozen Cortez girls couldn't resist the lure of the uniform, and fell in love and married GIs.

Once a boy and girl started formally courting, they were fair game for all sorts of embarrassing pranks and mischief. "As soon as a guy tried to take a girl out for a boatride, that's when the pranks would start," said Gene Fulford. "Several times my brother Grey found out that Tink and Edith was going out boatriding—this was before they was married—and he would slip down while they was getting ready to go and take some old women's drawers and some old wilted roses and put them in the boat. Edith'd say, 'What in the world are them roses and drawers doing in your boat? I know good and well they wasn't in here before.' Tink would say, 'Well, I swear I didn't know anything about it.' Oh, they had the worst times! Grey and different ones would do it for meanness, you know. They did it a couple of times after they got married and Tink and Edith like to got a divorce one time over it. Tink would never say nothing; he'd just sniff . . . but he knowed who did it."

Whether a couple got married formally or on-the-run, it didn't take long for the excitement to fade away and be replaced by the day-to-day struggle of trying to survive in a poor fishing village. Julian and Bessie's experiences are a case in point. Before the wedding, Julian had been fishing with his father Burns Taylor, who was the first Taylor to leave Carteret County and make the journey to Cortez. He and his wife Annie had settled in Cortez in 1901 with their two oldest children: Emma, who was three years old, and Julian, who was one.

After the wedding, Julian kept fishing with his father for a year, but then the '21 hurricane came along and changed the face of Cortez and the lives of the young couple. "Nobody knew this storm was a-comin' and it was right on top of us before we knew anything," said Julian. "It had been pretty dry and so the ground just soaked up the water, and it kept coming. The water was so high that the waves would have busted our front door if we hadn't put a 2x6 board across it. I stepped out in the front yard, trying to get down the road to get a boat, and the water was up to my waist. When I got down the road a piece, I wound up over my head. All of a sudden the wind picked me up and threw me into a barbed wire fence, and when I got out, I was all skint up. Oh Lord, I didn't have anything left but my britches. Well, I finally hunted me a boat and got Bessie and our two-month-old baby into it and headed up what road there was with the rope across my shoulder. I was wading—with no shirt at all and no shoes. It was blowing hard and a-raining and that wind must have been blowing 60 miles an hour. I got another woman, Miss Lonie Pringle, and her baby Stargell in that boat and pulled it clear up yonder to the other side of where the Paradise Bay Trailer Park is today. I couldn't see nothing, and when I'd come to a bridge, well, I'd just go in over my head and swim across and pull them over behind me."

Once they got past the flooded part of the highway, Bradenton residents were waiting with vehicles to take them to town. They caught a ride in a bakery truck, spent the night in town, and returned to Cortez the next morning.

"My daddy lost most everything he had," said Julian. "I helped him salvage everything we could, but the storm had cleaned off that whole waterfront. While I was helping him, I stuck a nail in my foot. I told Daddy, 'I've got all of this I want.' I went to Bradenton the next day and got me a job in the Ford shop, and we moved to town the next Saturday."

They lived in Bradenton for the next five years. During that time, Julian worked as a stock clerk at the Ford Company, a car salesman, a mechanic, and a machinist. They returned to Cortez in 1926 and he fished for a short while, until he started driving a truck for a fish company. He also opened a marine mechanics business in his garage. "I was fed up with fishing, so I went to motor working," he said. "Altogether, I put in about 50 years working on gasoline engines, and when I wasn't on the road driving a truck, I was working on a blamed old engine. I hauled fish in a semi-tractor-trailer for years—to Savannah, Mobile, and Atlanta. I could haul as many as 20,000 pounds of fish at a time."

Bessie often accompanied him on those runs as a helper, which allowed them to spend more time together and helped keep their relationship strong. "I'll never forget one time we was going across the Cooper River Bridge in Charleston, South Carolina," she said. "We had a full load, and just before he turned onto the bridge, he had a blowout—busted a rear tire. It was on a Sunday, and I don't know how far he had to walk trying to find a service station that would come change that tire. Well, he finally had to come back and do it himself, and I had to help him. By that time we were hot, tired and nervous, and when he pulled out and made a right turn starting up that bridge, well, it was so steep he was almost standing up in his seat with his foot on the accelerator trying to see. That bridge goes almost straight up and the truck was just barely moving. He was cussing that old truck, 'Come on here, get up this bridge,' and I was crying. I looked at him and I said, 'Honey, don't cuss . . . pray.' We got to the top and he said, 'Has your heart gone back in the right place yet? We're at the top.' I looked out and there's two spans of that bridge, and I said, 'Nope, yonder's another one.' " They made it across that bridge and through many hard times in their 60 years together. They are husband and wife, father and mother to two children, and perhaps most importantly, best friends.

Ten years ago, Julian sold the mechanics shop and they moved to a parcel of land in Highlands County. They still come back to Cortez every few months to visit old friends and relatives, and each time the changes in the village are more striking. "Oh Lord, I don't hardly know the place anymore," said Julian. "Most of the old-timers my age are already dead—my old friends Aaron Bell and Judge Millis and fellas like that are all dead. You might say I'm just kind of a lone wolf."

"It's not the Cortez we grew up in," added Bessie. "They used to say, 'Don't ever talk about anybody in Cortez because everybody's related,' but now there are so many new people who have moved in. It's just not the same."

For Julian and Bessie Taylor, much of Cortez is gone, but much remains. It was here that they met, courted, started their married life together, raised their children, and, finally, it is here that they'll return to be buried, side by side. Through it all, the sparks from that wild ride to Tampa in the Buick touring car have burned brightly.

Chapter 9

Roughnecks,
Drunks, and Drifters

IT TOOK GREY FULFORD A LONG TIME to loosen up. He was sitting
under a shade tree in his front yard with his right leg propped up, reweav-
ing the bottom of an old plastic lawn chair. I had heard that his emphysema had flared up and was giving him trouble, but he didn't seem to be
wheezing any more than normal. He seemed fine. A bit subdued, but fine.
Chronic discomfort from emphysema and a bum right leg that was shat-
tered in World War II would be enough to make anyone seem subdued.

I had come to talk to Grey because I thought there ought to be a place
in this book to just rear back and let fly with stories of famous fights, legendary drunks, and shows of strengths—the stuff that folklore is made of.
He seemed to be the leading representative of that tradition. His name
had come up numerous times in other people's stories, giving the impression that this man had been a wildcat in his day. And as Grey started telling old stories, slapping his thigh and letting out big rolls of laughter, and
squinting up his face as he spit tobacco juice on the ground after every
punchline, the impression was confirmed.

But when I left, there was another impression of this man, too: an
armchair philosopher who reflected on all the major issues of the day—
living and dying, the threat of nuclear war, and the future of the world.
Somehow the two images—wildcat and philosopher—seemed compatible
in this man who has had full shares of both joy and misery.

Grey knows about misery. When he was eight years old, his father
Clyde Fulford died in the 1918 flu epidemic. His mother Mamie was left
with four young children: Grey, the oldest; his brother Gene, age 2; D.D.,
who died in childhood; and his sister Margaret, who was only one month

old. Mamie made a living by keeping boarders, mostly single men who came down to Cortez from North Carolina for the fall roe season. "She'd charge them about $5 a week and another 50 cents a week to do their laundry," said Gene. "Sometimes she'd have six or seven of them at a time sleeping on cots in the old house we rented out. It was like a hotel. Momma had two old wood stoves and she hired two other women to help with the cooking, and Grandma would help make the biscuits and the cornbread. Wasn't no money around, but that's how she got enough to raise us."

When World War II broke out, Grey was one of 48 Cortez boys to enlist. He joined the Army, and two and a half years later, marching ashore on one of the small atolls in the South Pacific that the Japanese fought so fiercely to hold, he was shot in the knee. His leg was wrecked. Grey was carried to a field hospital, put in a body cast that covered his entire right leg, half his left one, and enough of his chest to make it difficult to breathe, and shipped home on a transport ship. "Yeah, I spent 30 months in the Army and 33 months in the hospital," Grey said, smiling ruefully.

Almost three years later, he was released from the hospital and returned to Cortez. He went back to fishing, but the stiff leg hampered him so much that he finally had to give it up. He and his wife Virginia have gotten by on her salary as a postal clerk at the Cortez post office and disability checks from the government.

The suffering from the leg and the added misery of emphysema have understandably dampened his spirits. "A lot of those wild things I did I just as soon forget, or wish I could forget," he told me. "I heard a preacher say that the Bible gives you 70 years to live and after that all the years will be misery, but my last 10 years have been misery."

But his friends in Cortez are not reluctant to recall Grey's past antics, which ranged from the mean to the mischievous. "Oh, Grey was always into something," said Woodrow Green. "One night me and Grey had been down at the poolroom having a little session of shooting pool, you know. Wasn't either one of us married at the time. We left to come home and we come by the barbershop. The barber used to keep a lot of flowers in the windowsill, and Grey said, 'Let's do something.' I says, 'No, let's go home.' And Grey says, 'Wait a minute.' And he went and pulled all the man's pretty flowers up, just for mischief."

"One night me and Grey was leaving Todd's Place over at the beach," said OK Drymond, "and Grey saw a laundry truck parked on the beach.

So he snuck over and took out a big bag of laundry, dug a deep hole in the sand, and buried that bag of laundry. I don't guess they ever did find it."

There are other stories: Grey cutting a plug out of some watermelons my grandma was growing, eating out the heart, replacing the plug, and Grandma never figuring out what was killing her melons; or leaving the women's underwear and wilted roses in Grandpa's boat. Grey never admitted to any of those pranks when I mentioned them, but he didn't deny them either, and I could swear there was a devilish gleam in his eyes when I recounted them. The pain of the past decade may have dampened his spirit, but it hasn't killed it.

Grey, or "Forty" as many people call him, may be the best representative of Cortez's wild side, but he is by no means the only one. For instance, I heard three stories about Cortez fishermen getting their shoes nailed to the dock, and each incident had a different perpetrator and victim. I can't vouch for the truth of any of them, but when I heard that it happened once to Albert "Gator" Mora, I figured that one had to be true. Gator Mora was a mountain of a man whose friendly nature, brute strength, and fearlessness are still legendary, even though he died in 1962.

Gator was about three ax handles wide, with massive arms and a sheaf of curly hair that almost stood straight up. He was strong all over—even his old leathery toes were like steel traps when he wrapped them around you. He fished with Grandpa Tink for many years and, when it was time to strike a school of fish, Gator would come lumbering into the cabin where us boys were sound asleep, poke a big, scaly foot into one of the lower bunks, and grab one of us on the fleshy part of the stomach and shut down on it. That's all it took to send us scrambling out of the cabin and jumping overboard with the end of the net, trying to escape.

Goose Culbreath told me the story about Gator getting his shoes nailed to the dock: "One day old man Pringle had gone out fishing and caught himself a big old pompano and, when he come in, he threw it up on the dock to take home to eat. While he was out pulling his net onto the spreads, Gator took some roofing nails and nailed down that pompano under the fins, so you couldn't even see the nails. Old man Pringle come back and went to pick up his pompano, and it wouldn't come. Well, he didn't say a word, just walked off the dock. Somebody said, 'Hey Uncle, you left your pompano!' He said 'It ain't my pompano' and kept walking. Well, he figured Gator had done it, so a couple of days later Gator was sitting down on the dock mending net. Now Gator was a great one for mending net, and he'd always take his shoes off and sit there and stick his toes in the mashes. Old man Pringle snuck up and drove a nail right through the sole of both of Gator's shoes. When Gator got up to leave, he walked over and slipped his feet in the shoes, tried to move, and fell right over on his face!"

Gator's physical strength was awesome. I heard several stories about him lifting the front of a car right off the ground. In one tale, Gator was driving home from town one day and the front axle of his car actually broke off. He got out, picked up the front end of the car, and walked it on home. In another, Wyman Coarsey had run his daddy's truck off the road and into a ditch. He was trying to figure out how to get it out and avoid a whipping when Gator walked up; he promptly picked up the front end of the truck and sat it back on the road for Wyman.

Some people think Gator could lift anything. "One time Uncle Tink and me and Gator and Grey and Dewey Capo was fishing down at Sister Key, putting in a stop," said Man Adams. "Somehow the old *Ralph*, Uncle Tink's boat, swung up there towards shore and the tide ebbed out and put her aground. I mean she was hard aground. Uncle Tink crawled in the cabin and said, 'I'm going to sleep until the tide comes in.' Well, it was a Saturday and we was drinking moonshine whiskey like nobody's business, and we wanted to go home. So Gator went and got a thwart out of the boat—it was about ten inches wide and two inches thick. He got overboard and shoved that thwart under her stern and picked up on her and we shoved her off in that channel. She was a 29-foot boat and he just picked her up! We tied that old mess of scows onto her and I got up there and started her up, and Tink hollered, 'What're you doing?' I said 'I'm going home.' When we got to the dock, he said, 'How in the hell did you boys get that thing off there?' Well, when we told him, he couldn't hardly believe it."

Gator was absolutely fearless. "You see that knuckle there?" said Man Adams, holding up his right fist and showing me a flat, concave knuckle on his middle finger. "Well I broke that knuckle on Gator's head. Used to we'd gather down on the shore in the wintertime and build a fire and the menfolk would sit around it and shoot the breeze. After they'd leave, all us kids would go there and sit around. We was there one time and Gator, he was three years older than me, he was so tough that he said, 'Now you guys can hit me anywhere you want, just don't hit me in the face. But you hit me anywhere else just as hard as you want.' So we started swinging at him—wham! We was hitting him in the chest and in the stomach, and one time he seen me draw back and just as I was swinging, he ducked his head. I hit him right on the top of the head just as hard as I could swing, and it drove that knuckle right back and broke it. Gator, he just laughed. He thought it was fun. I'm right-handed and I was going to school, and for days that knuckle was so swelled up I couldn't even write."

By the time he was full grown, Gator's natural strength was known far and wide. He and Ike Pearce, a Cortez fisherman who had the reputation as "the meanest man in Cortez," began supplementing their income by making and selling moonshine whiskey. They had a still out in the woods east of Cortez and another one on Anna Maria Island. Under the influence of corn whiskey, Gator's strength and fearlessness sometimes got him into troublesome adventures.

"There was a little building right behind Todd's Place, which was the hangout at the beach, where all of us would sit and play cards," recalled OK. "One time there was a bunch in there and they was all pretty drunk. Gator knew that one side of the building just had sheathing nailed to the frames, that was all, but the other side was built right up against a concrete wall. So he told one of the guys, 'I'll bet you that I'll run right through that wall over there if you'll run through the other side.' The guy took him up on it, so Gator lowered his head and started running and ran right through that sheathing. The other guy got up and ran into that other wall, hit that concrete head-on and it knocked him out cold. It liked to kill him!"

Man Adams recalled another incident: "Years ago, Les Guthrie used to run a little juke joint in his house, and one time we was in there shooting pool and drinking. Gator was drunk and he had done something to old man Les, I don't even remember what it was, but old man Les kept picking onto it and finally Gator turned around and slapped the stew out of him. Old man Les said, 'You big so-and-so, you better not be here when I get back!' He went to get his shotgun and he was gonna kill Gator! I knew it! Well, Gator had a head of hair that would stand straight up; it was kinda kinky 'cause he was Spanish. So I got that Gator right in the hair of the head and I said, 'Come on, let's go.' And I drug him all the way home and told his wife Stella: 'You better get Gator to bed or old man Les is gonna kill him.' That was on Saturday night, and on Monday when we went fishing, Gator said to me, 'Man, I don't know what's the matter with my head. It's so sore I can't even comb my hair.' I said, 'You ought not to! I drug you clear from old man Les's house to your house by the hair of the head.' "

Despite the wildness, Gator was one of the most friendly and jovial fishermen in Cortez, and he was well liked by almost everyone. His life ended tragically, however, in 1962, when worsening financial problems drove him deeper and deeper into depression, and eventually to suicide. "He come over to my house one morning and asked me if he could borrow my garden hose," said Gene Fulford, his brother-in-law, who lived next door. "I gave it to him, and I could hear him out there fiddling around with his car—he had an old 1960 Oldsmobile. I thought he was working on it or something. But he hooked that garden hose up to the exhaust pipe, stuck the end of the hose inside the car, and then got in there and started it up. He had all the doors locked from the inside. I finally went over to see what he was doing, and the whole car was all smoked up. I yelled to my neighbor and we broke the glass out of one window, opened the door and pulled him out. He was still breathing a little, but he died before they could get him to the hospital. I'll tell you, he's one of the ones I miss the most . . . him and Tink."

There is another Cortez fisherman whose strength and fighting skill are still legendary: Primrose Garner. Primrose was the brother of Gaylord "Gayboy" Garner, who owns the Star Fish Company. Like Gator, Primrose seemed almost larger than life; also like Gator, his life ended tragically.

"Primrose was a big old guy and as tough as a rubber ball," said Man Adams. "You'd hit him and just bounce off. And he loved to fight. They built a dance hall over on the beach in the '30s and there was four different outfits: Cortez, Palmetto, Bradenton, and East Manatee. All these guys would meet over there and we hated each other. One time there was two or three guys from Palmetto and they was all football players, 200-225 pounds, and three of them wanted to get on Primrose at one time. He knew he couldn't handle them all, so he got in the car and drove home. I was the first one he met, and he said, 'I want you to help me.' He got me and Curt Johns and somebody else and we went back. He said, 'All I want you to do is keep those other guys off me. I want them one at a time.' He walked there to the door of Todd's Place and said, 'Come on out. I'm ready for you.' Well, they come out and looked at us, and Primrose said, 'One at a time.' So he took one of them guys and he knocked him down two or three times, and he got onto him and beat his head on the pavement until there was blood running out of his ears. Finally the guy said, 'Pull him off me. I've got enough.' So we pulled Primrose off and said 'Don't kill him.' He turned to the other two and said, 'Okay, either of you guys are next.' And they said, 'Nope,' and they got their buddy and put him in the car. We told them, 'We don't want to never see you on this island again or you're gonna get just what he got. You stay on your side of the river over in Palmetto.' And they didn't come no more."

Fights were a common occurrence in local bars, and Primrose had a reputation for standing up for his friends. "He was really a nice guy, but meaner than hell when he got mad," said Hubert Horne. "During World War II, my brother Bill came home from the Navy on leave, and we went over to Todd's Place and sat down at a table. Bill wasn't old enough to drink and neither was I, but I told the waiter I wanted a beer. He said I wasn't old enough, but Primrose was in there in his Marine uniform. He had been in the Pacific when the war first broke out, and he'd been overseas for about four years and had ribbons from here to here. He'd just gotten back. He told the waiter, 'What in hell you mean he's not old enough? He just come back from the Pacific with me. Give him a drink!' So I got my beer that night."

"That was a mean place, especially during the war," Hubert added. "There was one guy over there they called 'Whitey,' and every time he got the chance, he'd whipped somebody. One time he started something with Dan Taylor and he cleaned Dan Taylor's clock. Next thing you know his buddies, who were motorcycle boys, all showed up and they ended up in a big fight with the Cortez boys. My brother Bill jumped right in the middle of it. Couple days later Primrose and Gayboy were over there, and Whitey started to pull something on Primrose. Primrose grabbed Whitey by the shirt, picked him up and slapped him three times, sat him back down on his stool and said, 'Stay there!' That ended that."

Primrose was killed in a traffic accident a few years after the war. "He had him a convertible and he drove like a maniac," said Hubert. "He went up to North Carolina to visit his relatives and coming back he had that thing floorboarded and a Greyhound bus stopped in front of him. He run right up under the rear of it and was killed."

Cortez fishermen have done their share of hard drinking over the years. As Charlie Guthrie describes it: "A lot of them fellas didn't drink . . . they funnelled it down." But one of the great ironies in Cortez is that half of the population drinks and the other half is fervently opposed to it. The conflicts between those two factions have produced some memorable episodes.

"One night Uncle Sanders Fulford was out fishing, and he got stuck by a catfish fin, and it just about killed him," said Toodle Green. "He was just about ready to pull his hair out. So when he came in, he went over to Uncle Nate's house 'cause he knew Uncle Nate always kept a jug of liquor. He told Uncle Nate what happened, and Uncle Nate went and got his bottle out, and Uncle Sanders just downed the house to kill the pain. Well, his wife, Aunt Lula, she wouldn't put up with any drinking at all. She'd just give him a fit. So when he got home, Aunt Lula wouldn't even let him in the house! He tried to explain about the catfish, but she wouldn't hear of it 'cause she thought he'd been out drinking with the boys."

"Earl Taylor's mother Julie used to whip him for going off and getting drunk," said Hubert Horne. "We lived right across the street from them, and I don't know how many times I've been woken up around midnight, when the Sailor's Haven bar closed, and all the guys would come back by their house and start yelling, 'Owww, Julie! No, Julie! Don't hit me, Julie! Oh Jesus, Julie, stop hitting me!' They'd go on like that for half an hour, just for meanness."

Cortez has always had at least one or two "town drunks"—harmless old men living in single-room fish camps on the shore. They earned a few dollars shoveling fish at the docks or depended on relatives or government assistance to survive. There's nothing quaint or funny about old alcoholics stumbling their way from one bottle to the next, but at least in Cortez they are accepted as part of the community, rather than being shipped off to state institutions. Other than occasional pranks the youngsters pull on them and occasional run-ins with the law when they get out of hand, the old drunks in Cortez still have a home.

Of course, the drinking stories have their tragic sides as well. There have been more than a few men and women in Cortez with serious drinking problems, and cases where "the fathers were off drinking and gambling while their kids had nothing to eat," says my mother.

One of the most tragic cases involved Uncle Neriah Taylor. "Uncle Neriah would go for months and months without drinking, and then he'd get started and wouldn't stop for two or three weeks," said Goose Culbreath. "Sometimes he'd get so drunk he couldn't turn a corner, and that's a fact. One night Marvin Carver ran into him walking down the street, and Marvin said, 'Uncle Neriah, you want me to help you get home?' 'No, son,' he said. 'If you can just help me turn his corner I'll be fine.' So Marvin helped him around the corner and the old man walked straight as an arrow all the way home.

"The way he died was that a 50-gallon drum of rum washed up on the beach one day and some of the boys got it down to Cortez in a boat. They had it over at Pig Guthrie's house, and old man Neriah come walking up with about three empty bottles and said, 'Boys, I want to get me some of that rum.' They told him, 'Now don't be doing that, Uncle Neriah. You don't want any of this stuff. It's so strong it'd even kill Gator Mora.' He stood there and thought about it for a minute and said, 'Boys, fill 'em up.' So he got drunk and must have been trying to walk home and fell overboard 'cause they found him the next day floating down at Bell's fish house, caught on a piling."

This chapter wouldn't be complete without talking about a group of men in Cortez's history with special attraction and mystique: the old bachelors. These old bachelors usually showed up unannounced, stayed for awhile, and left just as mysteriously. Some arrived by boat, others by land. They lived in old fish camps along the shore, with only a single cot, a kerosene stove and lantern, and a few tattered belongings. But they had a special magic for the youngsters in Cortez.

"There were always transients who came into Cortez from out of nowhere and nobody knew where they came from," said Momma. "Bill Ireland was one of them. He lived in the house that Grey lives in now, but it was out over the water on pilings and you could only get to it by boat. He was an old bachelor and he took care of himself, and he drank a lot and, of course, Mama would complain about that. Nobody knew where he came from except that he was from North Carolina. But he told me once that he had sailed on four-masted schooners up in Nova Scotia.

"Uncle Bill and Daddy were very good friends and he was very much a part of our family," Momma added. "Every Saturday night he would come over to our house and we'd make ice cream. And sometimes he'd cook fried chicken at his house and we'd go eat with him. One thing I really remember about him is that he'd order raisins and raw peanuts from somewhere and he'd give them to us when we went over. Mama would say, 'Now, don't eat all of his stuff,' but Uncle Bill would say, 'Go ahead, there's more where that came from.' And every Christmas he'd give Mama and Daddy money to buy presents for us.

"But one night he was in a bar on the highway," she continued, "and somebody took some of his money. Before daylight Bill got a gun and shot it through the guy's cabin. Well, he got embarrassed about it because everybody knew he'd done it, and right after that he packed up everything he owned and left town. He went off to Texas for awhile, and then back to Florida and ended up in Vero Beach, on the east coast. One of our family's big trips was loading up our car and going over to the east coast to find Bill 'cause he meant so much to us and to Daddy."

Pig added more details: "We drove over there in our 1933 Plymouth, and Daddy talked him into coming back, and then later Daddy went back over in the truck and loaded up Uncle Bill and moved him to Punta Rassa, down by Pine Island. Daddy moved him back to Cortez during World War II. For years, he lived in an old camp next to our house, until he got old and demented. They put him in the Arcadia State Hospital and he died there, and I remember Mama got in touch with his nephew in North Carolina and let him know that Bill had died."

There were other colorful characters, including one old bachelor called Old Lad. "He came sailing into Cortez in a big sailboat when I was nine or ten years old," said Momma. "Daddy let him live in a fish camp. He lived out there and he did carpentry work around town. He built a kitchen cabinet for Mama. What I remember most about him was that he subscribed to *National Geographic* magazine. I can still see those magazines out there. We used to play in his camp and read them. I don't think anybody knew much about him, but one time he decided to leave and was gone for months and months. He came back and he was so sunburned—he had big blisters all over his skin—and they had to treat him for a long time. I don't know what ever happened to him, because when I left to go to college, he was still living out there in that camp."

"Old Clamdigger" Joe Williams was another one of the bachelors. He got his name from catching clams and selling them to restaurants. Man Adams remembered his arrival in Cortez in a beat-up skiff: "We come in from fishing one day and Old Clam Joe was tied up at the seine spreads catching catfish. He asked Tink, 'Do you own this?' Tink said, 'Yeah, me and my Daddy.' He asked if it was okay for him to hang around there, and Tink said, 'Go ahead, but you don't have to catch catfish. You can have all the mullet you want.' We took him out fishing with us that night, and we saw a big school of fish, probably 25,000 pounds, and Clam Joe said, 'Neighbor, what in the world is that big black thing out there?' We told him, 'Uncle Joe, that's all mullet.' We hauled up there and caught about 11,000 and Uncle Joe got a share in it. He took his money and went out and bought a case of whiskey for about $50, and anybody who went to his camp, he'd say, 'Come on, have a drink.' Well, one time this doggone guy snuck in there and stole all of Uncle Joe's money. Joe knew who done it, and he said to Dick Posey, 'You tell that guy if he don't bring my money back I'm gonna leave him floating out there in the bay.' The next morning his money was laying right there on his bunk."

"That old man would have done just what he said," added Earl Guthrie. "He had come from Arizona and one day we was sitting there talking to him, and he was talking about how things were rough out west. Somebody said, 'Uncle Joe, what kind of law did you have out there?' He said, 'The only law you had was your carbine.' "

Clamdigger Joe, like the others, was a mysterious character to Cortez youngsters. "He used to call me Rosebud," said Momma, "and he told my mother that he had an insurance policy and I was his beneficiary. Of course, when he died, there really wasn't anything. When he was real old, about 85, somebody got to talking to him about going to church, and Clamdigger Joe said he wanted to go. He started going to church and was baptized, and it was like he had been looking for it all his life."

The other source of mystery and intrigue was pirate gold; every town on the Gulf inevitably had its legend about buried pirate treasure. Pirates did roam the Gulf coast of Florida, raiding Spanish treasure ships and stashing their loot along the swampy coastline. Gold fever afflicted several generations of young bucks in Cortez, luring them into what now seem, with hindsight, silly and preposterous treasure hunts. They seemed much more reasonable at the time.

Sid Guthrie, who died in 1980 at age 83, taped an interview with Toodle in which he talked about Cortez's pirate gold: "There used to be an old Indian shell mound on the other side of Cortez Road, and that's where the treasure was supposed to be. I often heard my Daddy and Capt. Billy Fulford talking about it. They thought there was some kind of treasure there. One time an old man came to Cortez with a map and talked all of them into quitting fishing and going out there to dig. He said they'd all be rich. Well, they dug and dug and dug, and they claimed they found something down there, but finally they got down so deep that the water was pouring in all around them and they couldn't dig anymore. They had to quit and go back to fishing and get something to eat. Then in later years some of us younger ones thought we'd try it out. So we got a couple of pumps and got down there and dug around in that hole. We dug way down in there for about a month and then we give up. We couldn't find anything but some big old conchs from the Indians. There were layers and layers of conchs. We finally all got disgusted."

Gold fever didn't die, and even the U.S. government tried to find Cortez's buried treasure. Wyman Coarsey, whose family lived on top of the shell mound, still believes there was something there: "A man from the government come in there after we bought it and he claimed that the records showed that there was a pirate treasure buried there. It was supposed to be one of Gasparilla's, the pirate that they have that festival for in Tampa. Those government men came around with metal detectors trying to locate it, but they never did. But that mound had been dug into by so many treasure hunters, and the county had hauled away thousands of loads of shell to put on the roads around here."

The shell mound was eventually destroyed and a canal dug in its place. So, we'll never know . . . or will we? All the metal detectors in the world can't kill a gold rumor once it gets started and, despite the years of fruitless digging, I wouldn't be surprised if another hardy band of golddiggers takes a stab at Cortez's buried treasure.

Grey Fulford would have gladly joined that search party 40 years ago, but not now. All he wants to do today is hold onto what he's got: his house on the water, what's left of his health, and, if possible, his way of life in Cortez. As for wild times and foolishness, his memories will have to do.

He has a fatalistic attitude about the future of the world and the future of Cortez—for him the two go hand in hand. "You look around at the world and it's scary," he said. "We've got more nuclear bombs than we know what to do with, and so do the Russians. It'd be suicide to go to war. And you look around here—the changes are coming so fast, they're coming everyday. But Mother Nature is a great leveler. They've built all these condos, but now they're running out of drinking water and the sewage is overflowing."

He feels the outside world impinging on his life but doesn't think much can be done to stop it. "Things are going to go along the way they go," he said. And yet, that fatalism is balanced by a stubborn resistance to fight back anyway, even if it's hopeless. Some of the old spark is yet in Grey Fulford.

"All I know is that I'm never gonna sell out my little place here as long as I live. I still hate the Yankees and a Yankee will always be a Yankee. They come down here and they think they're better than us, but they're not one bit better. You know, somebody told me once 'Grey, you either got to go along with everybody or you got to be a rebel.' Well," he said, leaning forward in his lawn chair to spit tobacco juice on the ground between his legs, "I guess I'll always be a rebel."

Chapter 10

"We Always
Had Something to Do"

HUBERT HORNE DOESN'T LOOK much like a hell-raiser anymore, but 40 years ago, this short, stocky man with the great big belly was a holy terror in Cortez, roaming the streets with a pack of hellions, all of them barefoot, sunburned, with patches all over their pants, a homemade sling-shot dangling from their back pockets, and a thick ring of black dirt around their necks. Today, after a career in the Army and raising two children of his own, Hubert Horne hasn't forgotten what it meant to grow up in Cortez.

"Everybody's gonna have their view of it," he said. "Some will say that there was nothing for the kids to do down here—no clubs, no recreation centers, no nothing. But a few years ago, Richard Roberts, my best friend growing up, made a very profound statement. He said, 'Kids growing up today ask "Who am I?" But when I was ten years old I knew who I was— I was that guy that was gonna have to get out and make a living. I didn't have to worry about who I was.' And that's really the way it was in Cortez. I grew up here in the middle of the Depression, and yet not one person in Cortez went hungry. Everybody was hardworking and everybody helped each other. If one family needed something then some of the others would make sure they got it. Hell, I didn't even know my family didn't have any money. I got my three meals a day. My pants might have had patches all over them, and when they wouldn't hold patches anymore then I wore short pants with patches on the seat, but everybody else's were the same way."

Everyone I talked to about growing up in Cortez expressed the same feelings of closeness. Modern psychologists talk about young people suffering from identity crises, but that was one childhood illness that Cortez youth did not catch. It was no romantic paradise, by any means, and there have been young people in Cortez with emotional and psychological problems, but identity has not been one of them. If nothing else, they knew they belonged . . . to the community, to the culture, and to the family.

The family has played a big part in the security of Cortez's children, and in this respect Hubert Horne was well blessed. His family wasn't one of the old-guard pioneer families from North Carolina—like the Fulfords, Guthries, and Taylors—but they made up for their relatively late arrival with numbers.

Hubert is my second cousin on the Green side, and it's been hard to track down much information about family roots. For the Green family, as for many other white working-class Southerners, family genealogy was not a high priority. All I knew about myself when I was growing up was that I was white, a Southerner, and a Christian. Somehow that was all that mattered. It wasn't until the summer of 1970, when I went to work at a resort hotel in Monmouth, New Jersey—an Irish-Catholic resort town—that I began to look beyond the South for my identity. People asked, "Are you Irish?" I had no idea. I knew all about race—it was burned into the forefront of my consciousness—but that's the first time I really thought about ethnicity.

When I started researching this book, I had little trouble finding out about the Fulfords, my mother's family, because they lived for 200 years in Carteret County, North Carolina. The Greens were a different story. All I know is that at some time prior to 1880, my great-grandparents Andrew Jackson Green and his wife Rebecca moved from Coffee County, Georgia, to Shady Grove, a tiny farming community in Taylor County, Florida. Andrew and Rebecca had 12 children in the piney woods north of Perry, although two died in childhood. Four sons survived: Millard Fillmore (my grandfather), Henderson, Elverton, and Sylvester; and five daughters: Kate, Florence, Lydia, Eva, and Evelyn (Hubert's mother). All of the brothers are now dead, but all of my great-aunts, except Florence, are still living together in Bradenton. Aunt Kate is the oldest at 93, and Aunt Evelyn, the youngest, is 81.

My great-grandparents both died when the aunts were very young, so Uncle Sylvester, a schoolteacher in Taylor County and later a noted history professor at the University of Florida, raised the girls. About 1915, Uncle Elverton and Uncle Sylvester bought some land in Highlands

County; Elverton moved there and began homesteading. When he came down with a severe case of rheumatoid arthritis, which eventually got so bad that he had to crawl on his hands and knees to get around, the doctor told him that he needed to move near the salt air of the Gulf. So in 1917, Elverton and his wife Lizzie and their two young sons Edgar and Woodrow moved to the eastern part of Manatee County, and shortly afterwards, to Cortez. They settled in the village and Elverton's arthritis cleared up enough for him to start fishing.

Later that year, Aunt Kate moved to Cortez with her first husband and their daughter Mary. The rest of the family began to make visits, and one by one, each of the aunts settled there as well. Aunt Eva and Aunt Lydia took jobs teaching at the school; Aunt Florence married Johnny Austin, a local fisherman; Aunt Evelyn and her husband Shorty Horne were the last to arrive, bringing their two young sons Billy and Hubert.

The aunts have been inseparable over the years. They're so close that when Florence split up with Johnny, Eva—the firebrand of the group— told him, "Johnny, when you marry one of us you marry all of us, and when you split up with one of us you split up with all of us, too." After her divorce, Florence moved to Bradenton and opened a beauty parlor. Eva, Evelyn, and Kate got their beautician's licenses and helped Florence in the business. Lydia was the only holdout; she taught elementary school until she reached mandatory retirement age—almost 50 years.

Florence died in 1965, but the other aunts kept the beauty shop open for a few more years, until they got too feeble to run it. Today, Kate and Eva live together in one house, with Lydia and Evelyn in another small house a block away. The closeness of the aunts was particularly evident when Eva became seriously ill in October 1982, and her doctor gave her only three or four months to live. The day after the doctor made his diagnosis, Lydia and Evelyn packed their suitcases, made Hubert and Daddy haul their bags and their favorite easy chairs to Kate and Eva's, and moved in to help take care of Eva.

It reminded me of a Faulkner short story, watching these old sisters rallying together to make Eva's last weeks or months more bearable. They talked very little with Eva about her illness. They didn't offer any counsel on "death and dying," as a professional therapist might. They never even told her that they knew the doctor's prediction. But they were there—solidly, silently—together. They never considered doing otherwise. It was family at its best.

Two months later, the doctors removed Eva's diseased gall bladder, and she immediately improved; the doctors revised their dire predictions. The day Eva returned from the hospital, Lydia and Evelyn repacked their suitcases, had Daddy and Hubert load up their easy chairs, and returned home, their job done.

In Cortez, those deep family ties gave children a sense of self, but it was at the fish houses that they gained a sense of others. "Us kids always had something to do—we'd go to them docks," said Hubert. "When I was seven years old, I was working on the docks, and all the kids were, it wasn't just me. We spent all our time at the docks. We carried knives on our belts, not for fighting, but for gutting fish. And if there was work to do, we did it."

Youngsters in Cortez are introduced to regular work at very young ages. In a fishing village, as in other working-class communities, children are an important part of the work force. Some might feel that working at the fish houses deprived the kids of their childhood, but compared to middle-class communities where children are isolated from meaningful work until their late teens, I'd choose the Cortez model. Cortez youngsters are part of the community, with important roles and responsibilities, and they know it.

They also learn about financial independence by the time they are ten. That was one of the biggest differences for me between summers in Cortez and my normal life in Tallahassee. During the school year, my friends and I had all kinds of ways to make money: we collected pop bottles, raked yards, and sold peanuts and hot dogs at college football games. These were jobs delegated to most middle-class kids. But in Cortez, I was a regular member of my grandpa's fishing crew, working side by side with grown men, and that was a completely different experience. When I was eight, I started drawing a regular paycheck of $10 a week—more than any of my friends in Tallahassee made. I went up to a half-share at age 12 and, when I was raised to a full-share at age 15, I knew I was a man. My friends in Tallahassee had nothing to compare to that.

Cortez youngsters worked hard for their money. "If I remember right, we was getting five cents for every 100 pounds of trout and mackerel we gutted," said Hubert. "We used to spend our nights down there during the mackerel runs 'cause they bring them in at night. We'd get in trouble for cutting school, and it used to make us mad because the kids from the strawberry farms in East Manatee got excused to pick strawberries, but they wouldn't let us off to gut mackerel."

The kids devised all sorts of schemes to earn spending money for cold drinks and honey buns. "We used to make our own boats out of tin," said Hubert. "We'd take a sheet of roofing tin and wrap it around a 2x4 to make the bow, wrap it around another board on the back end, put a board across the middle to keep the sides apart, pour melted tar around it to seal the cracks, stick a broomstick through a hole for a mast, put a sail on that dude and take off. If we wanted to go fast, we'd take wooden shingles, one in each hand, and paddle that dude. Now if somebody put in a stop in 'The Kitchen,' we'd go up there in our boats and grab the fish that were left up in the puddles near the mangroves. Grab what we could and sell them. Oh, we had all kinds of ways to make a dime.

"Some of the fish dealers would run us off their docks if we were just laying around, but most of them would put up with us because they sure wanted us there when there was work to do. When a boat would come in, we'd help unload the fish, except that we'd throw a lot of them under the dock instead of on it. Then when everybody'd leave, we'd dive the fish up and sell them. You're gonna lose a few anyway, right? So we just made sure we'd lose a few more. But the dealers knew we were doing it. That's why they didn't pay us much; they knew we were gonna get it sooner or later."

Toodle Green remembers that Woodrow, her husband, had a regular fish-house job when he was only six years old: "Just as soon as they got old enough to be of any help to the father in any way, they started working. Woodrow was just a tiny little fellow, and there was a man who ran the fish house who loved baseball, and when they started having baseball games in Bradenton, he would pay Woodrow ten cents to stay down at the dock and put ice on the fish if any boats came in. All of the kids had responsibilities like that. They weren't allowed to just roam all over town and play all the time; they had jobs and they knew they had to do them."

It's still true today. My teenage cousins Cheri and Susie Fulford have been helping their father Wayne on his shrimp boat since they were real young. One of my youngest cousins Troy Bailey, age six, comes home from school, puts on his Organized Fishermen of Florida cap, and goes down to the dock to help his grandpa Pig Fulford unload sardines. Troy's job is to operate the controls on a hydraulic hoist that lifts big boxes of sardines out of the boats. To him, the job is a lot of fun and hardly differs from playing, yet it is a useful job and he does it well.

Of course, life for Cortez youngsters was not all work, by any means; they had a freedom there that is rarely found. Not surprisingly, much of the fun centered around the water. They would go swimming every chance they got. "We'd be standing around and somebody'd say, 'Come on, let's go swimming,' and we'd go jump off one of them docks and swim all after-noon," said Gene Fulford. "We even used to swim over to the beach, in-stead of walking across the bridge. We'd swim alongside some of them old pilings and rest as we'd go, and if we had any money, we'd go to Todd's Place, at the foot of the bridge and buy a hamburger. We'd stay over at the beach all day. It's a wonder we didn't all get drownded."

Going swimming was just as big a deal for girls as for boys, and there were few inhibitions for either sex. "We were no different from the boys," said Toodle. "We'd go down to the bay—it was clean then, not like it is now—and as soon as the tide came in, somebody'd say, 'The tides's in! Let's go swimming!' And we'd jump off a fish house, no bathing suits or nothing, just an old dress and a pair of pants on—that was our swimming gear. We'd swim all around through that old slough out there and under the docks, just like a fish in the water. And nobody bothered us, nobody cared. When we got older, they built a bathhouse over on the beach, and it was really a treat to walk over on Sunday afternoon, and if you had ten cents you could rent a cubicle and change your clothes. We thought we were a big deal then, just like the kids from uptown."

Cortez kids often went swimming whether they wanted to or not. "It was common practice when a young kid came walking out on a dock for one of the fishermen to grab you and yell, 'Sink or swim!' and throw you right out in the middle of the bay," said Hubert. "They had to make sure you could swim or else you'd drown pretty quick around them docks. So they'd throw you in and then go in after you if you started sinking. One day, Richard Roberts, who we called Fido, come walking down there and Bernie Taylor grabbed him, knowing he could swim, and yelled, 'Sink or swim, Fido!' and threw him overboard. Well, Fido went 'glub, glub, glub' right under the water, and Bernie got scared and jumped in after him, in his clothes and everything, and about then old Fido come up laughing and outswam Bernie all over the bay.

"The fishermen had all kinds of tricks that they played on us kids" he added. "Normally in the summertime, we'd go swimming in our shorts, but if you happened to come down to the dock in long pants, you'd go in the old one-holer—the outhouse—and change into your shorts. You'd come back later and your pants would be tied in 900 knots—I mean hard knots that grown men had tied. You couldn't untie them so you'd have to carry them home like that and your mother would get mad at you. Oh, that sort of thing happened all the time."

When they weren't swimming, they were chasing fiddler crabs along the shoreline at low tide, gathering sea grapes on the edge of the bay, or playing make believe at the fish houses. "A lot of times after the dock closed us girls would play down at the dock," said Momma. "We'd pretend that the dock was a fancy hotel or a big mansion and that we were in love with a famous movie star."

As they got older, Cortez teenagers roamed farther from home, following romantic or hormonal urges—which were usually indistinguishable—but the water was still the focal point of their activities. They went on picnics to the beach, piled into old Model T's and drove up and down the beach, or, in that most sacred of all courting rituals, went for a boat-ride.

Cortez families had very little money to spend on entertainment, so when the children tired of playing around the water, which was free, they made do with homemade entertainment. "We'd raise hell to get our parents to go to the store and buy stuff, but none of our parents had any money, so we made our own junk," said Hubert. "And really, we had more fun with what we made anyway. We'd build rubber-band guns out of old inner tubes and play cowboys and Indians. Or we'd make slingshots. There's still no better handle in the world for a slingshot than a guava tree 'cause they 'Y' off almost perfect every time. Get one that fits your hand and cut it off, make rubber bands out of inner tubes, and go to it. We'd hunt birds and squirrels with them."

The youngsters exhibited their greatest creativity as pranksters, and Halloween was their crowning glory. One Halloween night, they rounded up every skiff in Cortez, tied them together, and strung them all the way across the channel in front of the Cortez Bridge. Other years they made giant pyramids by stacking fish boxes in the middle of the road, filled the fishermen's nets with horseshoe crabs, mixed up all of the poling oars, pushed Aaron Bell's fish truck into the bushes by The Albion Inn where it remained undetected for three days, or, the favorite trick of kids everywhere, turned over all the outhouses in the village and strung toilet paper all over town.

Hubert's favorite Halloween prank was even more elaborate. "One Halloween night me and Fido was roaming around and Bernie Taylor come driving up in his Model T truck. He was towing a great big old rotten boat, and he had about half a dozen kids pushing it from behind, trying to get it down the road. It was a big old scow that'd been on the beach for about six years, and the bottom was completely rotted out. Bernie said: 'Glad to see you. Get in there and push.' So we got back there and pushed that thing around Cortez for half the night. Finally we left it down at the Sailor's Haven beer joint—parked it right in front of the gas pumps so nobody could get by, and just left it. They had a terrible time getting it out of there the next morning, and the guy that ran the place was so mad he said he'd give a free Coke to anybody who'd tell him who did it. But he never got any takers."

True pranksters have to keep at it year round, not just on Halloween, and Cortez youngsters have been true to their calling. There's an endless parade of tricks, scams, and general mischief in the history of the village.

My uncle Wayne Fulford and his childhood buddy Wally Lewis, who is now, sadly, serving time in federal prison on a drug-smuggling conviction, would throw cherry bombs under the over-the-water outhouse of Talkin' Charlie, one of the village's harmless old drunks. Talkin' Charlie, who's dead now, is best remembered for having the fastest imaginary draw in Cortez. He would challenge anybody who walked down on the dock to a make-believe gunfight, snarling out his challenge: "You wanna draw? I'll shoot you dead if you blink." He lived in an old fish camp over the water, and Wayne and Wally would lie in wait for the right moment. "We'd wait till we'd see him go in and sit down in his outhouse," said Wayne, "and then throw a cherry bomb in the water right under him. That thing'd go off and blow water up all over him."

My grandma has such a serious nature that she's a natural target for pranks. "Poor old Edith," said Gene Fulford, "one time years ago she had some big old watermelons growing right out in front of the house. They was the prettiest things and she put fish boxes on top of them to keep the birds out of 'em. Well, some of these boys—my brother Grey and Clark Culbreath—they went out there one night and cut holes in the bottom of them watermelons and eat the heart out of them. They cleaned out the insides and then put the plugs back where you couldn't tell. Edith kept on watering them things everyday, and she'd say, 'Gene, I can't figure out what in the world's killing them melons.' The vines was dead, see, and I'd say, 'Well, Edith, it must be the worms.' And them durn boys done eat the insides out. I'll never forget it. She was mad about them melons for years, and she always blamed it on Major Hall, but it wasn't him that did it."

Cortez girls pulled their weight in the mischief-making, right along with the boys. Toodle remembered how three young girls once stole Bud Posey's ice truck. Posey, who made home deliveries in the days before refrigeration, always parked his Model T truck next to the ice house. The girls pushed it down the road so he wouldn't hear the engine when they cranked it and headed to town. "It was an old Model T truck with no doors on it, and all the girls knew how to do was make it go forward," said Toodle. "They didn't know how to back it up. So they got Bud's truck up to U.S. 41 and stopped it at a little juke joint. They only had enough money to buy them a candy bar, that was all. They got somebody to back the truck up for them and headed back home, but they got half way to Cortez and ran out of gas. Well, they couldn't do a thing but leave it there and walk home, and every time they saw a car coming they'd hide in a ditch. They were just terrified for days, because Bud was an old cowboy and he said that if he found out who took his truck he was gonna bullwhip them."

Needless to say, Cortez kids have had a passionate love affair with the automobile for generations. "I'd mow Uncle Tink's yard just to get to use his old truck on Saturday evenings," said Gene. "There was a place down at the old shell mound, about two miles square, where you could drive around. Just put some gas into it and ride all day, round and round. Run into a stump or something, just keep on going. It didn't hurt nothing."

For some reason—maybe it's from drinking so much artesian water or eating fish every day—most Cortez kids turn into raving maniacs on their sixteenth birthday. They have always been absolute fanatics about fast cars. During the 1960s, the Florida Highway Patrol's super speed patrol—the "Wolf Pack"—seemed to be permanently assigned to Cortez Road. But the Wolf Pack's sophisticated radar didn't really do any good. Every time one of us was stopped for speeding, the passion for fast cars grew even stronger. The boys were famous for passing six frightened carloads of Michigan retirees on Cortez Road, doing 90 mph in a 45-mph zone. The real trick was to avoid a head-on collision with oncoming cars by whipping onto the left-hand shoulder, waiting till the cars were past, and then pulling back onto the pavement.

The fascination with cars reached its peak during the 1960s. Being too young to drive, I spent most of those years on the hump in the back seat of other people's cars. Uncle Wayne had a 1958 Chevy with a "glass pack" and "three deuces," hotshot carburetion devices that he hoped would compensate for the fact that 1958 Chevys looked pretty strange and were never as popular as the 1955-1957 models.

The only time I got off the hump in Wayne's car was one winter night at four o'clock in the morning when he was driving Gary, Rusty, and me across the Sunshine Skyway to St. Petersburg, where Grandpa was waiting for us in his fishing boat. Wayne had it topped out at about 120 mph, driving right down the centerline of the bridge. When we got to the grating at the top, the tires started screaming like banshees, and Rusty and I were so scared we hit the floor and tried to crawl underneath the front seat.

But Wayne was eight years older than me, so I didn't really get to hang out with him very much. It wasn't until Rusty got a used Buick Special—which could get up and go even if it did have an automatic transmission—and Gary got a 1967 Camaro, that I got a true dose of car craziness.

I just about wore a hole in the back seat of Gary's Camaro—riding to town on Friday and Saturday nights to shoot pool at the Kue and Karom; pulling into the drive-in theater, with three guys stuffed in the trunk and two more squashed down in the floor of the back seat, and nonchalantly asking for three tickets; drag racing on 75th Street where a quarter mile had been carefully measured and marked with white stripes; or making our third visit of the night to Bradenton's only McDonalds, backing into a parking space, ordering a hamburger and french fries, and arguing about which of us "hardtails" would have to stay behind if we picked up any girls. We were much better at arguing than we were at picking up girls, so none of us ever got left.

When there wasn't anything else to do, which was often the case, we'd spend hours just driving around—cruising the beach, going over to St. Pete, racing up and down U.S. 41 between Bradenton and Sarasota. I always felt like something exciting was going to happen at any minute, but it almost never did.

There were exceptions, like the time we almost got run over by two guys in a Ford. We were stopped at a traffic light on U.S. 41, minding our own business, when these guys pulled up and challenged Gary to drag off the line. When the light changed, both cars laid rubber in all three gears and raced down the highway for about a mile. Suddenly, we saw Bobbi Jo Jones, another Cortez boy, driving in the other direction in his red Mercury Comet. We honked, turned around, and pulled off onto a side road with Bobbi Jo. Gary, Rusty, my brother Mark, and I got out of the car and were standing in the road talking to Bobbi Jo, when all of a sudden that Ford came barreling around the corner, heading straight for us. Everyone jumped in different directions—I landed on Bobbi Jo's hood—and the Ford missed us by inches. "Let's get 'em!" Gary screamed, and we piled back in the Camaro, cranked it up, and slid around the corner behind Bobbi Jo, who was already in full pursuit.

We chased those guys all over Bradenton for over an hour—through a dozen red lights, twice around the A&W Root Beer stand, across the parking lot of the Chevrolet dealership, and right through the front driveway of the Florida Highway Patrol station. We got close enough a couple of times for Gary to lean out with a Coke bottle in his hand, intending to throw it through their windshield, but the Ford broke away both times and ran another red light. We finally gave up the chase, but for months afterwards Gary kept that Coke bottle under the seat in case he spotted them again.

That happened during a summer vacation, and when Mark returned to school for the sixth grade, he was assigned the traditional essay on "How I spent my summer vacation." He wrote a rather subdued account of the summer's escapades, turned it in, and got it back the next day with an 'F' because the teacher thought he had made the whole thing up.

A lot of things happened in Cortez that schoolteachers wouldn't believe—or didn't want to. The entire summer of 1965 would come under that heading. That was the summer that Grandpa was dying and Wayne captained the *Anna Dean* in his place. His motley crew consisted of Rusty, Gary, Jimmy Guthrie, and me. Halfway through the summer, we were joined by J. G. "Jake" Culbreath, Goose and Maida's son, who was fresh out of the Army Demolition Corps. In what seemed a fitting tribute to the three years he'd spent blowing up dynamite and land mines, Jake stopped at a roadside stand in South Carolina on his way home and bought three boxes of cherry bombs.

Those cherry bombs kept us going that summer. We spent far more time blowing them up than we did shucking mullet. Our seining efforts could have been taken right out of the film library of "The Three Stooges."

One day we'd strike a school of mullet and the lead line would sand up—the tide makes the lead line roll up from the bottom—and the fish would swim out underneath. The next day we'd sit around the pier at Mullet Key all day, waiting for a school of fish to leave the pier and make a run down the beach. When they'd make their break we'd jump in the boat, crank up, and race down the beach, only to have the engine die on us, or the net get caught in the propeller, or some such foolishness.

We would have surely starved to death if we hadn't illegally snitch-hooked mullet every day from under the pier. Other than eating those mullet, our diet consisted of daily doses of Mountain Dews and Almond Joys, and, on one horrible occasion, an old rabbit that Rusty had shot two years before, which, after two years of cold storage in Grandma's freezer, was so tough and chalky that not even the pelicans would eat it.

We didn't catch many fish, but we did pull some great pranks. Midway through the summer, we abandoned Mullet Key to seek the greener pastures and, we hoped, more numerous women at John's Pass, a small beach town near St. Petersburg. Our fishing luck didn't improve any, but a whole new world of adventure opened up for us as juvenile delinquents.

Jake taught us how to make time-fuses by tying a lit cigarette to a cherry bomb. In five minutes, the cigarette would burn down far enough to ignite the fuse, and . . . kaboom! Late at night, bored, broke, and nauseous from our nightly meal at John's Pass Mushburger, we'd steer the *Anna Dean* down a narrow finger canal, pull up to one of the small boat docks, drop a cigarette-fused cherry bomb on the dock, and slip away silently. Five minutes later, the bomb would go off with a terrific bang, amplified so loudly in the night air that it sounded like mortar fire over Da Nang—just like on the six o'clock news. In two minutes, every light in the neighborhood was on, but by then we were long gone, laughing uproariously at our newly discovered power.

We developed all sorts of permutations: we'd light three cigarette bombs at the same time and drop them on three different docks, and then howl with laughter when they went off at the same time; or light three cigarette bombs at three-minute intervals, drop each one at a different dock, so that about the time the commotion died down from the first explosion, the next bomb would explode, and then the next.

We created our finest masterpiece one day while sitting 200 yards offshore, sunburned and nearly delirious with boredom, waiting for some mullet to leave the pass and run down the beach. We cut the top off of a

Coke can, strapped the can to the top of a flotation cushion, tied a 500-foot spool of fishing twine to the cushion, dropped a cigarette fuse and cherry bomb into the can, and voilà: a retractable floating powder keg. We waited for the incoming tide, dropped our patented bomb in the can, and watched breathlessly as the tide carried the floatation cushion right under the fancy restaurant that was built over the water next to the bridge. When the explosion hit, the folks in the restaurant came out running for their lives. We waited until they went back in, then wound in the string, reloaded our floating bomb, and did it again—did it several times that summer. It didn't make up for making only $15 all summer, but it helped.

Of course, Cortez youngsters weren't always jumping overboard, racing down Cortez Road in souped-up jalopies, or wreaking havoc in the retiree neighborhoods along the bay. When I went home in September to go back to school, my relatives in Cortez did the same.

The first schoolhouse in Cortez was established about 1895 in a small A-frame house that Earl Guthrie lives in today. In 1912, the county built a fine new brick schoolhouse; it would serve the village for the next 50 years.

Man Adams was there as a first-grader on the day it opened: "There were only two classrooms in the new school when it first opened and they taught up to the eighth grade there. One teacher taught up to the third grade and the other teacher had through the eighth grade. We'd sit at our desks and the teacher would ring a little bell and call each grade to come up for spelling or arithmetic or whatever. She had seats up front and maybe there'd be seven or eight kids up there for a lesson. Millard Brown's grandmother Mrs. Williams was my teacher, and I can remember how she'd wear an apron and take big safety pins and pin them to our clothes and then to her apron so she could walk around and us little kids would have to follow her."

The Cortez schoolhouse was the center of the community. It was where community fish fries were held, where the fishermen held union meetings, and where the villagers went for protection during hurricanes.

There were mixed emotions when the county decided to close the school in 1961 and bus the youngsters to Palma Sola Elementary School. Some parents thought that the closeness felt by the teachers, students, and parents was lost once the kids were bused to town. Because the teachers lived in the village and saw the students and parents on a regular basis, there was an established bond. On the other hand, educational programs were available in town that would never have been instituted at the Cortez School because of its small size.

The fishing families sent their children to the town school to get an education and improve their lot in life, but sometimes the educational system seemed more like an enemy than a friend. Education has been held out to these people as the avenue to upward mobility and a better life. But too often, the system has labeled working-class youngsters as dumb and stupid, tracked them into vocational programs because of their background rather than their test scores, and instilled middle-class values that made them ashamed of their families.

For many Cortez children, their sixteenth birthday was a day of liberation: they were old enough both to drive and to quit school. Prior to World War II, very few Cortez boys graduated from high school; most quit at age 16 and started fishing. More girls completed high school, but few went to college. The boys became fishermen and the girls got married; that was the norm. In either case, school just didn't seem very useful or relevant.

However, a person's intelligence is usually equated with years of schooling, and many people in Cortez still carry feelings of self-doubt and inferiority because of their limited education. "I only completed the ninth grade and I think I wasted a lot of years of my life because I didn't give myself any credit," said Wyman Coarsey. "I always felt that not having an education was a hindrance. We've got some smart boys here in Cortez who think they can't do nothing but fishing. I felt the same way. But I realize now that that attitude was forced on me. It wasn't until I worked for an oil company and then became postmaster that I realized that I could do work that college graduates had failed at."

Most Cortez kids didn't like school and didn't make any bones about it. They wouldn't settle down and act like the city kids, much to the chagrin of their teachers. At the Cortez school, students would climb out of the windows and run home when the teacher turned her back or would show up smelling like dead mackerel. When they started riding the bus to town, they'd walk barefoot to the bus stop in the morning, put on their shoes just in time to board the bus, and take them off again as soon as they got off the bus in the afternoon.

Sometimes the rowdiness was a reaction to the teasing they received because they were from Cortez. For generations, these youngsters have heard jokes about their smelling like fish. "When they first started running the bus from town out here to pick us up, the island kids would all hold their noses when we got on and act like we were stinking from fish," said Man Adams. "They'd start holding their noses and some of us Cortez boys would crawl onto them for it."

More fights have been started about the smell of fish, real or imagined, than anything else. Sometimes they really did smell like fish. "Lots of times during mackerel season the kids would be gutting fish all night and then go on to school the next morning," said Toodle. "Well, there's nothing any harder to get off than that fishy smell. I can remember kids going to school and you couldn't get near them. They'd gutted fish all night and maybe gone home and washed up, but they still had on their dirty clothes."

There were some other class differences that surfaced on those school bus rides. "The kids from the island and from town thought they were different from us—and they were different," said Toodle. "They were from the city and they looked and dressed different from us. I don't know if they actually looked down on us as much as we thought they did, but I know that a lot of times I felt like they thought they were better than me."

Even for those who were enthusiastic about going to school, there were obstacles in their way. "The kids from Cortez didn't have any advantages as far as school," said Toodle. "In my time, during the Depression, times were real hard and you were lucky if you got to finish high school. And up until the late '20s, there wasn't even a school bus that came out here, so once you finished the eighth grade that was it. Aunt Sissie said that the only way she could get to Bradenton High was in an old Model T truck that Jess Williams's daughter drove. She'd carry five or six passengers with her and charge about 25 cents a week to carry them to school. Aunt Sissie even boarded in town for awhile just so she could go to school. The county finally started sending a bus out here, but it was an old primitive thing with wooden benches the length of the bus and canvas awning to keep the cold and rain out. I don't see how it made it out here on that old bumpy road."

My mother Mary Fulford Green was one of the few educational success stories in Cortez. "We only had two books in our house when I was young: the Bible and Ethan Frome, and that's why I can't throw away a book, even today," she said. "Other than those two books, all we had to read was the *Grit*, which we subscribed to, and, on Saturdays, the *Atlanta Constitution* was delivered to Cortez and I'd read Flash Gordon and the funnies. That was it. But I always knew that I was going to go to college, even though we never discussed it. That was what was different about our family. Daddy never had an education, but he wanted his kids to. And Mama was pretty smart—if she couldn't figure out a math problem, it couldn't be done."

Momma graduated from Bradenton High in 1942 as the valedictorian of her class. She won several awards as the outstanding student in her class, but her biggest accomplishment was maintaining pride in her roots. "I always knew I was a fisherman's daughter and I was proud of it. There were clubs I knew I'd never be in and awards I knew I'd never win because of being from Cortez, but I always felt like I was just as good as any of the kids from the rich families in town." Ironically, on her graduation night, Grandpa got stranded out in a boat and couldn't get back in time for the ceremony. "Daddy was real proud of me being the valedictorian, but he ended up missing my graduation," said Momma.

She went to Florida State College for Women (now Florida State University) and got a B.S. degree in 1946. Years later, while teaching high school full-time and raising a family, she went back to FSU and, in 1966, received a doctorate in higher education. Grandpa and Grandma's desire for their children to go to college carried over to others as well: my aunts Belinda, Irene, and Anna Dean, and my uncle Gary graduated from college.

Cortez doesn't have a great track record for producing educated adults, but it has certainly produced an awful lot of happy childhoods—Hubert Horne's was one of them. He would have gladly stayed in Cortez his whole life, but in 1946, when he was in the ninth grade, his family moved to Bradenton. The move wasn't his idea: "My mother had to sell the house out from under me before I'd leave Cortez." But once he left, he never came back.

He joined the Army in 1948, and two years later was sitting in a foxhole in Korea, eagerly awaiting the fulfillment of General Douglas McArthur's promise that "our boys will be home for Christmas." However, the Chinese had threatened to enter the war if McArthur continued to push closer to the Yalu River, China's southern border with Korea. When he did, wave after wave of Chinese soldiers poured across the Yalu, surrounding Hubert's battalion on three sides. He didn't make it home for Christmas.

He did return to Bradenton after retiring from the Army, and now lives only five miles from Cortez. Although he isn't there in person, his roots and his memories are. And like all those who have grown up in Cortez, his heart and his soul are there, too. That's a lot to hold onto from a childhood.

PART III

Struggles

"Some of the hardest work awaited the fishermen when they got home . . . liming the nets and pulling them on the netspreads." But there was always time for the catch of the day (about 1920).

Chapter 11

"We Could Have Had It All
If We'd Stuck Together"

ON A MUGGY AFTERNOON IN JUNE, Bob Knowlton had just come back from trout fishing. A tall, lean man who looks nowhere near his 88 years, he was wearing a faded tan cap with an anchor emblem on the front, a well-worn pair of green work pants, and a v-neck t-shirt. It's the customary outfit that he can be seen in every day, walking along the shoreline. He was sitting in an easy chair in the living quarters of the firehouse, where he and his wife Ruth have lived since 1961 when Bob became the resident fireman for the Cortez Volunteer Fire Department.

Bob Knowlton knows more about putting out fires than anyone else in Cortez, and he knows as much about catching trout as anyone else in Manatee County. But today he wasn't talking about either topic. He was talking about the history of fishermen's unions on the Gulf coast of Florida, and he knows more about that topic than almost anyone else in the state. "A fisherman can jump in the boat anytime, day or night, and go when he likes, come back when he likes, and he doesn't have to go at all if he doesn't want to. They're the hardest people in the world to organize."

Lord knows, Bob Knowlton has tried. He spent 20 years, from the mid-1930s until 1958, helping organize the fishermen on Florida's west coast. There were some important victories during those years, some moments of unity and strength, but never a lasting organization. "You just can't keep them together," he acknowledged sadly.

The history of fishermen's unions in Florida is a little-known chapter in the history of the labor movement, but it includes an eight-year affiliation with the Seafarers International Union (1938-1945) and a six-year affiliation with the United Packinghouse Workers of America (1952-1957). Since 1967, Florida fishermen have had an independent, state-wide association, the Organized Fishermen of Florida.

In Cortez, it is history with a family twist. The battle lines between fishermen and fish dealers were often drawn right down the middle of families. Instead of Henry Ford, John D. Rockefeller, or the president of General Motors, Cortez fishermen had to organize against their first cousins, their uncles, and sometimes their fathers. Consequently, this labor history has a distinct quality of cooperation, as well as a viciousness that only family feuds can generate.

When Bob moved to Cortez in 1922, he didn't know anyone in the village and organizing a fishermen's union was the farthest thing from his mind. Born in 1896 on his family's farm in northwestern Pennsylvania, he moved to Michigan seeking warmer weather. He didn't find much of that, but he did get a job as a fireman on the Grand Trunk Railroad, which he worked for four years. "When I first started working on the railroad, they could keep you out there shoveling coal for 16 hours," he recalled. "Well, with one of those old coal-burning engines and a hundred cars behind you, you're gonna shovel some coal! But they got the union while I was there, and then they had to come relieve you after 8 hours. Once we got the union working, it worked fine, and that's what got me interested in a union when I come to Cortez."

Michigan proved too cold for him, so in 1921, Bob headed south. He ended up in Cortez in 1922. "I had heard about the fishing in Cortez, and I had always liked fishing," he said. "I got a job fishing with Elverton Green. It took me awhile to learn the bay, but after a couple of years, I got my own boat and crew, and I stayed right at it full-time until 1977, when I quit net fishing."

Bob was fishing when the Depression hit and all the mullet disappeared. It was a hard time for everyone. Earl Guthrie recalled: "It was a struggle back there in them there '30s, son. Good God in this world! The worst thing was there wasn't no fish. In 1936, me and Bill Guthrie and Jim Campbell fished 13 weeks down in Gasparilla and made $26.37 apiece. For 13 weeks! I'll tell you, when you drive a guy to the point he can't make a living for his family, he'll fight. And we was to that point."

During the 1930s, industrial workers across the country were organizing unions for the first time, and conditions were ripe for a fishermen's union in Florida. Cortez played a leading role in the union movements for two main reasons: Cortez was the second largest mullet fishery in the state and therefore had a powerful influence on the entire industry, and second, Cortez fishermen are closely related and stubbornly militant, with a reputation for sticking together, whether in a barroom fight or in the union. Fort Myers, the largest fishery in the state, provides an interesting contrast. The ports in Fort Myers are strung out along a narrow peninsula. Their geographical separation led to more competition among fish dealers, fewer family ties among fishermen, and, consequently, a harder job of building unity during union struggles.

The most obvious target for the fishermen's frustrations was the local dealers. In Cortez, the first organized action against the dealers took place in 1932. Fishermen were being paid a cent-and-a-half a pound for mullet, but at the start of the spring silver mullet season, dealers cut the price back to a cent a pound. The fishermen reacted quickly. Earl Guthrie recounted the events: "Well, we'd been expecting to make a few dollars during silver mullet season, and when they cut us to a cent a pound, we couldn't make it, that's all. So we all got together and formed a union and set a date for a strike if they didn't go back up on the price."

On the morning of the scheduled strike, most of the residents of Cortez were gathered in the empty lot next to Buck Parent's grocery store, one block from the fish houses along the shore. "Practically everybody in Cortez was up there that morning," Earl recalled. "There was a flagpole down there in front of the store, and one guy said, 'Let's put the flag up.' Another fellow said, 'By God, I'll go up there and put it up.' And by golly, he went up that flagpole just like a cat. We run the American flag up, and we said to the dealers, 'When you put the price back up, we'll take the flag down and go back to work. Until you get right and give us the price we're asking, we'll sit right here from now on.'

"Well, everybody was sore at each other, the fishermen and the dealers. And the dealers thought we'd go back to work in a couple of days. But we didn't! We sat right there! We'd gather up in that big lot every morning and sit around and play cards and cut the fool and had a good time. They didn't think we was as bullheaded as we was. I don't remember how many days we sat there, but finally they said, 'Well boys, we'll go it!' So we took the flag down and went back to work."

Today, reflecting on that first strike, Cortez fishermen agree that nobody was making any money during the Depression, not even the dealers. Woodrow Green, who ran a fish house in the 1930s and later became active in union efforts, remembered that quite a few dealers went bankrupt during those lean years. Dealers paid fishermen a cent-and-a-half a pound at the dock, and even after trucking their fish up into Georgia, they could sell them for only two-and-a-half cents a pound.

"We went back fishing after the strike," said Earl Guthrie, "but it wasn't too long after that until first one guy and then the other began to drop out [of the union], until we didn't have no strength at all. Well, the union just faded out like a cloud."

Cortez fishermen realized that they were at the mercy of the local dealers who bought their catch dockside. They also resented the fact that there were tremendous gaps between prices paid in different ports, even though their price was often on the up side. For example, Cortez dealers always paid more than dealers in Fort Myers, largely because Cortez fishermen knew the dealers well, knew how much they were selling the fish for, and were unified enough to demand a fair price.

The fishermen also realized that no matter how united they were locally, they would never increase the price very much in Cortez as long as the other ports on the coast remained unorganized. The need for a state-wide union and a standard price for fish was evident, and the opportunity presented itself in 1938, when the Seafarers International Union sent an organizer to Cortez.

"The Seafarers sent a fellow named Biggs in here and we formed a local," said Bob Knowlton. "We'd call a meeting down at the schoolhouse and talk things over, and the dealers usually gave us what we wanted. We got the price up to three cents a pound. Then after a while, Biggs put me in his place as local business agent and he went somewheres else." With SIU locals in east- and west-coast ports, the total state membership reached approximately 6,000 at one point.

After some initial resistance to an outside union, the Cortez dealers soon began to see some value in it. "The first time I ever joined the union, I was working for Tink Fulford, running his fish house," said Woodrow Green. "I didn't have no business joining 'cause I was a fish-house man, but I asked Tink, 'What do you think about it, Tink?' 'I think it's a good idea,' he said, 'let's get the price for them.' Well, he didn't do nothing but fish himself, seven and eight days a week. I said, 'Well, if you're gonna join, I'm gonna join, too.' He said, 'Yeah, let's help the boys out.' So the dealers cooperated with the fishermen. There was never no serious trouble of no kind in none of it with Cortez people. But the big trouble was that the dealers here couldn't really and truly raise the price much above what their competitors was paying in other places."

"I sat down and talked to Tink and the other dealers," said Bob, "and they saw that the union would keep Fort Myers from buying and selling fish cheaper than Cortez, and then putting them on the market and cutting [our] throats."

There were only a couple of one- or two-day strikes in Cortez from 1938-1945, and those occurred when the dealers unexpectedly cut the price. "There were only two or three times in Cortez when we had to let the dealers know we meant business," said Earl Guthrie. "Not many times, because they soon found out that we weren't just putting on a show. One time though, we quit fishing for a couple of days. Now we never put up pickets or such, we just wouldn't go. But one dealer here, he was a fisherman, too, and he said, 'By God, I'm going fishing!' We said, 'No, you ain't goin' fishing.' Well, he got his crew and pulled his seine on and took off. It was in the fall of the year, and we knew where he was going 'cause he had a spot up at Anna Maria Point where he stayed in the fall. So we all jumped in Model T trucks and anything we could get to ride in, and about the time he got there, we drove down on that shore . . . looked like an army! No, I didn't have a gun, but I wouldn't say there weren't any guns in the crowd. We marched down on that shore and asked him what he was doing. I don't remember what kind of remark he made, but it didn't hit us very well. We'd always appoint one guy to do the talking and the rest of us would keep our mouths shut, so the guy we had appointed, we knew he had the guts to back us to his dying day, he stepped out and said, 'Well, Cap'n, go ahead and strike anytime you want to, but when you put your net overboard, we're gonna help you get her in, and we will not promise you what kind of shape she'll be in when you get her.' He cranked up and come on home and that was the end of that. But oh, was he ill! Man, was he ill! But there wasn't a durn thing in the world they could do when the fishermen quit them, except tell us to tie their boats up, and they sure weren't making any money with them boats tied up."

When strikes did occur in Cortez, the dealers weren't above pulling some pretty devious tricks to try to break them. "The dealers were two-sided about the union," said Grey Fulford, holding up two fingers and crossing them to emphasize his point. "They'd join the union and pay their dues and come to the meetings and talk about how they were for the fishermen, but then they'd go behind our backs and try to bust the union. One time we went on strike at the same time as St. Petersburg and Sarasota. The dealers got one of their good buddies to go out fishing, and then they hauled them fish up to Petersburg on a truck and showed them around to all the fishermen, and said, 'See, them Cortez boys has done broke the strike and gone back fishing.' Then they carried them same fish down to Sarasota and showed them around. Just trying to make the other fishermen suspicious of us."

The SIU's pattern all over the state was to strike in individual ports, or in several ports at the same time if the dealers in both places cut the price. Securing a standard price for fish up and down the west coast was the union's main priority, although there were a few instances where local business agents helped settle grievances between individual fishermen and dealers. The SIU apparently did very little in the way of mobilizing fishermen for political activities, other than giving tacit support to the reelection campaigns of Franklin D. Roosevelt.

The only major confrontation in Cortez occurred in 1945, right at the end of World War II. A postwar strike wave swept through almost every industry in the country, as wartime profits had far surpassed the wage increases allowed by the War Labor Board. With the return of thousands of veterans and the expiration of no-strike pledges taken by unions for the duration of the war, picket lines blossomed all over the country. Cortez was no different. In 1945, Florida produced a record 55 million pounds of mullet (by comparison, Florida produced only 21.6 million pounds in 1977), and the fishermen wanted a bigger piece of the pie. When the dealers refused to grant it, a strike ensued.

"Forty-eight boys from Cortez went in the service during the war," said Woodrow Green, "and we was already on strike when most of them come home from the war. See, the dealers thought when them boys got home everything'd be different. I heard Tink say, 'When them boys get home, there won't be no damn union.' "

At first, it looked like his prediction might come true. "When some of them boys got home, they got sore as the devil with we guys," added Earl Guthrie. "We called a little meeting one night and some of them said, 'By God, we've been over yonder fighting a war and you fellas been home sitting on your ass on strike!' I said, 'Fellas, just wait. Let's get something straight. We were fighting for your interests so you'd have something when you came back. And you was making as much in the service as we was here. We sure wasn't making anything here.' Well, they saw it was so and from then on the dealers didn't get help from the servicemen."

In fact, once the veterans got involved in the strike, they wanted the union to demand an even higher price. "Yeah, some of them even said they wanted a union of their own 'cause our union wasn't tough enough," said Woodrow, laughing. "They didn't even want to associate with us. They said we weren't tough at all 'cause we were only asking for a little bit. But, finally, they come on in with us."

As is true with any strike, it was hard for the fishermen and their families to survive without a weekly paycheck, especially since many of them had no savings. The government had instituted a "20/20" program for unemployed veterans, under which they could draw $20 a week for 20 weeks. This helped some of the families, and the union members devised other ways to help each other. "Ones that didn't have money would borrow from ones that did," said Gene Fulford. "Buck Parent was helping the fishermen at his store. I bought groceries down there on credit and he knew that I couldn't pay him until the strike was over. And one time we had a big fish fry to help raise money for the union; boy, the dealers really got mad about that 'cause we went out and caught a boatload of fish."

In addition to the financial strains, there were plenty of emotional strains on families in Cortez, too, as the village was again split right down the middle between the dealers and fishermen. "You'd have thought somebody was gonna kill each other," said Gene, "but they was just mad, just mad. 'Judge' Millis, one of the dealers, why he was just like a daddy to me, and he got so mad that he wouldn't even speak to me. He'd just spit on the ground and walk away."

The strike lasted for several weeks; finally the dealers gave in and raised the price of fish. But the resentment between dealers and the union had reached the point where the word went out that Bob Knowlton and Woodrow Green were going to be run out of town because of their union activities.

"Yeah, I remember something about that," said Bob, chuckling as he told the story. "Somebody come and told me they was plotting all that, and I said, 'Well, all right, I lived a long time before I come to Cortez and I'm not gonna run too easy.' So then they said they wouldn't buy my fish. I was the local business agent, but I was still fishing my own rig full time, and one day Tink come to me and said, 'I can't buy any more of your fish.' I said, 'Why? What's the matter?' He said, 'I just don't want any more of your fish.' So I went around and told two or three guys, 'I can't sell anymore fish to Tink.' They said, 'Why? Just 'cause you're trying to keep the union going?' So every one of them that was fishing for him quit. They told him, 'When Bob can sell fish, we'll go back fishing for you.' Well, after a few days of that, one of the other dealers, Jim Guthrie, he said he'd buy my fish, so I told the guys, 'I'm gonna sell my fish over yonder,' and then they went back to fishing for Tink."

The attempt to run Woodrow Green out of Cortez met a similar fate. "They tried to ship Bob out first," said Woodrow, "and what happened with me was that one morning a good friend of mine, Gator Mora, came to my door and told me the dealers was fixing to railroad me. He told me exactly who it was and all. But how they was gonna figure on running me out, I do not know. I never asked Gator Mora anything about it, and I never did hear no more about it."

Despite victories like the 1945 strike in Cortez, the Seafarers Union was never able to achieve its main goal—a standard price for fish in all ports. Lacking that, and lacking the solid backing of all the fishermen on the coast, the organization collapsed by the end of 1945, as dealers cleverly played fishermen in one port against those in other ports.

For seven years, 1945-1952, there was not a fishermen's union in Florida. Major organizing drives continued in other states—particularly in New England and along the Texas, Louisiana, and Alabama coasts. A big stumbling block to those drives arose when dealers began filing court suits, claiming that the fishermen's efforts to raise the price of fish were in violation of the price-fixing statues of the Sherman Antitrust Act. Dealers won several landmark court cases on that point, which resulted in fines and imprisonment of some fishermen. This twisted use of the act effectively nullified the ability of unions to negotiate contracts and price schedules with dealers, and would prove to be a major factor in the next attempt to organize Florida fishermen.

By 1952, the United Packinghouse Workers of America (UPWA) was interested in organizing the fishermen. It had already organized the major companies in the packinghouse industry, such as Swift, Cudahy and Armour, and had also won contracts with many of the smaller, independent companies as well. The UPWA was interested in expanding to include other types of workers, and with a potential of 11,000 shrimpers and fishermen, Florida seemed a likely choice. After some initial contacts in 1952, the UPWA established a statewide fishermen's local in 1953, headquartered in

Osprey, near Sarasota. But when the union hired a former dealer as organizer, many fishermen grew suspicious, and the infant local collapsed completely by the middle of 1954.

The UPWA then assigned one of its national organizers, Ed Beltrame, to the Florida campaign. "The International sent me into Florida to put the pieces back together," said Beltrame, now retired and living in Lowell, Michigan, "and the first thing I had to do was establish better lines of communication. I started making the rounds of all the ports and set up six different locals, at Cortez, Everglades City, Homosassa, Fort Myers, Pine Island, and Cedar Key. Then I hired J. B. Roberts [of Osprey] to travel around and talk to the fishermen about the union. Everybody called him Prof because he was a retired schoolteacher, and he knew all the fishermen up and down the west coast. He was very instrumental in getting the union going again."

Beltrame began holding general port meetings every three months, at which fishermen from all over the state would assemble to discuss their problems. National UPWA leaders, like Secretary-Treasurer G. R. "Butch" Hathaway, came to those meetings to encourage the local organizing efforts. The UPWA's regional office in Atlanta began putting out a monthly newsletter for fishermen.

Beltrame and Prof Roberts traveled the state until mid-1955, when Bob replaced the elderly Roberts as a paid organizer. Beltrame covered the north end of the state, and Bob took Tampa south to the Keys. As Beltrame put 65,000 miles on his car in one year and Bob put 35,000 miles on his 1947 Chevrolet in one summer, the UPWA's membership climbed to 1,400 by the end of 1955.

It wasn't easy to get the union recognized in some places after the failure of the Seafarers, as local resistance was very strong. "I went down south one time," Bob recalled, "and there was a guy who was kind of a bully for the whole town. They said he'd hit a guy over the head with a gun barrel and bent the barrel. Well, that's a little bit strong. I said, 'Let's go talk to him,' but the other fishermen said, 'You can't talk to him. He's sitting right there on his porch with a shotgun, and he'll kill you if you go up there.' I said, 'Well, he won't haul off and shoot you for nothing, will he, before he knows who you are? Tell me where he lives, and I'll go talk to him.' So I went up there. He didn't have his shotgun; he had a big old dog sitting on the porch. I told him what we were trying to do, and he said, 'Let me tell you something, when you get that working like you say, I'll be in it. I'm just gonna wait and see.' 'All right,' I said, 'you go ahead and wait and see, but don't cause any trouble with these guys 'cause they're all going in it.' I don't know if he ever joined, but he never caused us any trouble."

Woodrow Green and other Cortez fishermen also traveled around the coast for the union, sometimes with Bob and sometimes on their own. "I bought a brand new Ford and I run that a good many miles up and down the coast," said Woodrow. "We worked those bays north and south of us and we had it going pretty good, although I think Cortez was the best place on the west coast. But I'll tell you the truth, there was some places where we was actually afraid to go into when we first started. One time down in Fort Myers, there was a guy [fisherman] who was brother to the biggest dealer, and the fishermen down there wouldn't even invite him to the meetings. But we went down and paid the gas for some of them to come up to our meetings in Cortez and see how the union worked, and eventually that brother to the dealer became the friendliest one of all. And whenever his wife began to catch on, she was a hot one! Boy, she was all right. See, the women was mainly the ones that was pushing the whole thing 'cause they wanted a living."

Although they pushed the union behind the scenes, women were not allowed to play any formal roles in the drive. "That was a mistake," said Beltrame, "because we never really gave the women a chance to support what we were trying to do. The UPWA set up women's auxiliaries in other places, but we never got around to doing it in Florida, and that hurt us."

The union pursued its goal of a uniform price in every port, and, in late 1955, Beltrame invited all of the dealers to come to a general port meeting to hear the union's demands. "Before the meeting, I had even drawn up sample contracts, showing what we wanted to negotiate," said Beltrame, "but the union's general counsel had warned me that the Sherman Antitrust Act prevented us from negotiating on the price of fish. At the meeting, the dealers listened to our proposals but turned thumbs down to them. Once they turned them down, the only thing we could do was try to force the issue in each port."

Early in 1956, the UPWA called a series of strikes in ports on the west coast, including one in Cortez. Despite resistance from some fishermen, the strikes were successful in raising the price of all fish: mullet went from 5-7 cents a pound to 8-10 cents, depending on the port; trout rose from 22 to 32 cents; bluefish climbed from 10 to 14 cents; redfish moved from 12 to 16 cents; and pompano jumped from 85 cents to $1.50.

In Cortez, the strike ended after nine days when the dealers agreed to raise the price of mullet to 10 cents a pound. But there were negative repercussions from the strike that would eventually drive the dealers further away from the local fishermen and closer to the dealers down south.

Pig Fulford of the Fulford Fish Company explained the dealers' perspective on the strike: "They [fishermen's union] started out to organize the whole coast and it would have been a good thing. The fishermen needed it. But then Cortez went on strike first, and we had trucks that stopped coming in here to buy fish and started going down to Pine Island 'cause they were still fishing down there. Well, it took us years to get those trucks to come back to Cortez, and some of them never did come back."

Cortez dealers eventually came under the influence of dealers in other ports and turned against the union. "When them dealers down south seen the union was growing and doing some good, they began to kick pretty heavy," said Woodrow. "They got onto Tink and Judge and Jim Guthrie, and they turned turtle. They had been 100 percent for the fishermen until that clique south got in with them, but then they was one of them. We'd go down to Fort Myers; they'd go down to Fort Myers. We'd have meetings together; they'd have meetings together. Yeah, they turned turtle upside down."

The UPWA had two other obstacles to overcome before a lasting organization could be built: racism and internal disunity. Like other CIO unions, the UPWA had taken strong stands on the importance of organizing all workers, white and black, and, at its 1947 national convention, one-third of all delegates were black. But the fishing villages' populations were completely white in the 1950s (except for St. Marks, which had two black fishermen according to Ed Beltrame), and many villages, including Cortez, still have no black residents. The UPWA's tenure in Cortez was the one time in the village's history when the prejudices relaxed a little and the common economic interests of the fishermen and the UPWA's black members overrode the Jim Crow attitudes of the time. The divisions were still there, but not as sharply as before.

"The Seafarers didn't have any blacks," said Bob, "but the Packinghouse Workers had plenty of them, and lots of officers that were black. In fact, they had a black organizer named Don Smith who was a troubleshooter for the union. He came here to Cortez one time and stopped in front of our house. He didn't get out and come in, so I went out and got him and we come in and had breakfast. My wife Ruth said, 'What are people around here gonna say?' I said, 'I don't care what they say. He's all right.'

"And one time I got a couple of guys to go with me to Tampa for a meeting, and Smith was up there at that. He got up and talked and told them some things, and when we was coming home one of them said, 'If you had about half a dozen like Don Smith, it wouldn't take long to organize the whole state.' I never heard any complaints about blacks in the union, not here anyway."

Ed Beltrame and Bob Knowlton never encountered any direct prob-lems because of the UPWA's racial policy, but there were grumblings under the surface that they never heard. "When we went up to that meeting in Tampa, there was a great big fellah, black as tar," said Gene Fulford. "He was the head organizer from Chicago. And for some of them that stopped it right there. I heard some of them say that if he was the head of it then to hell with it. But he knowed his union, that's for sure."

In any case, racism was not as harmful as the disunity within the ranks of the fishermen. Stubborn individualism hurt the union repeatedly in key struggles. "We could have all got more money for our fish," said Hal Cul-breath, "but this bunch of fishermen here would go to that schoolhouse [for the meeting] and swear they didn't have the $3 to pay their monthly dues, but then they'd come right down here to the Sailor's Haven beer joint and get drunk. They had enough money to get drunk! And when we went on strike some of them'd swear they wasn't going fishing, but they couldn't wait till they got out of the schoolhouse 'fore they'd go."

Despite the obstacles, the UPWA kept inching ahead. It finally achieved its long-sought goal of a standard price for fish in all ports, although the union did agree to a small differential for the southern-most ports, because of the greater distances they had to truck their fish to market.

But the UPWA came to an abrupt and nearly bloody ending in the spring of 1957, when a long and turbulent strike broke out at Fort Myers Beach. "Everything was going the finest kind," said Bob, "but then down at Fort Myers Beach they cut the price on the fish. We couldn't see any reason for it, they didn't need to do it, so we called them out on strike. It went on for weeks—four to six weeks if I remember right, and every week me and Woodrow carried $1,000 to $1,500 down there from the national strike fund so the fishermen could live.

"But there was one guy there, a fisherman, and he was the one that started all the trouble and kept it up. He said as long as he could sell his fish, he was gonna keep fishing. He said he had to keep fishing, that he couldn't afford to stop, that he had to live, see. Well, in a way that was true, but what was he gonna live on later on? He didn't think about that."

With the one fisherman refusing to support the strike, tensions in the community built to a fever pitch. There was talk of killing or dynamiting to get him to quit fishing. "It came to the point where some people thought there had to be a little bit of killing," said Woodrow, "and that's what really and truly killed the whole deal. Nobody wanted it, and that's why they just threw the union overboard. Now I'm telling you like it was. And the main one to be killed was this young fellah—he's been in my house, had a family, had a real good boat—he had everything, that fellah did. And everybody liked him 'cause he was real friendly. But he was on the opposite side of the fence, and the dealer was paying him a premium to be the ass that he was, and some of his brothers were beginning to get just like him. And he had a lot of influence away from Fort Myers Beach because he was so friendly. Well, my estimation of the whole thing, buddy, is that nobody wanted nobody there killed, and that just set everybody afire. There was no other way around it 'cause they had pleaded with that fellah and everything else."

The union men seriously discussed other options, besides killing the man, such as blowing up a fish house or some trucks. "There was one guy who was willing to go in there and blow up a fish house," said Bob, "but there was only one road into that place and one road out, so he would have had to go in by boat, and he didn't want to do it. Well, I don't like that kind of thing, nobody likes it, but that one guy was hurting everybody in that whole town. You have to do something, as a last resort, if he refuses to cooperate. That's what that rough stuff is for, and the earlier you do it, the better."

Unable to reach a consensus on violence, the end came quickly for the UPWA. "That one guy went on fishing and pretty soon the dealers got another one to go, and first thing you know the whole works fell apart," said Bob. "They produce a lot of fish there, and we just couldn't keep the rest of them out. Once that strike failed, we tried to keep the union going for a little while and took a lower price for the fish, but then other dealers cut their prices, too, and that ended that." In November 1957, Bob wrote to Beltrame, who had been reassigned to an organizing drive in Tennessee, and told him that the union was a complete flop, that the price of mullet was down to three or four cents and was expected to drop even further.

The UPWA made two attempts to put the pieces back together. About a year after the Fort Myers Beach strike, Ruth Knowlton and Elizabeth Jones, the wife of another Cortez fisherman, traveled up and down the coast collecting signatures of fishermen who were willing to rejoin the union. "We got over 100 names and sent them to Hathaway [secretary-treasurer of the UPWA] and he tried to schedule a meeting to talk it over, but the people just wouldn't come," explained Ruth.

As a last-gasp effort, the UPWA offered to establish cooperatively owned fish houses that the fishermen would run themselves. These co-ops, called "crow-hops" in Cortez, were rejected, largely because repeated failures had discouraged the fishermen. "When they seen the whole thing folding up, the union said they'd put us in crow-hops," said Woodrow. "They would have financed every dime of it if we just said, 'Yeah, we'll go together.' And they come down begging, long after it was all blowed away, wanting to help the fishermen out that way. They said they'd even build freezers in the crow-hops, so they'd have the advantage over other fish houses 'cause back in them days there weren't any freezers anywhere around here. But we couldn't get the fishermen to even talk about it. Well, that just busted it, brother."

It stayed busted, too, until 1967, when the Organized Fishermen of Florida was formed to counteract a rising tide of anti-netting legislation which threatened to destroy commercial fishing in Florida altogether. OFF is an association of both dealers and fishermen and is a different kind of organization altogether from the earlier unions.

To Bob Knowlton, sitting in his living room and reflecting on the past, the future doesn't look good for fishing in Cortez. "If things keep going like they are now, I don't believe there'll be any fishing five years from now. All those party boats, yachts, and kicker boats are racing up and down the bay all the time, and they keep it so stirred up the fish can't even feed. And the condos just keep going up everywhere—I think the county commissioners could stop it if they wanted to."

Bob Knowlton isn't a union organizer anymore, but his 30 years in the Volunteer Fire Department and the 125 foster children that he and Ruth have kept in their home over the years attest to his community spirit. He is part of the legacy of the labor movement in this country, albeit an unrecognized and unknown part of it. Yet he feels no bitterness about all the years he put into the union, only sadness. "When the last one failed, I said 'Well, that's the end of it for me. Nothing more.'"

But he has too many years of his life wrapped up in the labor movement to turn loose of it completely, and there are memories of those years that he's still attached to—like the time he met John L. Lewis in Fort Myers. And when all is said and done, those memories remind Bob Knowlton of what could have been. "John L. Lewis had a house down in Fort Myers and I met him one time and talked to him for quite a while. He was just the nicest guy you'd ever talk to. Well, look at all he did for the miners." He shook his head slowly, shrugged, and said, "We could have had all that, too, if we'd stuck together."

Chapter 12

"The Finest People on Earth"

M. C. "MAC" McCARTER WAS STANDING out on the netspreads by my uncle's shrimp boat, working a big chaw of tobacco in his right cheek and leaning over every few minutes to spit a thin stream of tobacco juice into the water. It was a hot day in June, the sun was bearing down, and Mac was reflecting on what it was like to be one of the first black men ever to work in Cortez. What he said caught me somewhat by surprise. "I'll tell you, I never felt the people here treated me like I was black. They treated me like I was a human being. I've often said that the people in Cortez are the finest people on earth."

Mac McCarter came to work at the Fulford Fish Company in 1956 and stayed for 13 years. When he took the job, his salary was $50 a week; when he left it was $75. There had been only a few black men to work in Cortez prior to Mac's arrival. Only a handful have worked there since he left. Cortez has never had a black resident. It will probably be many years, if ever, before there will be one. That's why Mac's words surprised me.

During his 13 years in Cortez, all of the great struggles of the civil rights movement took place: the Montgomery bus boycott, the sit-ins in Greensboro and dozens of other cities, the Freedom Rides, the Selma-Montgomery march, and voter registration drives all over the South. During those same years, Martin Luther King, Jr., went from obscurity to national prominence to the balcony of a Memphis hotel where he was killed by an assassin's bullet. During all of that, Mac came to work six days a week at the Fulford Fish Company and never spoke of any of it. He spent each day shoveling, weighing and packing fish, loading 100-pound fish boxes onto refrigerated trucks, scraping and painting the bottoms of boats, fertilizing and hoeing Grandpa's coconut trees, and doing anything else that needed doing around the fish house.

Mac's years coincided almost exactly with the years when I was spending every school vacation in Cortez—summers, Thanksgiving, Christmas, and Easter. During those years, I spent more time with Mac than with any other adult. He was the supervisor of a raggedy work crew that consisted of my uncle Gary, my cousins Rusty Fulford and Jimmy Guthrie, and me. It was Mac who set the pace for our work. It was Mac who did the things that we weren't strong enough or knowledgeable enough to do. And it was Mac who gave the word that it was time to load up in the old battered Chevy pickup truck and make a run to Hoot Gibson's store for an RC cola and a honey bun.

Mac was my model of what it meant to be a man. He was strong, confident, friendly, and skillful. He could split and clean mullet faster than anybody in Cortez. He could work as hard and as long as anyone, including my grandpa, which is saying something. He was as strong as any man in the village. And he was as fun-loving as anyone I've ever known. He laughed long and hard, with a great booming eruption from the back of his throat—at his own jokes, our jokes, and anyone else's jokes. Every now and then, usually just around us boys, and never in front of strangers, Mac would break into "playing the hambone"—slapping out a rhythm with both hands on the back of his legs and singing an old blues chant. It was pure entertainment, with no trace of the Uncle Tom shuck-and-jive.

Mac's reputation for hard work is still intact. One day last summer, Gene Fulford was complaining that it had taken the county almost two years to four-lane a stretch of Cortez Road. "I've often thought," he said, "that if they'd had Tink Fulford and old Mac working on that road, they'd had it done in six weeks."

I knew it was important to this book, for a number of reasons, that Mac McCarter be in it. First, no book on Cortez would be complete without looking at the attitudes toward and treatment of blacks. Second, the years that I spent working with Mac played a major part in shaping my own attitudes about race. In spite of the many racial stereotypes, jokes, and slurs that I heard as I was growing up, the actual reality of Mac McCarter outweighed them all.

When I arrived in Cortez, I looked up Mac's phone number and added him to the list of people to interview. But just a few days later, I looked out of my grandma's living-room window and there he was, walking out on the netspreads next to the dock. I went down and said hello, told him that I was writing a book about Cortez, and spent the next 45 minutes reminiscing with him and Uncle Wayne.

My memories of Mac are of a tall, lean, well-muscled man. Today, other than a few flecks of gray in his hair, he looks exactly the same. I told him he looked like he could still outwork anybody in Cortez, and he laughed, saying, "Well, in my time I could work with any of them. But I'm turning 50 this year, and I've quit a lot of that hard work like I did down here. I figure by the time a man turns 50, if he ain't got it, he ain't gonna get it."

Many of Mac's memories of Cortez had to do with Tink Fulford. It was Grandpa who hired Mac in 1956, and he was the one who set the tone of how others would treat him. "There's nobody else like Tink Fulford and there never will be," said Mac. "He was a real character, and he pushed everybody real hard—himself more than anybody. But he was as fair with me as he could be. He never had a bad word for me. He didn't show any partiality to me—he worked Wayne and Mr. Pig just as hard as he worked me. Yep, they threw away the mold when Tink Fulford died." At Grandpa's funeral, Mac sat with the family in a private room in the funeral parlor's chapel.

I asked Mac how other people in Cortez treated him and about incidents of racial prejudice or discrimination. "Now there were some things I didn't like," he said, "and every now and then somebody'd call me a name, but in all those years here I didn't have a bad word with anybody but one time, and I just chalked that one up to that person's ignorance."

But there were obvious ways in which Mac was treated differently because he was black. Mealtime was when it was most evident. We would work together all morning hoeing Grandpa's trees, but when lunchtime came, we'd go to the house and Mac would go the dock. One of us would fix him a plate and carry it down to the dock, but he was not allowed to come inside to eat. We never questioned it.

"There were certain things I knew I couldn't do, like going inside to eat," said Mac, "but I never let that kind of thing bother me. See, I was raised up under that system, and I knew there were things that was wrong about it, but there really wasn't anything you could do about it as one man. Now black kids today, they would think it was terrible and they wouldn't stand for it, but that's the way things were when I was growing up. And there were some people in Cortez, like Miss Letha (Leeper) who'd invite me to come in and sit down at the table with them. Boy, that woman was the best cook in Cortez! Anything she cooked was good."

There have always been distinctions between blacks and whites in Cortez as far back as anyone can remember. No blacks have ever lived in the village, and, until recent years, there were tight restrictions about them even working there. "Oh, no black people were ever allowed to live in Cortez," said Toodle Green. "My mother told me a story that happened years ago, about Aunt Lula Fulford. She and Uncle Sanders had a big house down on the water, and one time a black man came in on a boat there. I don't remember all the details, maybe he was waiting to catch the steamer. But the people thought that just because he was black he'd do terrible things. So he was out on this dock waiting, and Aunt Lula, she was always a very brave sort of person, she just went out and told him, 'Don't you let the sun go down and catch you here. You just better get going!' And he did."

There were several times in Cortez's history when black laborers were hired to work in the village, but even then the prevailing attitude was "be out of town before sundown." "Back in 1908, when they started building the old shell road to Bradenton, there were a bunch of colored people working on that," recalled Julian Taylor, who was a young boy at the time. "The foreman of the crew was white, but all the laborers was black. They rented a big barn from Mrs. Bratton and the colored guys stayed in the loft of that barn. And I remember when they first started trying to hire them to work in the fish houses, some of the boys went to them and said, 'Now when the sun goes down we want you out of town. You can work in the daytime, but you can't be here at night.' There was a black family lived down at what they used to call the Wyman Place and when I worked at the fish house, I'd carry them home in the truck so's they'd be out of Cortez before night."

There is no question that many of the people in Cortez, if not most, have deep-seated prejudices towards blacks, which is a tribute to the thorough conditioning of white Southerners. Since the end of Reconstruction, most attempts by working-class blacks and whites to get a fairer shake from the Southern power structure have been effectively blocked by divide-and-conquer tactics. Waving the bloody shirt of race hatred has been a powerful weapon for keeping whites and blacks from joining together to fight for common goals.

It's worked so well that in Cortez, where residents have had little contact with blacks and few opportunities to generate stereotypes and prejudices on their own, the message of race hatred still prevails. Racism is so institutionalized in the culture that Cortez residents picked up more from the press, the school system, and the church than from their own experiences.

"I guess it's just a holdover attitude of a lot of whites towards blacks," said Toodle. "Just because a person was black, they'd look down on them as a nigger. That's all you were in their opinion. And that just galls me, because the whites were just as poor and just as uneducated and ignorant as the blacks, but because their skin was white, they felt superior to someone whose skin was black."

In Cortez, racism has apparently been more an attitude than a practice. The elements of fear and mistrust that fueled bombings and lynchings elsewhere have been present in Cortez, but there hasn't been much of an opportunity to act them out.

"Back in the '20s, I remember that the Ku Klux Klan held a big meeting out between Palmetto and Parrish," said Man Adams. "The klan got real strong back there in the '20s and I guess they was trying to get more members here in Manatee County. I wasn't nothing but 17 or 18 years old at the time, and I rode out to that meeting. I guess most of Manatee County was there, and every Model T in town was there. They burnt the cross and everything, but I just wasn't interested in it. I don't know but one guy in Cortez that was ever a member of the klan, and he was a member of the church, too. One time somebody said they seen him open his billfold and there was a card with three big K's. They was all real surprised about it."

During the years that Mac McCarter was driving his green 1961 Chevy to Cortez, I never heard him talk about the civil rights movement, nor did I hear anyone mention it to him. But I certainly heard a lot about it around the dining room table at Grandma's house, only 100 yards from where Mac was eating his dinner. Race was a very hot subject in my family. Other than money, it was the number one topic that my parents fought about.

The battles really cranked up when my aunt Belinda and her husband Oliver Porterfield were visiting from Montgomery. Oliver was a Church of Christ preacher who had a license tag on his car that read: "Member, Governor's Personal Staff." The governor, in this case, was George C. Wallace—not the repentant George C. Wallace of 1982, who was re-elected as governor of Alabama with the endorsement of many black groups, but the shrill, nasal-voiced banty rooster who stood in the door-way of the University of Alabama in 1962, confronting a squad of U.S. marshals. During the Selma demonstration, Oliver went on television in Montgomery to denounce the protesters for "urinating in the streets." I don't think he said a word about the police dogs and billy clubs employed by "Bull" Connor.

After supper at Grandma's house, the arguments would really heat up, with Momma, my sister Cathy and me on one side, and Daddy, Oliver, and Grandma on the other. We would yell and scream at each other for hours, each side quoting scriptures to justify positions. Oliver's final stand, when he had said everything that a good Christian could say to someone in his own family, was to turn to Cathy and me and say, "Well, I'm afraid that your mother has ruined you kids—turned you into nigger lovers." At that point in the argument, it was the finest thing he could have said to me.

Looking back, I've been thankful on many occasions for those raging family arguments, although a price was paid in closeness with some family members. For many Southern whites, racism was not a subtle discussion topic discreetly raised in an otherwise liberal household. It was a storm of rage and venom poured out among blood relatives. To emerge from those flames and still be both a friend to blacks and a proud Southerner is an important accomplishment. My mother's stubborn commitment to racial equality and the forceful reality of Mac McCarter have stood me in good stead over the years.

I think that when racism is finally laid to rest, there will be a new ap-preciation for the struggles that white Southerners will have waged within their own families. This is even more crucial because two of the most im-portant bonds within Southern culture are at stake: family and regional identity. There are no greater values, other than God, perhaps, that make up the traditional identity of Southerners.

At times, the easiest route out of that trap was to disown those South-ern roots and, possibly, the family as well. It seemed easier to deal with the guilt and shame of racism by casting it all aside and declaring yourself free of all connections to the past legacy. But there are few things more pathetic in the world than a Southerner pretending not to be one. A bet-ter solution for Southern whites is to reclaim pride in the good qualities of Southern life—and there are many—without accepting racism as a part of it. The South and racism are not irrevocably bound together.

There is actually a history to be proud of. It's not the history we were taught in school, but in many ways I think it's more important to the future of the region, and the country as a whole, than the legacies of prejudice and fear. By retrieving those incidents of unity from the pages of history, and there are many of them, we can find something to build on for the future.

There were several waves of black-white unity in the decades after the Civil War. The Southern Farmers' Alliance, the Knights of Labor, and the Populist party were most noteworthy. Heroic battles took place on the New Orleans waterfront at the turn of the century and in the piney woods of the Delta in the 1910s, with blacks and whites fighting the timber bosses, the goon squads, and the klan. If Southern working people are ever going to get off the bottom of the wage scale—and truly "rise again"—those same kind of unified battles will have to be fought once again.

When Mac McCarter left Cortez in 1969, he did so because of money, not because of racial mistreatment. Sometimes it's hard to tell the difference. "After 13 years I was only making $75 a week," he said. "I asked Mr. Pig for a raise and he said he couldn't afford it. Well, I just had to have more money. I had a family and I wanted to buy a house and I knew I'd never be able to on $75 a week. Since I left Cortez, I've realized that I can make more money. I've paid off my house and I'm going to build an addition on it. I never would have had nothing if I'd stayed at $75 a week." After leaving Cortez, Mac worked for a year at Moore's Seafood Restaurant on Longboat Key, and then had his own lawn-mowing business for about a year and a half. He's been working for Palmetto Federal Savings and Loan ever since, making deliveries to the bank's six branch offices and doing their lawn and maintenance work.

It's clear that the civil rights movement has brought some changes to Cortez. Black men work at most of the fish houses and make considerably more than $75 a week (although usually not as much as their white counterparts). Black truck drivers pick up fish every day at the Cortez fish companies. Black families drive to the village to buy fresh seafood. Cortez youngsters go to integrated schools where they are taught by black teachers and, in some cases, make friends with black children.

But there is a long way to go before the old attitudes are gone and black families are welcome to live in Cortez. If that day finally comes, Mac McCarter should get some credit. Neither a black militant nor an Uncle Tom, he is simply a man who takes pride in himself and delight in others.

In the process, he never stooped his head, lowered his gaze, or surrendered one shred of personal dignity.

After 45 minutes of swapping stories with Wayne and me, Mac had to leave to get back to town. As he was driving off, Wayne told me about the first time his daughter Cheri, now 21, met Mac. "He quit working here when Cheri was pretty young, so she never really knew him. But one day when she was about 7, Mac came down to the dock and I said, 'Cheri, this here is your cousin Mac.' She went to school the next day and told the class, real proudly, that she had a black man for a cousin."

"You know," Wayne added, "if all black people were like Mac, it'd be a better world."

"What you mean," I said, "is if everybody was like Mac it'd be a better world."

"You got it there," he agreed.

PART IV

Facing the Future

"The first schoolhouse in Cortez was established about 1895 in a small A-frame that Earl Guthrie lives in today." Bearing its own historical marker, Earl's home is the oldest one-room schoolhouse still in existence in Manatee County (1910).

Chapter 13

"The First Thing
A Yankee Learns to Say"

BLUE FULFORD AND I WERE DRIVING home to Cortez in his pickup truck after delivering 15,000 pounds of Spanish sardines to Ruskin, a small community 30 miles north of Bradenton. We had hauled the fish up there in big fiberglass iceboxes, 800 pounds per box, stacked two-high on Blue's flatbed trailer.

At the J. O. Guthrie Fish Company in Ruskin, my second cousin Jimmy Guthrie, who took over the fish house when his grandpa died, used a forklift to unload the boxes—screeching, squalling, and sliding over the wet floor of the dock the way he used to drive hot rods on Cortez Road. Jimmy dumped the bait into a huge washing bin. The conveyor belt attached to its side carried the fish up to the packing crew—six young men wearing "J.O. Guthrie Fish Company" uniforms—who weighed out 25 pounds of bait into flat cardboard boxes, stapled the boxes shut, and stacked them in a cavernous freezer.

Coming home, Blue Fulford talked about the future of fishing in Florida. He is probably the best-known commercial fisherman in the state, having served for eight years as the executive director of the Organized Fishermen of Florida. Depending on who you're talking to, he may be called Blue, Sonny, Tommy, or any combination of the three.

As we passed a new subdivision on the outskirts of Bradenton, Blue pointed at two elderly Yankee gentlemen fishing in the canal behind their house and said ruefully, "Yeah, the first thing a Yankee learns to say after moving down here is 'what are they doing out there catching my fish?' That's the first thing they expropriate—the fish."

The commercial fishing industry in Florida is full of contrasting images. On the one hand are Jimmy Guthrie's fork lifts, conveyor belts, and deep freezers—common tools of the trade in the 1980s—and on the other hand are Blue's words of warning about "Yankees expropriating the fish." Watching the fork lifts scurrying back and forth across the floor of Jimmy's dock and listening to the roar of the giant compressors running the freezers, it was easy to believe that the fishing industry was on a roll, expanding to meet the demands of the future. But listening to Blue's haunting words, I wondered if the industry will survive at all.

Which image is believable? The only choice, in my mind, is to believe both. In some ways, the fishing industry in Florida has never been better, and, in other ways, it is on the brink of collapse.

Blue Fulford has stood at the center of those contrasts for over a decade, and he understands both the promise and the threat to commercial fishing as well as anyone in the state. "The modern era for Florida fishermen began in 1967," said Blue, a short, muscular man with big forearms and a deeply tanned complexion. "That was the year that a group of developers, politicians, and some neighborhood associations tried to do away with commercial fishing altogether." These groups proposed local legislation to ban all net fishing in Manatee County within 1,700 yards of shore. There are few places in the county that are not within 1,700 yards—almost a mile—of some shoreline. Similar anti-netting laws were proposed in other counties.

"I'd like to think they didn't intend to kill the fishing industry, but I'm not so sure," said Blue. "The ringleader of the group in Manatee County said to me, 'Well, Mr. Fulford, it looks like you people are just on the way out.' It looked so bleak in the late '60s that I didn't encourage my two sons to become fishermen. I figured if the bays weren't declared off-limits by law, then dredge-and-fill would get us anyway. I thought within five years our way of life would be gone forever. But we had to do something. We'd been here too long and too many people were dependent on these bays."

That same year, the Organized Fishermen of Florida was formed in Everglades City, and that one event changed Blue Fulford's life and the lives of most Florida fishermen as well. OFF grew out of a local dispute in Everglades City over a state-sponsored experiment with the use of purse seines to catch king mackerel. Local fishermen were afraid that the more effective purse seines, which were too expensive for most fishermen to buy, would put them out of business. OFF initiated a campaign to outlaw purse seines for all food fish and had accomplished that by 1969. OFF was the fishermen's way to fight back. To build support for the Everglades City struggle, Jimmie Robinson traveled to other ports and organized local chapters. She became the first statewide executive director of the organization.

As anti-netting legislation began to proliferate around the state, OFF's resistance to it grew accordingly. Blue Fulford became head of the Cortez chapter, then state president, and served as executive director from 1972-1977. He was replaced in 1978 by Jerry Sampson, who still holds that position today.

Although OFF was new and financially weak, having any kind of statewide organization at all was a big step forward. But OFF received added impetus from an unexpected quarter; coinciding with its organization was the growing national environmental movement that was sweeping the country. Florida fishermen learned to work cooperatively with the long-haired activists, whom they had once distrusted, in organizations such as "Save Our Bays." That unholy alliance between fishermen and environmental groups helped to slow the ravages of "Mr. Bull Dozer, Mr. Dredge Boat, and Mr. Drag Line," which Blue called the three main threats to commercial fishing. "It was like a miracle—the entire nation suddenly became environmentally conscious," said Blue.

Several landmark environmental bills were passed in Florida during the late 1960s and early 1970s, including: the Air and Water Pollution Control Act (1967), the Beach and Shore Preservation Act (1970), the Water Resources Act (1972), and the Environmental Land and Water Management Act (1972). Combined with federal measures such as the Coastal Zone Management Act (1972) and the National Environmental Policy Act (1974), these laws helped slow the destruction of Florida's coastal ecosystem and thus helped stabilize the future of commercial fishing.

The biggest lesson OFF had to learn was how to play the game of power politics. In the spring of 1972, Blue left Cortez to go to Tallahassee and spend the next eight legislative sessions as the lobbying voice for OFF. What he found when he got to Tallahassee shocked him. "It was a real education for a country boy, I'll tell you that. I had been so isolated in Cortez that I hadn't even taken a vacation for 13 straight years. I had just stayed there and fished and never got out anywhere else. When I got up there to Tallahassee, I was about the most disillusioned person you've ever seen in your life.

"I'd go up there and sit in that legislative gallery and think to myself, 'These are the people who are supposed to be taking care of the business of Florida.' I couldn't believe what I saw. A bill would come up for a vote and four guys would be standing over in the corner talking and not paying any attention, a couple of others would be reading the funny papers, somebody else would be talking to his girlfriend on the phone and trying to get a date, and some of them would be asleep. Half of them wouldn't be there and half of the ones who were there wouldn't vote. They're the biggest bunch of monkeys you've ever seen. They're not doing the business of Florida, they're just up there taking care of their own business. I was so disillusioned. Then I realized that's the way politics works. But it just makes you sick when you think about it."

OFF's top priority was fighting the local anti-netting regulations, and, in 1972, it succeeded in getting a bill passed that made fisheries regulation the responsibility of the state, thereby voiding all local anti-netting laws passed by county or city commissions. However, local regulations could still be enacted by the legislature as "special acts" and about 220 such bills are still on the books. In 1975, Blue and other OFF members filed suit, challenging those local bills as unconstitutional because they denied fishermen the right to make a living. But in 1981, the courts ruled against OFF's claims; that ruling is under appeal.

Today, OFF claims 1,400 members in 30 local chapters. Unlike earlier organizing efforts that pitted share fishermen against dealers, OFF includes both in its ranks. "I think OFF is a real good thing, but it doesn't have anything to do with the price of fish," said Woodrow Green, who was active in earlier unions in the 1940s and 1950s. "It was the dealers that built it and they didn't give you any choice about belonging—they just went up a little bit on the price of gas and took that out for OFF dues, which made some of the fishermen mad. But they were right to do that. It was an emergency and they needed to do it. I was shrimping back then and I kept paying my dues long after I retired, because I believed in it. If the dealers had been on the other side it would have been just like our earlier unions. The dealers would not cooperate with us 'cause they was gonna run everything or have nothing—that was the theory of the whole business. But OFF is the only thing the fishermen have got now, and if they don't hold onto it, commercial fishing is gonna be wound up."

One of OFF's main goals has been the development of a statewide fisheries management plan based on sound ecological and biological principles, rather than on arbitrary political deals and maneuvers. In 1980, the Florida legislature established the Saltwater Fisheries Study and Advisory Council, composed of representatives from government, science, commercial fishing, sportfishing, and fish dealers. During 1981, the council held 15 meetings around the state to take testimony from citizens and expert witnesses and presented the 1982 legislature with a 174-page book of recommendations. But the 1982 session was dominated by squabbles over a new reapportionment plan for the state, so the recommendations were never passed.

The 1983 legislature did enact them and, in June 1983, the new Marine Fisheries Commission was given full rule-making authority over marine life, with the exception of endangered species. The seven-member commission is composed of scientists, sportfishermen, and commercial fishermen, and all rules which they pass must be approved by the governor and the cabinet before becoming law.

The commission is in the process of developing options papers for each marine species, which will eventually be translated into state regulations. Testimony from marine biologists, commercial fishermen, and sportfishermen is being taken in an extensive series of public hearings. As of August 1984, options papers have been developed for scallops, clams, cobia, spearfishing, snapper/grouper fisheries, king mackerel, and stone crabs. The commission is already embroiled in its first controversy: a recommendation to ban netting of king mackerel in major portions of the state. Commercial fishermen have complained bitterly about the proposal.

Blue Fulford thinks that, overall, the Marine Fisheries Commission is a tremendous improvement over the confused and sometimes contradictory regulations of the past. "There will probably be some places where we can't fish at certain times of the year, but it will have to be done for biological and environmental reasons," he said. "That will be a great thing because we've never had any sort of planning in Florida regarding fishing. We've just gone along until a crisis hit or somebody got upset about something and then the state would do something. But this thing can work. It can be done! We're going to have to take everybody's needs into account—the commercial fishermen and the sportfishermen and everyone else. And fishermen are going to have to be reasonable, too. We can't have commercial fishermen up there in some finger canal banging and hollering and waking people up at night, but it can work."

OFF's most vocal opposition on the Marine Fisheries Commission and in the halls of the capitol isn't the big real estate developers, but the Florida League of Anglers, representing sportfishermen. As the tourist industry has grown in Florida, so has the importance of sportfishing as a lure for vacationers and tourists. Sportfishing, water skiing, white sand beaches— such are the amenities that travel brochures are made of.

In recent years, the Florida League of Anglers has pointed an accusatory finger at commercial fishermen, blaming them for the decreasing numbers of trout, redfish, mackerel, kingfish, and other species. The animosity between the two camps surfaced most noticeably in the fall of 1981, when Jerry Hill, the sportfishing columnist for the *Bradenton Herald*, proposed a statewide ban on all net fishing for three years, with fishermen to be paid a yearly "pension" out of state funds. Although this proposal "never had a chance in hell of passing," as Executive Director Jerry Sampson put it, the idea was hotly debated throughout the state.

"If the sportfishermen had their way, there wouldn't be any net fishing within three miles of shore, and only then with a hand dip-net," said Blue. "And the only difference I can see between a commercial fisherman and a lot of these sportfishermen is the sportfisherman takes a picture of his fish before he sells it."

The founding of OFF in 1967 signaled the beginning of a political awakening for Florida fishermen, which has culminated in their equal status on the Marine Fisheries Commission with marine biologists and sportfishermen. They still have other battles, such as the one with sportfishermen, but at least now they know how to play the game.

While fishermen were experiencing a political revolution of sorts during the 1960s and 1970s, there was a parallel revolution in fishing technology and marketing. The opening salvo was the development of monofilament nets in the late 1960s. Unlike cotton and linen, monofilament required no daily liming and spreading, and thus eliminated the major source of drudgery from the fisherman's life. Today's fisherman can leave his net on the boat until the end of the season. Furthermore, monofilament is a "clean" material that doesn't catch as many crabs, pinfish, or seaweed as the old nets did.

The other major technological advance was the development of the kicker boat in the late 1960s. Mercury, Johnson, and Evinrude outboard motors gave birth to this new creature when they replaced the six-cylinder inboard marine engines that had been used since the turn of the century.

By the late 1970s, kicker boats had become the dominant craft on the inland waters of the Gulf coast and had revolutionized fishing techniques. "These kicker boats can get up into waters where nobody ever fished before," said Blue Fulford. "They can go up so shallow, right up into the mangroves, that there's no place for the fish to hide."

Monofilament nets and kicker boats changed forever the methods of catching fish, but the most dramatic innovations have been in packaging, shipping, and marketing. Clearly, the best news for Cortez fishermen is in the marketplace. "Today you can sell anything you can catch. The markets are fantastic," said Blue. Fish that were once considered trash, such as jacks, can now be sold at a profit. Mullet gizzards, which used to be thrown overboard or fed to the fish-house cats, are now frozen and shipped in bulk to Taiwan. There's a demand for anything and everything that's caught, if not in the U.S., then in the expanding overseas markets.

These markets began opening in the early 1970s and have resurrected an industry that was stagnant a decade ago. Prior to this, Florida fish dealers depended on small domestic wholesalers to truck their fish to southeastern and northern markets. At the height of the fall roe season when mullet were most plentiful, it was common for Cortez dealers to cut fishermen off, refusing to buy any more fish, because they had nowhere to sell them. Many times when we had caught a load of fish and found out too late that we were cut off, I've helped split thousands of pounds of mullet, remove the roe, which could be sold to local restaurants, and dump the fish in the bay. The price of mullet had dropped so low by 1970—10 or 12 cents a pound—that fishermen were receiving only a few cents more than they were in the 1920s. But all of that changed when state and federal officials put Cortez dealers in touch with buyers in Taiwan, Japan, and Hawaii who wanted all the mullet and mullet roe they could get.

Because of the great shipping distances, the mullet had to be frozen first, which brought an end to the era of fresh fish in Cortez the same way the railroad ended the era of salted fish in the 1890s. And with this change, some of Cortez's most familiar landmarks have disappeared. The big coolers, with 100-pound boxes of iced mullet stacked to the ceiling, have been replaced by gigantic freezers, some of them two stories high. With profits now measured by how many fish can be packed, frozen and stored, dealers have sunk thousands of dollars into the construction of new, larger freezers. The Bell Fish Company, Cortez's largest dealer, has a block-long freezer that's big enough to put all three of the other fish houses inside.

The biggest market for frozen mullet is Hawaii. "We ship frozen mullet by air freight in big containers called LC-3s," said Pig Fulford, owner of the Fulford Fish Company. "We can put 2,500 pounds of fish in each one. We freeze the fish real good and then truck them to the Tampa airport early in the morning, load them on a plane, and they arrive in Hawaii that same day. Those fish have only been out of the water for 36 hours by the time they arrive in Honolulu."

The overseas markets have also made mullet roe more valuable than the fish themselves—red roe brings as much as $4.30 per pound. Sometimes the fish are more trouble to get rid of than they're worth. Two years ago, Pig placed notices in the *Bradenton Herald* telling people to come down and get all the mullet they wanted for free, because he could only sell the roe.

Removing and packing the roe is a full-scale operation involving a dozen workers, many of them women. The mullet is first split open, then the roe is removed, placed in individual plastic baggies, and packed in five-pound boxes. Other workers remove the mullet gizzards, which are also sold to Taiwan (Pig sold over 1,100 pounds of frozen gizzards in 1982). Mullet roe is considered a delicacy in Taiwan and is a popular dish on special occasions such as the Chinese New Year. It is salted and cured in the sun before eating.

At the height of the roe season in December and January, 50,000 pounds of roe are frozen each week in Cortez, and, at $4.30 per pound, the fish houses gross more than $200,000 per week. "People drive down here and see these little old wooden fish houses and they don't realize how many fish are being produced," said Pig.

Although roe has displaced mullet as Cortez's most important product, the fish themselves are still vital to the village's economy. Cortez is second only to Lee County in mullet production and, in 1981, the Fulford Fish Company alone produced nearly a million pounds of mullet.

In recent years, other fish have begun to rival mullet in importance. The most profitable of these are bait fish—Spanish sardines and thread herring—which are caught with purse seines during the summer. After freezing, the fish are shipped to bait shops on both coasts of Florida. In 1982, almost two million pounds of bait were sold by Cortez fish houses.

Bait shrimp, which were first caught in Sarasota Bay 40 years ago using small beach seines, have now become a year-round industry. Cortez bait shrimpers supply most of the bait shops on Anna Maria, Longboat Key, and in Sarasota. Uncle Wayne gave up fishing for bait shrimping ten years ago and says he will never go back. "The only thing I miss about fishing is looking at the pretty girls on the beach. Other than that, if somebody gave me a fishing boat, I'd try to sell it the next day. You just can't make a regular living anymore at it. If I'm not making $400 a week shrimping, then I'm falling behind, and there's no way you can do that fishing. And one of the best things about being a shrimper is that I'm independent. I get my own customers and none of these fish dealers have anything to do with how much money I make."

The Bell Fish Company has a fleet of grouper boats that make regular journeys to the Yucatan Peninsula, off the coast of Mexico. Over 600,000 pounds of grouper are caught by Cortez boats each year.

That's the positive side of the fishing industry in the 1980s: expanding markets, better gear and equipment, and technological advances. But the one thing missing from that list of positive factors is the only ingredient that really counts—fish. New technologies and new markets are useless if the supply of fish is endangered, and Florida's fishing industry faces serious threats to its most important commodity.

Environmental damage to the fishes' feeding grounds is the most serious. Marine biologists are nearly unanimous in their belief that the major destructive force on all species of fish is the combined effects of dredge-and-fill operations, sewage and industrial waste pollution, the construction of seawalls, and the violent destruction of the wetlands along Florida's coast.

Sarasota Bay is a case-in-point. In 1980, Dr. William J. Tiffany headed a study called "Environmental Status of Sarasota Bay: Selected Studies," which was sponsored by the Selby Foundation in Sarasota, under the supervision of Mote Marine Laboratory. Tiffany concluded:

> Vast areas of Sarasota's barrier island/low-flow estuarine complex have been exploited and stressed to the point where we are now experiencing environmental problems in these areas. Many are pollution related problems which could translate to health problems affecting the human population residing in this coastal zone. Problems such as sewage effluent entering Sarasota Bay, urban runoff into the estuaries, loss of grassflats and other marine nursery habitat, all contribute to continuing the degradation of the systems which have been the backbone of this area's economy. . . . On 26 May 1974, Mr. Harmon Shields, former Director of the Florida Department of Natural Resources, stated that Sarasota Bay is a "dead bay." Although, this has not yet come to pass, the bay water quality continues

to decline. One can only wonder why we blatantly continue to abuse Sarasota Bay and ignore the existent problems, while there is such an overall feeling of "environmentalism" in our area. It is, however, certain that our bay only has a finite capacity to assimilate man's abuses, including improperly planned growth and its associated pollution problems. When that limit is exceeded, nature will not be kind to our local economy.

Tiffany also noted that the seagrasses in Sarasota Bay, important breeding and feeding grounds, have decreased by 20 percent in the past 30 years and that the lowly pinfish has become the dominant fish species in the bay, which is "a severe sign of stress in the ecosystem."

Other studies reached similar conclusions. Steven C. Sauers and Rob Patten of the Office of Coastal Zone Management in Sarasota found that seagrass beds in one section of Sarasota Bay—Whitaker Bayou—had decreased by 54.5 percent between 1949 and 1979, a loss of more than 100 total acres. Poor water quality was identified as the main culprit, although dredging and filling operations, propeller cuts from boats, and trawling by fishermen also contributed.

In a study sponsored by the Sarasota Board of County Commissioners, researchers concluded that dredging and filling operations had destroyed approximately 655 acres of grassbeds in the past 25 years. They estimated that boaters had wiped out as much as 40 percent of the grassbeds in some areas. These researchers compared aerial photos from 1949 and 1974 and concluded that over 22 miles of mangrove shoreline had been destroyed and more than 50 miles of seawalls had been constructed during that period.

Why is the destruction of the estuaries so serious? This study described their importance: "Estuaries are extremely productive areas for plants and animals. . . . Many animals enter the estuary at the larval stage and use the area as a nursery, while others enter to feed or spawn. . . . Estuaries and associated wildlife have a large economic value because of the recreational and aesthetic benefits they provide to residents and visitors. Also, since many fish use these areas, the commercial and sports fisheries are dependent on them. Coastal wetlands also play an important role in shoreline stabilization and flood control. The mangroves and marsh vegetation at the mouths of rivers, tidal creeks, and along bay shores absorb seasonal flooding and dissipate wave energy."

Blue Fulford put it more simply: "I think it's very serious when we talk about destroying our bays and estuaries and building houses where fish used to swim. People think these mangrove swamps are just slimy and smelly, and full of mosquitoes and snakes, but one acre produces seven times more basic organic protein than the best acre of wheat field, twice as much basic food material as the best corn land, and it's the equal of the best acre of rice land or sugar cane."

A full 30 percent of Florida is wetlands, which includes swamps, flood plains, mangrove shorelines, and the Everglades. Not only are they important habitats for wildlife, but they also recycle wastes and filter pollutants out of drinking water, protect against stormwater flooding, control erosion, and contribute to Florida's mild winters.

Over 11,000,000 acres of Florida's wetlands have been lost to agriculture and development, and they are still being drained at the alarming rate of 215,000 acres per year. The bulk of the drainage is for agricultural use, but much of that land is then sold off to developers for residential housing. An estimated 241,000 acres of farmland are lost each year to development.

Florida's legislative leaders declared 1984 "The Year of the Wetlands," and, after a tremendous fight, the first major piece of wetlands legislation in Florida's history was passed by this legislature. The final version of the bill placed wetlands regulation in the hands of Florida's five water management districts which have been criticized for their ties to agricultural interests, rather than with the watchdog Department of Environmental Regulation, as originally proposed. That compromise, along with concessions to agricultural and limestone mining interests, led to a split among the state's major environmental groups. The Audubon Society supported the bill, claiming it was a valuable step in the right direction, while Johnny Jones, lobbyist for the Florida Wildlife Federation, claimed that the final bill was "worse than no bill at all." The water management districts are in the process of developing enforcement policies for the new law, so the real test of the state's commitment to wetlands preservation won't be known for several years.

There is no clear consensus among scientists or fishermen of how extensively the fish population has been decreased by this environmental damage. Most Cortez fishermen think there are about as many mullet as there ever were; the mullet's scavenger nature has probably shielded it somewhat from the effects of pollution. But fishermen also believe that bottom fish—redfish, trout, flounder, and sheephead—have decreased significantly in recent years because they are more vulnerable to pollution and dredging. Shellfish—scallops, oysters, and clams—have been hit hardest by pollution. All of the waters of Sarasota Bay have been declared unsafe for shellfish harvesting because of high coliform counts—a result of years of dumping raw sewage in the bay.

However, environmental problems are not the industry's sole concern; it is facing another threat that it unwittingly brought on itself: the kicker boat. The invention of the kicker boat allowed fishermen to strike fish anywhere in the bay, but as with many technologies, it has created a new set of problems. "I know it's the kicker boats that have killed off the redfish, flounder, and sheephead," said Blue Fulford. "These young kids get up there in those mangroves and chase them and herd them up, and the fish don't have a chance to feed. They can go right up in the woods almost and catch them." Some fishermen have gone so far as to propose that the boat be outlawed.

The boat is a symptom of what may be the most dangerous threat of all to commercial fishing: part-time fishermen. "It used to be that kids from up north would come down to the dock and they'd see that it was a lot of hard work to be a fisherman," said Blue. "You had to pole a skiff to get up in shallow water; you had to invest a lot of time and money to keep your boat running; your nets were always tearing up and rotting if you didn't lime them. It was a lot of work, so they wouldn't do it. But now they come down here and see these little old kicker boats flying around all over the place, and it doesn't cost that much for an outboard engine, so Daddy buys them a boat and a motor and a monofilament net that will last forever, and off they go. Most of them don't know what they're doing—they're part-timers and fly-by-night fishermen, but there are so many of them that the bay is full of fishermen 24 hours a day. Used to be everybody'd come home once in a while, but now there's somebody out there with a gillnet constantly. Every time they see one or two fish they strike them and, if they don't catch a couple of them, they run them off so nobody else can catch them."

The kicker boat has created a tidal wave of part-time fishermen whose total numbers now far exceed the number of full-time fishermen. That influx has changed the fishing industry more than anything else.

"There's only so much resource that the bay can produce, and there are so many people putting pressure on the bay, I don't know whether it can take it," said Blue. "The part-timers in their kicker boats are making it hard for the serious commercial fisherman to make a living. You used to be able to come home every now and then, but now you have to be out there all the time if you want to get them, or else some part-timer will get them. It used to be that it really mattered about the tides and knowing the bottom. I can remember fishing with Uncle Tink and maybe we'd wait a week for the fish to get right before we'd go after them—waiting for them to get in the right place with the right tides before we'd strike them. But maybe those things don't matter anymore. These part-timers just get out there and run around and strike one every time it pops its head up, and they seem to catch some fish."

In an effort to discourage part-time fishermen, several Florida counties, including Manatee, passed bills in 1983 which require anyone who wants to sell fish to buy a $300 annual license that has to be bought between August and October each year, prior to the roe season. Although some full-time fishermen objected to the cost of the license, the purpose is to try to drive some of the part-time fishermen off the bay.

All in all, the fishing industry in Florida at the end of the twentieth century is a perplexing and illusive creature. Is it booming and expanding to meet the demands of the new markets and new technologies of the 1980s? Yes, certainly that is true. But is it, on the other hand, an endangered species trying to hold its own against the threats of pollution, development, and overpopulation of the Florida coast? Yes, that is true as well.

Which will prevail? I don't think anyone knows the answer. But I do think that the future of fishing in Florida may be foretold by what happens in Cortez. All of the contending forces are operating in this small village, and whatever happens here will very likely be a harbinger of the rest of the state. "Cortez is one of the few places left in Florida where all of the family members are still living off the sea, still totally dependent on the sea," said Blue. "It's one of the last places where that kind of culture is still preserved. But in a lot of ways Cortez is already dead. It's changed so much in the last ten years with all of the people moving in, I don't know whether it can last another ten years or not."

If it doesn't, Blue Fulford and the fishing families of Cortez will find other jobs and other places to live. Whether they end up in Florida's urban centers or the faceless suburbs of Bradenton, it will not feel or smell or taste like home. Deep inside, where only they can tell, a piece of their soul will have died. And even deeper, where no one can tell, a piece of Florida's soul will have died with them.

Chapter 14

Prodigals Returned

OH BOY, THEY'D NEVER BELIEVE IT in New Jersey!" said Charlie Mora, as he adjusted the string tie under his chin that held his big straw cowboy hat on his head. "They'd never believe this was me." The sun was just going down behind Anna Maria Island as Charlie finished filling his ice chest and gas tank, pushed the bow of his boat away from the dock of the Fulford Fish Company, cranked the motor, and slipped away down the channel on another gillnetting expedition. It was just another normal workday for Charlie Mora, Cortez fisherman.

What they wouldn't believe in New Jersey is that this is the same Charlie Mora who spent 32 years running a lathe in the UniRoyal plant in Passaic, New Jersey. Charlie Mora, lathe operator, is now a commercial fisherman.

Actually, it's just the final step in the cycle. Charlie is no Yankee transplant trying his hand at fishing, but a born-and-bred Cortez native. He left home in 1940 seeking more money and a more secure future than what he could expect as a commercial fisherman. He found some of each, but the yearning to return home brought him back to Cortez in 1973 and, eventually, back to fishing. The prodigal son has returned.

It's a familiar story in small Southern towns. Charlie was part of a mass exodus of whites and blacks who left the South during the first half of the twentieth century seeking higher wages in the North. The thousands of young Southerners who rode the rails and buses to the industrial centers of the northeast and midwest were fleeing the dire poverty and hopelessness of the region. For decades, the South has had the lowest per capita income of any region in the U.S., and it still holds that honor, despite the recent economic expansion of the Sun Belt. Southern blacks had an added motivation for leaving: escaping the lynchings, fire bombings, and "separate and unequal" confines of the Jim Crow South.

As the Southern emigrants streamed into the factory towns of the North—Chicago, Pittsburgh, and Detroit—Southern culture took root. The Delta Blues moved up the Mississippi River and became the Kansas City Blues and then the Chicago Blues; Dixieland moved North and evolved into jazz; Appalachian music stayed alive in the hillbilly sections of Baltimore and Detroit. However, other parts of their culture were lost. Accents were usually the first to go. Charlie talks in a smorgasbord accent—part Southern drawl, part Jersey nasal whine. "When I got up North, everybody made fun of the way I talked, so I made a conscious effort to get rid of my accent," he said.

Most left the South for practical reasons: money, opportunity, jobs. "I was 23 years old and I had grown up here and fished here all my life," said Charlie. "But back in 1940, it was real rough times for fishermen. There were hardly any fish. I had an uncle in New Jersey who kept asking me to move up there, but I couldn't make up my mind. But one night we went fishing across the bay; there were two boats and we stayed out there nine hours, made six strikes, and only caught 300 pounds of fish. I decided that was it. I came back home the next day and told everybody that I was going to New Jersey."

He moved to Passaic in 1940 and got a job in the UniRoyal plant. "We made hoses—big fire hoses and suction hoses for dredge boats, that sort of thing," he said. "I ran a lathe. I'd take a big pipe the same diameter as the hose I wanted, put it on the lathe, and wind the rubber around it until I got the outside thickness I wanted. Some of those hoses were huge—two or three feet across."

Shortly after arriving, he met a local girl and married her and, by the time World War II broke out, they had two small children. But every summer, from 1940 to 1973, Charlie and his family came back to Cortez on vacation. "I'd come home and go fishing with my brother Vernon, and I used to think sometimes about moving back," said Charlie. "My wife loved it here, but I had put in so many years in the plant that I didn't want to lose my pension."

But in 1973, UniRoyal helped him make up his mind: the company announced that it was closing the Passaic plant. "Boy, it was rough when they said they were closing down," said Charlie. "But we had a real good union—the United Rubber Workers—and it was great. The union negotiated a deal where you'd get your full retirement pension if you had 30 years of service or were 57 years old. I was only 56 when the plant closed, but I had 32 years of service, so I got a full pension. It was tougher for the younger ones 'cause some of them just got a couple thousand dollars in severance pay. We could have had it a lot worse though. Just down the road a few miles, in Clifton, there was a rubber plant that closed six months after ours did. All they had was a little old independent union and those people didn't get anything."

When he first got back home, he took a job as the bridge tender on the Cortez Bridge. He did that for six years, but got bored with it and, in 1980, bought himself a kicker boat and started fishing. So, after 40 years, the circle has been completed.

Charlie Mora is not the only Cortez native who left home and returned. A lot of young bucks have sworn they'd never get on another fishing boat as long as they lived and moved away to try another line of work. They are usually back home two or three years later. The lure of the water and the bond of family are strong indeed.

In my family, Uncle Gary went off to David Lipscomb College in Nashville, got a degree in business, stayed there for several years selling funeral plots, and then chucked the big city and came back to Cortez to be a bait shrimper. Uncle Wayne also quit fishing in the late 1960s, went to Bradenton and worked for two years as a milkman, but ended up back in Cortez as a bait shrimper. My cousin Hazel, Pig's daughter, also left in the early 1970s. She moved to Tennessee, became a social worker, then moved back home two years ago with her new husband.

Of course, there are some who have left and have never returned—or not yet, anyway. My cousin Rusty, Hazel's brother, finished a hitch in the Navy and moved to a tiny farming community in northern Virginia. But even that has its ironies. "Rusty didn't like Cortez because it was such a small town, but now's he living in a place that's even smaller than Cortez," said Sylvia Fulford Bailey, his younger sister.

If it was just the returning prodigals moving back to Cortez, there'd be no problem. But new arrivals, primarily Northern retirees, are moving to Florida at the rate of 1,000 per day. Despite his years in New Jersey and his adopted Jersey accent, Charlie Mora resents the changes brought by the Northern influx: "I hate the way Cortez is being squeezed out. It seems like there have been more changes since we moved back in 1973 than in

214 / Ben Green

all the years I was gone. I tell you what I hate the most is these Yankees come down here and act like there was nothing here before they came. And they act like it all disappears when they leave in the spring. I saw an article in the paper a few weeks ago where a woman from up North was saying that she remembered how all this was swamp in 1947. Well, she's crazy! There were plenty of things here in 1947."

Charlie Mora should know. On summer evenings like this more than 100 years ago, Spanish fishermen from Cuba and Key West were roaming these shores and bayous, catching mullet and selling them in the Havana markets. Before the turn of the century, Charlie's grandfather Joe Mora moved north from Cuba to Key West and then to Manatee County. Moras have fished the length and breadth of Sarasota Bay ever since.

As Charlie revved his throttle and headed down the channel, the sun slipped behind the western lip of Anna Maria Island and sent a deep red glow of fire across the surface of the bay. The factory whistles and narrow, crowded streets of Passaic, New Jersey, were far away. Charlie Mora was home.

Chapter 15

The Next Generation

FROM THE INSIDE OF TONY AND SYLVIA Bailey's new cedar house, you would never guess that you were in Cortez, Florida. It's a two-story house built on top of creosote-treated pilings, with a spacious carport and patio underneath, and a new swimming pool in the back yard. Inside, the living room has an open, airy look, with high ceilings, lots of windows, and watercolor seascapes and ferns arranged on the white plaster walls. A huge fireplace of rough-hewn stone dominates the back wall. There's a spacious kitchen, a downstairs family room with a color TV, and three bedrooms upstairs.

On this evening in June, Sylvia and Tony were hosting a dinner party for two other young Cortez couples: Bobbi Jo and Stella Jones, and Larry and Sharon Fulford. After feasting on Sylvia's homemade spaghetti, tossed salad, hot rolls, and chocolate cake and ice cream, the guests settled in the living room and talked about Stella's pregnancy, plans for summer vacations, and the latest news about friends and relatives.

It was a perfect evening that could have been taken from the pages of *Family Circle* or *Southern Living*—in any one of a thousand suburban neighborhoods. But the evening suddenly turned mean when I mentioned my plans to write a book about Cortez. From that point, it was painfully clear that this party was happening in Cortez, Florida—and nowhere else.

These young couples, and others like them across the country, are products of the postwar baby boom and share many of the same goals and dreams of others from their generation. They are the couples who postponed having children until their thirties and are now making up for lost time; that trend is evident here in Cortez, where a flurry of new babies has been born in the past two years. These Cortez couples are taking out loans to build new suburban-style homes; they're buying color television sets on credit from Sears and J.C. Penny, and are borrowing from savings to take two-week vacations to North Carolina. There is a new interest in educational enrichment programs and after-school care for their children.

But in other ways they are very different. While young urban professionals—yuppies—are staking out a fast-track, independent life-style, these young couples are living in a small, old-fashioned community that is trying to hold onto its past. In the face of a high-tech revolution that is displacing skilled workers at an alarming rate, they've chosen a career that has changed little since their great-grandparents did it 100 years ago. And while young people by the thousands are marching in the streets of New York, Bonn, and Stockholm demanding a freeze on nuclear weapons, these folks are fighting a more immediate threat in Cortez: the destruction of their community.

The question of whether Cortez will survive affects all those who live in the village, but it has a special bite for the younger ones. Whereas the older residents are worried about holding on to what they've had in the past, Sylvia and Tony and the other young couples are at a different stage in their lives, a planning stage. Their worries stretch into the future: will the community still exist in 10 years? 20 years? 30 years? If it does, will it be the kind of community that they will still want to live in? Will their children stay here once they're grown?

When they ask themselves those questions, the answers do not instill great hope. Many young people think it is a lost cause. "Cortez is finished," said Larry Fulford, a bait fisherman. "All these outsiders have moved in already, and once they get one of those condominiums in here, it will be all over."

Much of what Cortez meant to them when they were growing up has already been lost. "It's pretty well gone," said Bobbi Jo Jones, a foreman in the motor repair shop at Tropicana. "A lot of the things that I took for granted as a kid are gone. I remember when you could get in a boat and go all the way across the bay and maybe see one pleasure boat out there, but now they're all over the place. We used to go up to Palma Sola Bay, and it was just like wilderness. We'd see redfish showering so thick they'd turn the water red. But that's all gone now from the dredging and filling. And we used to be able to drive to town without it taking all day, but the

traffic is so thick now on Cortez Road that I don't get out there unless I
have to."

Ironically, some of the changes were welcomed at first. "The funny
thing is that I thought I'd like all the changes when they started," said
Sylvia, who runs a beauty shop in addition to being the full-time mother
of three. "It was really nice to have more restaurants and stores to shop
in, and to not have to drive all the way into town to get to them. But now
it's gotten so out of hand that I'd rather have it the old way."

The onrush of condos and shopping centers is the most obvious threat
to Cortez, but not necessarily the most dangerous. There are financial
pressures that might cause the community to collapse long before the bulldozers and draglines arrive. "There's gonna be so much pressure on people
to sell their land, I think eventually a lot of people here will sell out," said
Larry. "Now, some of the old-timers might not sell out, but most other
people will be forced to sell because somebody will offer so much money
they won't be able to turn it down. And the way property taxes are skyrocketing because of all the development, some people will have to sell
because they can't pay their taxes. The taxes on that little old house I
bought have gone up from about $100 three years ago to $500 this year."

Cortez is also under siege psychologically—by the unaware, unthink-
ing attitudes of many newcomers toward existing communities and culture. In some ways, those attitudes are the hardest to stomach. "What really
gets me going is when people come down here and buy a place and then
start saying how they've 'upgraded the South,' " said Bobbi Jo. "That's
when I really lay into them. I tell them: 'What do you think? You think
you're the first person to ever enjoy the warm weather, or going fishing,
or to the beach? We'd been doing that a long time before you came here,
in fact we used to do it a lot better.' "

But while they talk negatively about the future of the village, their actions reflect a commitment to stay. They continue to build new houses,
invest in new fishing boats, pickups, and small businesses. Their actions
reflect, if not confidence in the future, a stubbornness to stick it out for
as long as they can. It is not easy to give up on one's home, and in many
ways they have no choice but to stay and fight. What holds them closest
to Cortez are their roots. Uncrowded beaches, virgin schools of redfish,
and dove-hunting expeditions in the marshes along Cortez Road may be
things of the past, but fathers, mothers, great-aunts, and grandparents are
not. More than anything else, it's blood that makes them stay.

"Tony and I talked a lot about moving to Bradenton a few years ago, but we realized that we'd be leaving all the things that we love about it here," said Sylvia. "Brian and Troy [their two oldest children] can walk next door and see their great-granddaddy Earl [Guthrie], and they can walk down to the dock after school and see their daddy and their grandpa [Ralph Fulford]. It's nice for me and Tony, too, 'cause he can come home for lunch every day, so we get to see more of each other. Almost all of our family lives right here in these three or four blocks: my mother and father, Grandma Edith [Fulford], Granddaddy Earl, Aunt Letha [Leeper]. It's a real important thing to have so much family here."

These young couples have revitalized a tradition that had just about died out in the village: regular socializing. Many of the older residents don't get out much, except for church, grocery shopping, or doctor's appointments, but the young couples have started getting together on a regular basis for dinner, movies, or going out to eat. The forms of that socializing have changed—families no longer walk down the streets at dusk, braving the mosquitoes to sit on their neighbor's porch and visit. Today, the socializing takes place in air-conditioned living rooms with color TV sets droning in the background. But the content is much the same.

There is only one group in Cortez that is not trapped by memories of the past or worries about the future: the children. They are free of the "used to be's" and the "what might happen's" that plague the grown-ups and, therefore, might have the clearest view of what Cortez is really like today. When you ask an adult about Cortez, you'll hear about the past; when you ask a child, you'll hear about today—and what you hear is pretty good. For children, Cortez is still a mighty fine place to live. They can still catch pinfish off the front of the dock with just a hook on a string and a piece of mullet gizzard for bait. They can still jump overboard at a moment's notice and go swimming in the bay. They can still chase fiddler crabs along the shoreline at low tide, row out to The Kitchen in a beat-up dinghy, or gather excitedly on the docks to watch a big catch being unloaded.

Of course, the adults will mutter that none of these pleasures are as plentiful, clean, safe, or accessible as they once were. "So what," the youngsters reply. When I asked Troy Bailey, age six, how he liked living in Cortez, he gave me a straight answer: "Well, what can I say . . . I can ride my bike and I have a pair of roller skates and a favorite baby sitter." Enough said.

Clearly, the fate of Cortez is largely in the hands of its young adults. Their parents and grandparents must help them carry the fight now, but ultimately, these young couples are the ones who must maintain the fight— 20, 30, 40 years from now. Without them, the battle to preserve Cortez has no future. It is a fight they must win—for themselves and their children.

Chapter 16

"The Smugglers Might Kill Me, But They Sure As Hell Can't Eat Me!"

SCENE ONE: ON A DREARY, OVERCAST AFTERNOON in November 1980, four women gathered nervously on the shoulder of Cortez Road, adjacent to the old Cortez School. The cold, drizzling rain that had fallen all day had slackened temporarily. The women talked quietly for a few minutes, discussing their strategy, then reached down, one by one, and selected a hand-lettered picket sign from the pile at their feet. They spread out in single file along the roadside, ten feet apart, and the waiting began.

Several minutes passed in silence. Finally, a single car came around the last bend in Cortez Road, passed the Paradise Bay Trailer Park, and approached the women. Sue Maddox, 48, a thin, bespectacled bookkeeper, took a deep breath, raised her sign above her head, and turned to face the oncoming vehicle. The three other women—my mother Mary Fulford Green, my aunt Irene Taylor, and Sue's sister Betty Lou Turner—followed her lead. The car slowed to a crawl as the driver craned his neck to read Sue's sign: SMUGGLERS AND PUSHERS ARE KILLING OUR CHILDREN. DEMAND TOUGH PENALTIES. Puzzled, the driver glanced quickly at the signs of the other women, then sped on toward Anna Maria Island. The women laughed nervously about the man's reaction, then turned to watch for the next car. The picketing had begun.

Scene Two: Junior Guthrie's trial began in a nearly empty federal courtroom in Tallahassee on 22 August 1983. It was an unusually pleasant afternoon for August, and the slight coolness in the air brought hopes that the summer inferno might be ending. Soft sunlight streamed through the high windows of the courtroom, casting golden shadows across the polished hardwood floors and maple pews. The Great Seal of the United States, five feet in diameter, hung on the back wall behind the judge's bench, dominating the room with its one-eyed message: *E Pluribus Unum.*

It was a majestic setting for one of the biggest drug smuggling trials in Florida history. Junior Guthrie, a 34-year-old Cortez fisherman, was charged with importing 246,000 pounds of marijuana, valued at $23 million, between 1977 and 1981. Another Cortez fisherman, Wally Lewis, was on trial with him, charged with two counts of conspiracy to import and possess marijuana.

Junior and Wally had actually been indicted six months earlier, but Junior had evaded the six agents who were sent to arrest him and had spent four months on the run. "I drove by his home and he was standing on his balcony talking to his father," said one of the agents. "Five minutes later we went back and his family said they hadn't seen him in weeks." An anonymous tip to the police led to his capture in late June in the little town of Sebring, Florida, where he had been living under an assumed name. He had also lost 45 pounds, frizzed his hair, and shaved his beard. He was taken before a federal judge in Tampa for arraignment and bail was set at $2 million.

With all the pretrial publicity, I expected the courtroom to be jammed with spectators, reporters, and television crews. Images of other famous trials—the Scopes Monkey Trial, the Lindbergh kidnapping, the Chicago Seven—filled my head as I pushed open the heavy wooden doors of the courtroom and went inside. Instead, the courtroom looked like the setting for a small family wedding. Junior's mother and father were sitting in the second row; near the back, two reporters from the Bradenton and Sarasota papers were scribbling on notepads; and several young legal aides sat behind the tables of the prosecutor and defense attorneys. That was all.

Junior looked up from the defense table when I walked in and stared hard at me, wondering, I assumed, "which side are you on?" It's a question he's been asking a lot lately. He was wearing a pale maroon shirt with a white striped tie that clashed horribly. The millions he allegedly made from smuggling obviously hadn't been spent on clothes. Wally Lewis sat with his lawyer at an adjoining table, looking dapper in a gray pin-striped suit, but so stiff and pale that he could have been on display at the Griffith-Cline Funeral Home.

I sat down behind Junior's parents and listened while the judge gave final instructions to the jury and suddenly found myself engulfed by a feeling of great sadness. Junior's mother and father were enough to break anyone's heart. Old Pig Guthrie was sitting there with his hearing-aid cocked toward the judge so he could hear; he had his arm around his wife's shoulders, comforting her in a way I guessed he had seldom done in their years together. I found myself staring at his old gnarled hands, bloated and ruined from a lifetime of fishing, and at his wife, who kept pushing her designer glasses up on her nose, trying hard to maintain her composure.

The whole thing turned my stomach and, try as I might, I couldn't shake the feeling of personal involvement in this trial. I knew all the facts—that Junior was no longer the harmless, swaggering cousin with whom I had fished those summers I was growing up, but that he had been involved in major smuggling operations for years, and that the prosecutor would portray him as the kingpin of smuggling on the west coast of Florida. I knew, too, that smuggling has hurt Cortez badly. It has brought fear, murder, and a bevy of desperate men to the village, eroding much of the closeness and reputation of the community.

I knew all that, yet sitting in that straight-backed pew behind Pig Guthrie, I felt a rush of protectiveness towards Junior and Wally that caught me completely off guard. I was struck by how much they looked like my uncles, with the same complexion and bone structure. They were still family—that's what it was—and, more than the questions of guilt or innocence, what obsessed me throughout the trial was: How could this have happened? How could Junior Guthrie have gone from the blustering, small-time fisherman I knew to a dope kingpin with $2 million on his head? And I wondered that, if Junior and Wally were guilty, was Cortez guilty, too? Were all of us on trial?

The judge finished his instructions to the jury, motioned to the prosecuting attorney, who stood up, approached the jury, and began his opening argument. The trial had begun.

Drug smuggling has brought one thing to Cortez that nothing else in its 100-year history ever has: fame. The village never got much recognition for being the second largest fishery in the state and never made the front page of the *Bradenton Herald* for being the last fishing village on the Suncoast. It took smuggling to put it on the map.

When former Cortez fisherman Floyd "Bubba" Capo and six boys from St. Petersburg were arrested in 1973 with nine tons of marijuana—the largest pot bust in U.S. history at the time—Cortez achieved fame. Front-page stories and a wealth of jokes and stereotypes about the village have come with it because dope smuggling makes good copy. In the bland, shopping-mall world of south Florida, smuggling stories have become the modern-day equivalent of the western novel. The good guys—prosecutors, undercover agents, and crusading politicians—wear white hats. The bad guys—scruffy fishermen and corrupt sheriffs—wear black.

Like all myths, this one depends on stereotypes: ignorant, squinty-eyed fishermen; backward, incestuous communities; fiercely protective kin-folks resentful of outsiders and the law. Some of the media's reports on Everglades City and Steinhatchee—fishing towns with national reputations for smuggling—seem to have drawn heavily on "The Beverly Hill-billies," "Lil' Abner," and the Hollywood film *Deliverance* for inspiration.

One effect of this stereotyping has been to glamorize the smugglers. Shortly after his capture, Junior Guthrie was described by the *Sarasota Herald-Tribune* as "a fearless, powerfully built man and Robin Hood-style character in many smuggling legends of Southwest Florida." However, the Junior Guthrie who walked into that Tampa courtroom after four months of hiding was a short, pudgy fisherman in cutoff shorts, a surfer t-shirt, and boat shoes.

The only legends Junior is associated with in Cortez have to do with how many grades he flunked in school and the stupid dares that he was always willing to take as a kid. If you wanted to challenge somebody to dive headfirst off the roof of the dock at low tide, Junior was your boy. The only thing that Junior was ever good at, and he was very good at that, was catching fish. And as the testimony unfolded about his smuggling career—bungled attempts, shortchanged payments, mechanical failures—one could argue that fishing was still the only thing he did well.

The truth about smuggling is not nearly as black and white as the media stereotypes it. In Cortez, a total of perhaps three dozen fishermen have been involved in smuggling since the early 1970s; about half of those were homegrown boys, the rest were drifters and recent arrivals. Some stayed in it for just a few months, long enough to make a small bundle, others were full-time operators who made millions. A half-dozen people have disappeared, have been murdered, or have died from drug-related activities. A dozen Cortez fishermen have been indicted; two-thirds of those have been convicted. Another dozen have been implicated.

The other 400 residents haven't benefited from smuggling in any way; they feel that they've lost a great deal of safety, closeness, and community feeling because of it. They have spent the past decade doing just what their parents and grandparents have done for generations—working hard every day to earn a modest income from fishing and shrimping.

Even at the height of the smuggling in the late 1970s, their lives were about the same as they were before it arrived. They got up each morning and went to work, came home in the evening, read the paper, watched the six o'clock news, laughed at Archie Bunker's abuse of the English language, waited in suspense to find out who shot J. R. Ewing, and went to bed early.

The smuggling was a silent backdrop to their lives. They heard the boats coming in at odd hours, saw the new vans and Lincoln Continentals parked in front of Junior's house, and gazed suspiciously at the burned-out derelicts who descended on Cortez like locust, hoping to get a job on a fishing boat and get in on a few runs. This was the one thing that most of the residents were guilty of during those years—burying their heads in the sand and hoping that the problem would simply go away. That puts them in the same boat with most people in the country; not wanting to get involved seems to be a national disease.

The most interesting story about smuggling in Cortez has been largely overlooked by the media. It isn't how many millions Junior Guthrie allegedly made, or the grocery sacks and PVC pipes stashed with hundred-dollar bills, or the sophisticated radios that directed boats and vans to off-loading sites along the coastline. No, the real story is about the people who did get involved, who did speak out publicly against both the smugglers and the stereotyping.

Primarily, it's about Sue Maddox. The story of how a slightly built, demure bookkeeper ended up on Cortez Road with a picket sign in her hand is at least as interesting as tracing Junior Guthrie's steps from small-time gillnetter to dope kingpin. Ten years ago, no one would have believed that either event was possible.

Sue Maddox is a latecomer to Cortez, arriving in 1965. Her mother Myrtle Fulford Turner was born and raised in Cortez, but moved to Mulberry in Polk County when she got married. Sue was born in Mulberry and grew up there. "We'd come back to Cortez in the summers and for vacations, and Mama always referred this as home."

Sue got married, had two children, and worked as a secretary in Mulberry. But when her marriage failed and pollution from nearby phosphate mines began showing up in the drinking water, she decided to relocate. Cortez seemed like a natural choice. "Maybe I had overglorified Cortez in my mind, but I saw it as a utopia," Sue said. "Cortez to me was honest, smiling people and lots of great memories as a child."

When she moved there, she bought the old Walter Taylor home and got a job as a bookkeeper at Bell Fish Company. Junior Guthrie, 15 at the time, lived just three houses down the street. "Junior is a distant cousin, and I liked him so much when I first moved here," she said. "You know, everything he touched just seemed to fall apart, but he had the best personality and was really a good kid. A few years after I moved here, a group of us got together and tried to buy the old Cortez School for a community center, because the kids here didn't have anything. Junior had gotten married by then, and he and his wife Judy were both really interested in getting that community center. They did a lot of work on it. We never could raise enough money, but, you know, I've often wondered what would have happened to Junior if we'd succeeded."

By 1970, Sue Maddox's utopia was starting to go sour. Bubba Capo, who had fished with my grandpa for many years, started building big storage compartments on his fishing boat, saying he wanted to go after deepwater mackerel and needed the extra space. Bubba moved north to Horseshoe Beach in Dixie County and, in March 1973, law enforcement officers discovered his boat near Steinhatchee with 17,000 pounds of marijuana in his storage bins. Bubba ended up in deep water all right, but without any mackerel. Instead, he'd caught a boatload of "square grouper"—marijuana bales—Florida's most profitable species.

Bubba, Mike Knight, another Cortez fisherman, and five men from St. Petersburg Beach were arrested in what was the largest pot bust in U.S. history at the time. The defendants, who became known as the "Steinhatchee Seven," hired Percy Foreman, the flamboyant Texas trial lawyer, to represent them. But all of them were convicted, including Bubba, who still claims that he didn't know the other defendants were using his boat to haul pot.[1]

---

[1]"Successful fishermen or Dixie's drug 'godfather'?" St. Petersburg *Times*, 15 April 1981, B:7.

He served two years in federal prison, returned to Dixi(1976, and went on to become the godfather of smuggling on th(... .... coast. In a 1980 sting operation, undercover agents for the Florida Department of Law Enforcement secretly tape-recorded Bubba boasting that he could buy the Dixie County sheriff for $10,000. "I can give you that county," he claimed. "It's just like taking a little baby and saying, 'Here, honey, here's a piece of candy,' and they walk over and get it. I got it made in Dixie County." Later that year, Bubba received a combined sentence of 38 years for smuggling 28,000 pounds of marijuana in several counties. [2]

By the time Mike Knight returned to Cortez in 1976, after serving two years for his "Steinhatchee Seven" conviction, other local fishermen were heavily involved in the smuggling. The next four years were boom times for smuggling, and the string of murders, indictments, and convictions that followed would destroy any remaining utopian illusions for Sue Maddox and eventually force her to take action.

• In February 1978, David Capo, Bubba's son who still lived in Cortez, was convicted with three other men for conspiracy, attempted smuggling, and possession in the "Sandy Creek Massacre." The defendants had attempted to unload their cargo of marijuana from the *Gunsmoke*, a 60-foot shrimp boat, near Panama City in January 1977, but were scared off by an approaching barge. Several weeks later, the *Gunsmoke* sank off the coast of St. Petersburg; it was recovered in November 1977 with more than 20,000 pounds aboard. [3]

The "massacre" occurred when four innocent people walked up unsuspectingly on the Sandy Creek operation. They were killed and dumped in a Taylor County sinkhole; their bodies were discovered eight months later. Walter Steinhorst and David Goodwin were charged with first-degree murder; Capo and Raymond Parker, Jr., another Cortez fisherman, were two of six men charged with third-degree murder. The third-degree charges were later dropped, and David Capo was given immunity and became the prosecution's star witness against Steinhorst, who was convicted

---

[2]Ibid.

[3]"Four guilty, 4 innocent in smuggling trial," Tallahassee *Democrat*, 25 February 1978, A:1.

228 / Ben Green

in May 1978.[4] Capo himself was indicted again for smuggling in 1984 and is awaiting trial.[5]

• In February 1978, Mike Knight's Cortez home was firebombed and burned to the ground. Previous attempts had been made to blow up his fishing boat and his pickup truck, and Knight claimed that all three incidents were the work of a St. Petersburg extortion ring, which had been pressuring him and other smugglers to cut them in on their profits.

Knight told several Cortez residents that "People from across the bay are trying to extort money from me and I won't pay. I went to prison and paid taxes on the money I got, but they won't leave me alone." Four months later he was dead. He and his girlfriend were sitting on Indian Rocks Beach when Knight suddenly jumped up, started running around frantically, and then charged out into the Gulf and drowned. The mysterious circumstances of his death led to a murder investigation. The autopsy uncovered several unusual puncture wounds on his body, and police speculated that he might have been shot with some sort of dart gun which made him go crazy. However, no suspects were ever arrested.

In August of that year, St. Petersburg police did arrest six men who were charged with heading a robbery and extortion ring, with Knight and several other smugglers among their victims.

• On 2 June 1978, Joe Mora, a lifetime Cortez fisherman, disappeared and was never heard from again. The rumor was that he had been involved in a smuggling deal with some Cubans, but they had refused to pay him his share. When he went down to try to get his money, he never returned.[6]

• In August 1978, a statewide grand jury handed down the first indictment against Junior Guthrie, charging him with directing the unloading of ten tons of marijuana—worth $8 million—near Panama City on 15 November 1977. FDLE agents said that Mike Knight's death had been the key to the indictment against Junior, as several of Knight's friends had been enraged by his apparent murder and had started cooperating with investigators.

---

[4]"Jury asks death for Steinhorst," Tallahassee *Democrat*, 5 May 1978, A:1.

[5]U.S. District Court records, Clerk of Criminal Division, Tampa, Florida, case number 84-76-CR-T-8.

[6]"Where has Cortez man gone to?" Bradenton *Herald*, 26 August 1978, B:1.

However, in January 1979, all charges against Junior were dropped hours before his scheduled trial; a St. Petersburg circuit court judge ruled that the prosecution had obtained evidence from an illegal wiretap. A part-time police informant had illegally tapped Junior's phone and then turned over the tapes to police, trying to barter his way out of kidnapping, extortion, and assault charges.[7]

• Raymond Parker, also known as Rainbow, whose third-degree murder charge in the Sandy Creek Massacre had been dropped, was indicted in 1980 by a Wakulla County grand jury for smuggling 20 tons of marijuana. Parker disappeared from sight until February 1981, when he surrendered to police. He pleaded guilty to the charges and was placed on probation for three years and was fined $20,000.

His troubles weren't over; in June 1983, the Internal Revenue Service sued him for nearly $300,000 in delinquent taxes, reaching back to 1977. The IRS confiscated and auctioned most of his personal property, including his $75,000 fishing boat, air boat, speed boat, trailer, jeep, pickup, and Mercedes. When they went to get the Mercedes, they had to go look for it; Parker had driven it into a swamp, turned it upside down, and removed the wheels. The IRS dragged it out of the swamp and sold it for $27,000—considerably less than it would have brought without the swamp treatment.[8]

• Smuggling in Manatee County had become so rampant by 1980 that a state grand jury was convened in Bradenton in July of that year. It began investigating politicians, law enforcement officers, and financiers with possible smuggling connections. Several prominent figures were eventually indicted, including Jerome Pratt, an attorney and former state legislator, and Afton Pyles, a former Palmetto police lieutenant.

By August 1980, Sue Maddox was fed up with the whole mess. When Harold Goncho, a crewman on the Bell Fish Company's offshore grouper boats, was killed in an apparent drug-related boating accident, she decided to do something about it. "I counted up that it was the seventh drug-related death in Cortez, and it really made me mad," she said. "I realized that kids I had watched grow up were willing to kill other people to make a dollar. And I was really mad at the community, too. I was dumbfounded

---

[7] "Guthrie at large following indictment," Bradenton *Herald*, 5 March 1983, A:10.

[8] "IRS sells fisherman's boat for back taxes," Bradenton *Herald*, 25 June 1983, B:1.

that the community would allow it to happen. But it was business as usual—most people continued to party and socialize with the smugglers because they were afraid. I felt like if their families had refused to associate with them maybe they would have stopped. Well, I didn't really think it out very well, but I decided I had to do something."

She went to Bradenton and rented a portable sign, had it towed to Cortez, and placed it in her front yard with the message: ANOTHER DRUG RELATED DEATH. SMUGGLERS DON'T CARE. DO YOU? The *Bradenton Herald* sent a reporter and a photographer and printed a photo that evening of Sue standing next to the sign.

Her question brought an immediate reply. "I told the man when I rented the sign that I fully expected it to be damaged—stones thrown at it, and that sort of thing," she recalled. "I put it up in the yard at noontime, and about ten o'clock that night I thought I heard a rock hitting the sign. I went out to look and flames were 20 feet in the air. They had doused it with gasoline and set it afire." The *Bradenton Herald* dutifully sent their photographer back the next morning and ran a picture of the gutted sign.

Sue's action was the first crack in the wall of silence that had surrounded and protected the smugglers. Other cracks followed. The firebombing also showed clearly that the silence had been maintained more by the threat of violence and retaliation than by family loyalty and protectiveness. Now that she had broken the silence, the threats of violence escalated. "A lot of people told me they were surprised the smugglers hadn't firebombed my house," said Sue. "I'll tell you, I was really terrified the night they burned the sign. I thought sure the house would be next. I used to go out walking at night with my children, or take the dogs for a walk, but I stopped doing all of that. I didn't feel it was safe anymore. We had already lost quite a bit of freedom in our own town."

Once she had taken that first step, there really wasn't any way to go back, even if she had wanted to. She had become notorious in Cortez and in Bradenton as a result of the news reports. Local residents divided into two camps: those who were glad she had taken the risk to speak out, and those who thought she was a damn fool who would be dead if she kept it up.

Both camps would soon have the chance to find out. Two months after the sign-burning, in November 1980, Sue Maddox took her protest to the streets. A new restaurant was opening—the first large commercial restaurant in the village proper—and there were allegations that it was financed by laundered drug money.

"That restaurant was like pouring salt in the wound," said Sue. "It would have been bad enough to have any big restaurant in Cortez, but to have a commercial restaurant backed by drug money, that was even worse. The owners sent out engraved invitations to the grand opening, and that was the final straw. I decided to set up a picket line on Cortez Road."

Nothing in Sue's life had prepared her to take such a drastic step. Again, none of the stereotypes fit. Sue Maddox is not a "battling little lady" taking on the smugglers, nor a longtime activist fighting for her home. She certainly doesn't think of herself as heroic. She's just a woman who had had enough and decided to do something about it. "I had always had an orderly existence and I'd never been on a picket line in my life," she said. "But I think this drug thing would have upset me no matter where I was living."

She found out she would be risking a libel suit if she tried to directly link the new restaurant to drug money, but she could hold a general informational picket against drugs. "On Monday morning the owner of the restaurant came down to the dock to see me and said he had heard I was going to picket his restaurant. He wanted to know why I was doing it. I told him the law wouldn't let me picket his restaurant, but I was just generally picketing against drugs. He asked me not to do it and said he was afraid people would identify his restaurant as having been built with drug money. I told him, 'Well, I'm sure it was!' "

She phoned other people asking them to help and stayed up most of the night making hand-lettered signs. On the afternoon of the restaurant's grand opening, she arrived several hours before dark with plenty of signs for other people. She never needed them. "It was cold and drizzling and not a soul showed up," she remembered. "I stood out there anyway for about two hours. I had signs saying: 'Do Business With Honest Businesses,' 'Drugs Kill, While Smugglers Get Rich,' that sort of thing. Not long after I got there, the owner called the sheriff, so a deputy came out and looked at my signs and said, 'Lady you can stay out here forever if you want to.' "

The local papers reported on her lonely vigil; she told the *Sarasota Herald-Tribune*: "I'm sick of fat cats making money off killing kids. I may be the only one here, but if we can stop just one child from falling into the drug trap, it will be worth my time and effort."

She got some heckling and taunts from carloads of Cortez teenagers, but most of the people who drove by were simply curious. "One big car pulled over, with a bunch of people dressed up inside, and wanted to know what made me decide to get out there," said Sue. "Overall, I got a good feeling that people were glad to see me trying to do something about it."

She had openly defied the smugglers twice, and rumors of what might happen to her continued to surface. One concerned relative told her, "Sue, don't you know they're gonna kill you if you keep this up?" "Well, they might kill me," Sue replied fiercely, "but they sure as hell can't eat me!"

But other than one minor incident with Junior Guthrie, she was never harmed. "Junior lived just a couple houses down from me, and one night he harassed me in his car on my way home," she said. "We were both trying to turn off of Cortez Road and he had the right-of-way, but he just sat there waiting for me to turn, acting like he might try to hit me when I did. But I wouldn't turn until after he did, so all the way home he crept along real slow, and made sudden stops, just trying to bother me. He pulled up and blocked my driveway, but I just waited and he finally went on home."

Her picketing did cause some friction within her own family. Her two grown sons, Richard and Tad, both live in the area. "Rick thought it was proper for me to be picketing, but Tad would have preferred I stay home," said Sue. "Tad's wife ended up taking a waitress job at the restaurant, and I wouldn't let her come to my house as long as she was working there. It created some hardships in my family, and it took a long while to straighten things out."

Emboldened by the success of her first picket, she planned another one three weeks later, and this time she got some help. "I talked to a lot of people who were opposed to the smuggling, and some of them said they'd come," said Sue. "Others said they supported what I was doing but were afraid the smugglers would burn them out. And a few women wanted to come, but their husbands absolutely refused to let them. I notified all the newspapers and TV stations 'cause we wanted to get as much publicity as we could."

Three other women showed up: my mother, my aunt Irene Taylor, and Sue's sister Betty Lou. That it was women, and not men, who were willing to stand up to the smugglers didn't really surprise Sue Maddox. "That's been the story of my life," she said. "My mother was always real strong, and I've been divorced for a long time and always called the shots. You know, women aren't as worried about personal injuries as people think they are, and I don't think they're as concerned about what other people think of them as men are."

It was raining on the day of the second picket, just as it had been for the first one, but that did not deter the women. There also seemed to be more enthusiastic support from those who drove by. "Lots of people waved and gave us the thumbs-ups sign," said Sue. The women also felt a strong sense of family kinship with each other. "It was exciting because all of us were cousins, and we were unified through Grandpa Billy and Uncle Nate [Sue's grandfather]," said Momma. "I told one person that the blood of my grandfather cried from the ground to vindicate this town. Honest, hard-working people built Cortez, and we wanted to restore that reputation."

How much good did the picketing do? It's hard to say. There was no public uprising against the smugglers. They weren't ridden out of town on a rail. But slowly, their unchallenged domination of the village began to crumble. Letters applauding Sue Maddox's efforts trickled in to the local papers. Small groups of local people began meeting secretly with law enforcement agents, reporting on any suspicious activities in the village.

By mid-1981, momentum had shifted away from the smugglers. The grand jury that had been convened in Manatee County in 1980 had handed down indictments on a number of prominent people. Wally Lewis and a Bradenton man were indicted in July 1981 for conspiracy to import and distribute marijuana and cocaine. Raymond Parker was arrested in February 1981. In Cortez, the smuggling appeared to have tapered off as operations were shifted further north to the Florida panhandle and Louisiana.[9]

In October 1981, when Judge Gilbert Smith ruled that several convicted smugglers could pay $50 for each day of their sentence, rather than go to jail, there was a flood of hate-mail against his "Pay for Freedom" plan. He also had a mild-mannered bookkeeper named Sue Maddox to contend with. She pulled out her magic markers and poster board, made a collection of signs, and picketed Judge Smith at the county courthouse.[10]

By 1982, Junior Guthrie was the only "big fish" in the Cortez smuggling business that the FDLE hadn't landed. When the Internal Revenue Service filed suit against him in March 1982 for $483,220 in back taxes on unreported income, it looked as though Junior might fall victim to the

[9]"Guthrie at large following indictment," Bradenton *Herald.*

[10]"Cash register justice a shameful disgrace," Bradenton *Herald*, 30 October 1981, A:5.

same fate as Al Capone. Based solely on his visible expenditures, the IRS figured he owed that much in taxes. When Junior paid them the money, thinking that would shut them up, the IRS immediately wanted to know how he got the money to pay it. Discretion in spending money was never one of Junior's strong suits, and there had been rumors in Cortez that his outlandish spending might get him killed by other smugglers who feared that it would call attention to them, too.[11]

During his 1983 trial, there was lengthy testimony about his wild spending sprees. One witness told about a man pulling up to a Cortez dock in an Excalibur speed boat—one of the fastest boats on the market—and Junior offering to buy it on the spot. The man declined, but Junior kept jacking up the price until the man agreed to sell the boat for $50,000. Junior sent someone to fetch a grocery sack of money from his house and calmly counted out $50,000 in cash.

Witnesses testified that in 1976, before the alleged smuggling operations, Junior only could afford a $16 down-payment for a $160 television set at Sears, which he paid off in small monthly payments. Yet two years later he walked barefoot into a Sarasota bank and handed over a grocery bag with $200,000 in cash.

His own financial records showed an astronomical increase in net worth, from $47,392 in 1976 to $1.7 million in 1980. In 1976, his assets included a $20,000 home, $18,000 in fishing gear, and two used cars worth a total of $5,500. When he applied for a loan in 1980, his assets included: his Cortez home, valued at $160,000 after being completely rebuilt in cedar; other real estate valued at over $1 million, including a $383,000 farm in Virginia, a $350,000 fish house in Cortez, a $90,000 duplex on Anna Maria Island, and another home in Okechobee County worth $60,000; fishing boats worth $203,000; and $77,000 in cars, including four late-model vans, a $15,000 Lincoln Continental, and a $30,000 Mercedes.[12]

It was obvious that FDLE investigators wanted Junior Guthrie very badly, particularly after the 1979 charges against him had been dropped. In March 1983, when the indictments against Junior and Wally Lewis were handed down, they got a second chance. Of course, it would take another four

---

[11]"Guthrie belongings sold," Bradenton *Herald*, 29 May 1983, B:1.

[12]"Guthrie traded cash for loans, bank says," Sarasota *Herald-Tribune*, 31 August 1983, B-M:2.

months to catch up with Junior, but in August 1983, the *Sarasota Herald-Tribune's* front-page headline announced: "Junior Guthrie Will Finally Get His Day In Court."

The seven-day trial provided a revealing glimpse into the inner workings of a smuggling ring. There were descriptions of Colombian natives paddling out in the dead of night to "mother ships," their canoes filled with bales of marijuana; of payoffs in dingy motel rooms, with hundreds of thousands of dollars stuffed in PVC pipes and grocery sacks; of highly sophisticated radio equipment used to synchronize pickups between boats and trucks up and down the coast.

The government called dozens of witnesses, including some of Junior's cousins, to testify about Junior and Wally's involvement in the smuggling operations. Many were smugglers themselves, having agreed to testify in order to avoid jail, or, for some who were already serving time, to gain an early release.

Junior's defense hinged on the credibility, or lack of it, of the prosecution's witnesses. Clifford Davis, one of his attorneys, charged that "the prosecutor will play the Pied Piper and parade a jailhouse full of rats in front of you." The second point of contention was Junior's position in the smuggling hierarchy. The government charged that he had been a major kingpin as far back as 1977, and Davis suggested that Junior was "nothing but an errand boy and a flunky" for Mike Knight, Bubba Capo, and others who were "the real kingpins."

The trial had elements of the absurd about it. Eight different prosecution witnesses, including his own father-in-law, could not identify Junior when asked to point him out. Granted he had lost 45 pounds, shaved his beard and frizzed his hair, but anyone who ever watched Perry Mason knows that the defendant always sits at the front table. Eight different witnesses couldn't remember that. Several pointed to a man sitting in the audience who looked like Junior had before his dramatic change in appearance. In another bizarre twist, the motor home of one government witness exploded into flames in the parking lot of a grocery store the day before he was scheduled to testify. No evidence of arson was ever found.

When the government completed its case, the defense rested without calling a single witness. In his closing argument, Davis urged jurors to reject the testimony of the prosecution's "rats." "The government bought and paid for this testimony . . . with immunity, money, and threats," Davis said. "I hope you will weigh the testimony of these rats, see the kind of people they are, and ask: Would I cash them a check?"

David McGee, the prosecuting attorney, rebutted Davis's charges: "The defense has said our witnesses are bad people. Of course they are. They are drug smugglers. Who else is going to do that kind of work. If Junior Guthrie hired the choir from the First Baptist Church, we'd have called them. If he had unloaded his boats at St. Peter's Cathedral, we'd have called the pope to testify against him."[13]

Evidently, the jury decided that it would cash a check from the government's "rats," but only a small one. Junior was found guilty on two charges—conspiracy to import and conspiracy to possess marijuana—but was acquitted on five more serious charges, for which he could have received a life sentence without parole. He was sentenced to five years and $15,000 on each count. He won't be eligible for parole until he's served 40 months. Wally Lewis was convicted on the same charges.

In addition to his criminal conviction, local banks and businesses have lined up to get a piece of Junior. A string of civil suits has been filed against him since his March 1983 indictment. While Junior was hiding in Sebring, the bank foreclosed on his fish house, Gulf to Bay Fisheries (known in Cortez as "Gulf to Colombia Fisheries"), and his Cortez home. His wife was forced to sell some of their household belongings at a highly publicized garage sale.

Prior to his capture, the IRS had filed another suit against him, claiming he owed an additional $3,000 in back taxes. The IRS may yet prove to be his worst nemesis, as it has filed two additional claims since his conviction. In April 1984, it put two liens on his estate, one for $10,082 in back taxes for 1982, and a second for a whopping $484,485 in back taxes for 1977 and 1978.[14]

The final chapters for Junior Guthrie and Sue Maddox have yet to be written. Junior is in federal prison in Kentucky and may still have to face smuggling charges in Louisiana. His financial problems appear staggering,

---

[13]"Prosecutor: Find Guthrie guilty of criminal enterprise," Bradenton *Herald*, 2 September 1983, B:1.

[14]"The IRS joins the list of creditors seeking money from Guthrie," Bradenton *Herald*, 24 March 1984, B:1.

at least on the surface, since no one knows how much money he has buried underground.

And what about my initial question: How could this have happened to Junior Guthrie? I never found the answer. When I started the book in 1981, I thought many times about walking over to his house, knocking on the door, telling him I was writing a book about Cortez, and asking him to give me the inside story. I figured I had a better shot at that story than anybody in the state—after all, we're still cousins. When I asked other people in Cortez about the idea, they all said the same thing: "You will die." It was enough to change my mind.

My guess is that it all happened in small doses, one at a time, until Junior was so far into it he couldn't pull back. I haven't seen any indications that he deliberately planned this course or understood the pitfalls ahead of him. He seemed to charge pell-mell into smuggling with the same blind ferocity that he jumped off those docks at low tide. Other people were able to make one or two runs and then return to a normal life, but Junior always went whole-hog—whatever he did.

Could the family have prevented it? I'm not sure of that either. I've fantasized that if Tink Fulford had still been alive he might have squashed the smuggling by the sheer force of his own will. He was a strong enough personality to have gone to Junior and Bubba, before they'd reached the point of no return, and possibly convinced them to get out of it. But that's only speculation.

Cortez is severely hurting for leadership, to stop both the smugglers and the condos from overrunning it. The community has never really needed that kind of political leadership before. Cortez has only faced one other threat from outside—and the smuggling was certainly started by outside financiers—and that was the anti-netting legislation in the 1960s. At that time, when their backs were against the wall, Blue Fulford and the Organized Fishermen of Florida provided the leadership that was needed. Only time will tell if similar leadership will emerge in the 1980s.

Sue Maddox came closest to providing it against the smugglers, although she had two disadvantages to overcome, both of which are very real in Cortez: being a woman and being an outsider. "I've been living here for almost 20 years and I still feel like an outsider," she said.

Today, she continues to work as a bookkeeper at the Bell Fish Company. It's been almost three years since she last carried her picket sign. But she is different from what she was before, in a way that anyone who has ever crossed a threshold is different. She'll never be the same person she was before, in her own mind or in the minds of Cortez residents. "I feel that most people supported what I was doing, but I know there are some people who still think I am absolutely bonkers because of what I did," she said. Since the smuggling tapered off, she has stayed active in other battles. In August 1984, she testified at county commission meetings about preserving the four public accesses to Sarasota Bay in Cortez, one of which was eventually given to the Bell Fish Company.

Overall, the smuggling has left some wounds that may never heal. "There's some damage that will never be repaired," said Sue. "There are members of the family that I'll never feel the same about. If you don't have a good name, it doesn't matter what else you have. But there are still a lot of honorable people here, and I feel close to them."

The wound that may take longest to heal is the damage done to Cortez's reputation. With condominiums and housing projects pushing ever closer, the smugglers' village stereotype has made it easier to excuse destroying the village. "It's just a bunch of smugglers anyway" is the attitude of some people.

Others aren't even aware it exists. "When you mention Cortez, a lot of people in Bradenton think you're talking about the Cortez Plaza Shopping Center," said Sue. "They don't even realize there is a fishing village here. I think it's just a matter of time before Cortez is gone. With all the people moving here and the trucks rolling in to pick up fish, it's not a quaint, picturesque fishing village anymore—it's a factory! I grieve a little bit about it each day, because one day Cortez will just be a memory to those of us who care about it."

Because of everything that's happened to Sue Maddox during the past decade, Cortez is no longer the utopian paradise that it was when she first arrived. She has witnessed bloody events that she never thought possible and, in the face of them, surprised herself with her own courage. But because she stood up when she did, perhaps some of that utopia still remains.

Chapter 17

Waiting on a Southwester

THE CORTEZ ROAD SIGN WAS GONE. That was the first thing I noticed when I arrived in April 1981, and it confirmed my worst fears in an instant. "Oh my God," I thought, "Cortez is already lost."

It was a small, unpretentious county road sign with only one word: "Cortez." There was no "Entering Cortez" at one end of the village or "Leaving Cortez" at the other—just "Cortez." For many years that sign was the only clue to thousands of tourists on their way to the beaches of Anna Maria that they were passing through a community of sorts.

Now even that was gone, and I was afraid that it meant much more than anyone else imagined. Had the Manatee County Commission, in some late-night meeting, already pulled the charter on this tiny community? And with the sign gone, how would the multitude of tourists know that this cluster of white frame houses and old fish houses was different from the other developments that now litter Cortez Road from Bradenton to the Gulf? How would they know that this community had a history, had bloodlines stretching back to the 1700s, and hadn't just been created by a fleet of dredge boats and draglines?

The new housing developments along the seven miles of Cortez Road have road signs. You better believe it! They have big concrete monuments bordering the entranceways, 5 feet high and 15 feet wide, with designer logos saying "Coral Shores," "San Remo Shores," or "Sunny Shores," with seagulls and palm trees in the background.

All Cortez ever had that declared its existence to the world was that thin metal sign, and now even it was gone. I asked my grandma and several cousins about its disappearance, but no one seemed to know how long the sign had been missing. Deciding I was getting alarmed over nothing, I dropped it. But two months later, when the sign was still gone, I called the Manatee County Road Department to find out why.

"Don't worry about it," said the man who answered, laughing, "one of them Cortez boys probably yanked that sign up and stuck it in his fishing boat. He's probably got it with him on his smuggling runs! Ha! Ha! Ha! You know what I mean?"

"Yeah, right," I said.

"Yes sir, them boys making some kind of money fishing, ain't they? Whooee! 'Bout that sign, though, we've already ordered another one and we'll have it up in a couple of weeks."

Four months later when I went down for Thanksgiving, the sign was still missing. It was still gone at Christmas and again at Easter. Finally, in September 1982, it was back in place.

With or without a sign, Cortez is in deep trouble—and so is the rest of the state. Florida is growing faster than any other state in the country, except for Arizona, and the phenomenal growth has created problems that have never been faced before. Trying to understand them on a statewide level, one is forced to deal in statistics, demographic trends, and political rhetoric. But here in Cortez, all of Florida's problems—except for the influx of Haitian and Cuban refugees—are being played out, not on charts and graphs, but in flesh and blood. In Cortez, the statistics are reduced to names and faces, to people who, through no fault or choice of their own, find themselves on the cutting edge of change in Florida. This tiny village is a microcosm of Florida's future, and by listening to its voices—rough, unsophisticated voices seldom heard in the halls of the capitol or on the nightly news—a true picture of where this state has come from and where it is going may emerge.

The loudest voice in Cortez belongs to Wyman Coarsey. He has been more vocal and visible in the battle to save the village than any other person. He has been called a rabble-rouser and a troublemaker, but he doesn't look like either one. He looks like a small-town postmaster with a big smile and a booming laugh—and that's exactly what he is.

He greets the residents every day as they drift in to pick up their mail. Home delivery has not yet come to Cortez, and Wyman likes it that way: "I do a good job because I know the local people. If you get a greenhorn in here from out of town, that person will not care personally about Edith Fulford or Doris Green. He'll just care about getting his salary and trying for a bigger job somewheres else. Being postmaster in my own hometown gives me a lot of pride because the locals had to vouch for me before I got this job. I try to do right by my own people."

A combination of civic concern and old-fashioned stubbornness has prompted Wyman Coarsey to become involved in the fight. He has seen Cortez go full-circle in his lifetime, in more dramatic fashion, perhaps, than anyone else in the village:

"My family didn't have nothing, and if it weren't for the people in Cortez, we never would have survived, and that's the truth. I was born out on the Mixon Fruit Farm, and in 1931 my family lost our home, so we moved right out on top of the old shell mound off Cortez Road. It was right in the middle of the swamp. The last people to live there were the Timucan Indians, and I've got the relics to prove it. We lived just like the Indians. We lived and slept in an old boat on top of the shell mound. It was surrounded by water every day at high tide and we had to wade in and wade out. We'd park our old '27 Dodge truck at the end of the road and my dad would roll up his pants, wade ashore, put his shoes back on and go to work.

"We did all our cooking and eating ashore. All our pots and pans was hung in the trees, and at night the coons would smell the fried fish and track all through the pots and get sand all in them. That's the way we lived for many years.

"Eventually we tore down a couple of old houses in Bradenton and got the lumber out of them to build a house. I lived in that house till I was 16 years old and it was just as primitive as it could be. People in Cortez all had electricity and I thought they were rich, because I never used an electric light until I went into the Navy. We didn't have a well for years—we hauled water in wash tubs and carried them home in the truck. And all we ever had for a bathroom was a little john down in the swamp. There was no pollution 'cause every day at high tide the chubs would come up there and eat everything up. Now this wasn't back in prehistoric times! This was in 1945 and 1946!"

Wyman was one of 48 Cortez boys who enlisted when World War II broke out. After the war, he worked at the Fulford Fish Company and fished with Tink Fulford, but when stopnetting was outlawed in 1950, he went to town and got a job driving a fuel-oil truck. He did that for 18 years, until 1967 when the Cortez postmaster position opened up. Wyman got the job and has been there ever since.

Being the postmaster is his vocation, but his passion for the past seven years has been the battle to save Cortez. His battleground has been the chambers of the Manatee County Commission. His weapons have been the county's zoning ordinances. And his enemies are the high-rise condominiums that he fears will blot out his view of Sarasota Bay and his way of life.

It has not been an easy battle, or a hopeful one. "I have fought like hell at those county commission meetings for the last seven years trying to prevent this high-rise mess from coming in here," he said. "And I've tried my best to fire up the people here and get them to raise enough hell to get that county commission to pass some laws to protect us from this crap. To put a stop to it! Hold Cortez the way it is, and say 'Hey, zone out any further buildings except residential homes.' Now I'll admit that having a few people moving into a community is bound to help. It's like a dry stream that's laid dormant for years—you need some fresh water, but you don't want the flood! And that is what's gonna happen to Cortez, I'm afraid. The flood's coming!"

That flood has already arrived for much of Florida. *The Florida Experience*, as Luther J. Carter dubbed the state's explosive growth in his 1974 book by the same name, has given rise to a litany of problems. These include:

• Population Explosion. In 1950, Florida had 2.7 million residents and ranked twentieth among the 48 states. By 1970, the population had grown to 6.7 million, making Florida the ninth largest state. By 1980, it had ballooned to 9.7 million and Florida had moved up to number seven. The population is expected to reach 14.6 million by the year 2000, as newcomers are moving to Florida at the rate of almost 1,000 per day! The state's warm climate and white sand beaches also attract 25 million tourists a year, who spend $22 billion annually, making tourism the state's biggest industry.

• Drinking Water. Environmentalists fear there could be critical shortages of drinking water in the next decade. Freshwater supplies are already being stretched, and an additional 1.5 trillion gallons of water will be required each year to meet the needs of new residents. Increased demands on freshwater aquifers have resulted in saltwater intrusion into coastal well fields and the Biscayne Aquifer, the major water supply for south Florida.

• Coastal Zone Development. Florida's 1,300 miles of coastline comprise only 28 percent of the state's land area, yet by 1978, it contained over 78 percent of the population. Fourteen percent of all barrier islands are classified as urban. Each year the state and federal government spend $10 million on beach renourishment projects, and still fall far short of what is needed to solve the state's erosion problems.

On 7 June 1981, the Associated Press reported that "construction has been so complete in some areas that rain rushes to the sea, denying a refill to the underground supply. . . . Wetlands have been drained, streams have been re-routed and lakes have become sewage disposals in the rush to cash in on the mass migration to the Sun Belt. Many environmentalists blame Florida's government for smiling down upon a growth-at-any-cost attitude that is mortgaging the state's future."

Florida continues to lose 215,000 acres of wetlands and 241,000 acres of productive farmland each year to development.

• Water Pollution. Years of dumping raw sewage into Florida's bays and estuaries and massive dredge-and-fill operations have created pollution problems in many areas. Shellfish have been declared off-limits in some bays because of high coliform counts. Run-off from phosphate mining and pesticides have polluted numerous rivers and lakes.

• Pesticide Contamination. Florida citizens were shocked in 1983 when the pesticide Temik was discovered in shallow drinking wells and groundwater. This highly toxic chemical has been used for years to control nematodes in citrus and potato crops. In January 1983, state Agriculture Commissioner Doyle Conner banned the use of Temik during the remainder of 1983. That ban was lifted in 1984. In February 1984, Temik was discovered for the first time in a deep well fed by the Floridan Aquifer, which stretches from the panhandle to Lake Okeechobee.

In late 1983, the discovery of high levels of ethylene-dibromide (EDB) in flour, grits, and dozens of other products on Florida grocery shelves set off a nationwide panic to remove contaminated products from the marketplace. EDB was also discovered in Florida groundwater. The state Department of Agriculture, citrus farmers, and golf courses had been injecting this toxic pesticide into the soil for 20 years to control nematodes. EDB gas had also been routinely sprayed in grain and corn silos, and on citrus.

In early 1984, Commissioner Conner ordered EDB-contaminated products removed from the shelves, and Florida's action prompted the federal Environmental Protection Agency to issue standards on safe levels of EDB in foods. The state Department of Environmental Regulation has begun statewide testing for EDB contamination of drinking wells, and the 1984 Florida legislature passed a $3 million EDB clean-up bill to buy carbon filtering systems for private citizens whose wells have been affected.

• Housing and Energy. New residents will require two million new homes and an additional 600 million BTUs of energy each year. Property values are increasing statewide at an annual rate of 18 percent, and beachfront property is increasing by as much as 100 percent annually.

• Toxic Dumps. Florida has more toxic-dump sites than any state in the nation. In response to this problem, the Florida Consumers Federation and the League of Conservation Voters initiated a petition drive, "Clean Up '84," to put a constitutional referendum on toxic substances on the November 1984 ballot. If passed, "Clean Up '84" would give citizens a constitutional "right to know" about toxic substances used or dumped in their communities.

In the late 1960s and early 1970s, public alarm over the destruction of the state's environment led to the passage of several landmark bills, including: the Air and Water Pollution Control Act, which regulated sewage treatment and industrial waste disposal; the Beach and Shore Preservation Act, designed to protect dunes and beaches by establishing coastal-construction setback lines; the Water Resources Act, which established five regional water boards to set and enforce policies on water use; the Environmental Land and Water Management Act, which required large-scale development projects to be reviewed by the state and established "areas of critical state concern"; and the Local Government Comprehensive Planning Act, which required local governments to develop comprehensive plans for land-use, transportation, and coastal preservation.

But by 1980, successful lobbying by developers to water down the new laws, the failure of local officials to vigorously enforce them, and increasing pressures from the hordes of new residents had combined to put Florida's fragile ecosystem in more danger than it had been in 1972, Florida's "crisis year." As a result, there has been a revival of environmental concern statewide, which has led to the passage of new protective legislation. Governor Bob Graham, who had drawn criticism in his first term for waffling on environmental issues, has spearheaded three special state-acquisition projects: Save Our Coasts, Save Our Rivers, and Save Our Everglades.

The Save Our Coasts project, approved in 1982, established a $200 million bond program to purchase sensitive or endangered coastal lands. The project has been embroiled in controversies over the administration of the funds, charges of political influence-peddling in the selection of which beaches to purchase and the prices paid for them. But despite the problems, by the summer of 1984 the cabinet had approved $50 million for the purchase of beach property throughout the state. The Save Our Rivers project will be used to purchase environmentally sensitive river frontage. The Save Our Everglades project will fund purchases of wildlife habitats and major portions of Florida's "river of grass."

On other fronts, the 1984 legislature passed the state's first major wet-lands protection bill, although it drew heavy criticism from some environmental groups because enforcement powers were given to the state's water management districts, and compromises were made to agricultural and mining interests.

The legislature also grappled with, and ultimately failed to pass, the Growth Management Act of 1984, a package of bills recommended by a 21-member Environmental Land Management Study Committee formed by Governor Graham in 1982.

Public opinion polls have shown that growth management is the number one concern of state residents. Governor Graham called it "our greatest challenge." State newspapers have urged legislators to adopt a comprehensive plan. In a 1 May 1983 editorial, the *Tallahassee Democrat* wrote: "Although Florida's leaders keep recommending their sunny paradise to northern neighbors, they now also issue dire warnings to the home folks about the consequences of being unprepared for massive population growth. During the past decade, the state's lawmakers have met those warnings with little more than empty promises."

The growth management bills proposed in 1984 would have required stricter local land-use plans and special building requirements for coastal areas, provided a streamlined review process for large developments, and expanded the right to sue over land-use decisions. Despite the support of Graham and House Speaker Lee Moffitt, only one bill survived. Intense lobbying by developers and real estate interests and the preoccupation with the wetlands bill doomed the rest. As Moffitt said at the end of the session, "We're going to wake up some day and regret tremendously that we let the special interests defeat a strong growth-management package."

Cortez sits in the middle of all this. Its own backyard, Manatee County, has grown from a population of 34,704 in 1950 to 145,984 in 1980, with estimates that it will climb to 242,300 by the year 2000. In 1980, Bradenton was listed as one of the 25 fastest growing cities in the country. Sarasota to the south and the Tampa-St. Petersburg area to the north were also on that list, making the four-county Suncoast region surrounding Cortez one of the greatest growth areas in the country.

There are other factors. The vast majority of the county's new residents are white retirees; in 1980, 40 percent of the population was 65 or over, and 60 percent was over 45. In the 1960s, many of those newcomers settled in mobile home parks, and Bradenton boasted of having "the world's largest trailer park." But when land prices skyrocketed in the 1970s, developers converted to multi-family units—read that as condos—which jumped from 9 percent of the county's total housing units in 1970, to 19 percent in 1977. Thirty-eight percent of all housing units built during that time were multi-family.

As the developers' noose slowly tightens around Cortez, some local residents have given up—feeling that it's hopeless to "fight city hall." Wyman Coarsey isn't one of them. "I don't think enough people here really see what's coming, or, if they see it, they feel like they can't do anything to fight them people up there on the county commission and the zoning board. But I don't feel that way. What we have to do is go up there and make those people do their job—and they are not doing it now—which is to protect this area."

The hopelessness that Cortez residents feel is understandable—they've watched the steamrollers and tractors ram ever closer to the outskirts of the village. But those attitudes are still hard for Wyman to accept. "I was up there at the zoning hearings one time, talking about how the people of Cortez didn't want these high-rises in here, and one of the commissioners asked me bold-faced-out: 'Well then where are they? Where are all these people you're talking about?' What could I say to that?"

Unfortunately, the local residents who are willing to fight have little experience at fighting political battles. But there are groups of people who know how to fight politically, already have effective political organizations, and are willing to fight to preserve Cortez. Neighborhood associations in Sunny Shores, San Remo Shores, and Paradise Bay Trailer Park, the oldest developments on Cortez Road, are now the most outspoken critics of further developments near Cortez. Ironically, only a few years ago these same groups were Cortez's most feared enemies, as they were leading the fight to ban commercial fishing in all Manatee County waters. A Cortez fisherman whose livelihood was threatened has a long memory, and some of the old wounds still haven't healed.

When I was growing up, there was no question that the residents of San Remo and Coral Shores were the enemy. It was open class warfare. In 1967, they got a law passed that banned net fishing in the bayous and finger canals bordering their neighborhoods. Their reasoning was that when a fisherman struck a school of fish in one of these narrow cuts his nets blocked the passage of other boats—namely, their yachts and pleasure boats.

Cortez fishermen had a different perspective. They had been fishing in those bayous for nearly 100 years, while the finger canals were recent creations of draglines and dredge boats. So who had the rightful claim? Besides, they were usually fishing at night, when the party boats were tethered snugly to their docks, and they were gillnetting mullet, which aren't a game fish and generally won't bite a hook. The closest those San Remo residents came to catching a mullet was when they drove down to the Cortez fish houses and bought some for dinner—and where did they think those were caught?

It seemed clear that the real issue wasn't the mullet or the blocked canals, but the resentment and arrogance of Northern retirees towards Cortez fishermen with patched khaki workpants and two days' stubble on their chins. What really galled the emigrants was the idea of Cortez fishermen invading their placid retirement paradise.

When the new anti-netting law was passed, both sides adapted. Cortez fishermen nailed pieces of carpet to the stern of their boats so the lead line wouldn't make noise when the nets were run overboard. They covered their exhaust pipes with nylon stockings to muffle the engine noise. They slipped into the canals at low throttle late at night, made their strike, and hurriedly roped the net back in the boat. The law stated that a fisherman had to be caught with his nets in the water, so instead of clearing the fish as the net was pulled back in, the fishermen roped it into the boat and cleared it later.

San Remo residents had their strategies, too. When a fishing boat puttered into the canal, porch lights started blinking all around the basin, signaling to the other houses to begin the watch. As soon as a net was spotted in the water, a call was made to the Game and Fish Commissioner, who was in charge of enforcing the law. However, what the residents didn't know was that the game commissioners were local boys, and they had an informal agreement with the fishermen that they'd wait 30 minutes after receiving a complaint before leaving their office. That was usually enough time for the fishermen to rope their nets back in the boat.

Between their own slyness and the stalling of the game commissioners, Cortez fishermen won far more of those battles than they lost, and the anti-netting regulation never stopped commercial fishing in Manatee County. On many occasions I have helped rope a net full of mullet into a skiff, crouched low in the boat so the seawall would shroud us, while a card party was taking place on a well-lit patio 25 feet away. We were close enough to hear every word that was spoken and see the winning hands of the players, yet they never knew we were there.

The fishermen didn't win all the battles, though, and the ones they lost had steep prices. A fisherman caught in an off-limits area could lose his boat, his net, and hundreds of dollars in fines.

Outside the constraints of the law, each side also had "extra-legal" enforcement methods. I've had a gun pulled on me only twice in my life, both times by elderly gentlemen in banlon shirts and bermuda shorts. The sight of a fishing boat in their backyard canal sometimes triggered a weird Matt Dillion fantasy in otherwise gentle grandfathers. They would suddenly pull .38 caliber revolvers out of the back pocket of their shorts, wave them in the air, and shout wild threats about what they were going to do if we didn't "leave and never come back." It never worked. One time, two old men pulled guns on me and Uncle Gary, who jumped out of the boat and, in one of the most powerful displays I've ever seen, chased them all the way down the street to their houses.

When a fisherman did get caught by the law, Cortez teenagers took their revenge in the only way they knew how. We'd find out who made the call to the game commissioner, drive to their house in a fleet of souped-up Chevys, and peel wheels and spin donuts all over the poor guy's freshly mown lawn, leaving nothing but mud and tire tracks in our wake. If we still weren't satisfied, we'd go home and call every pizza place in town and have pizzas delivered to his front door, then stay up late that night making long-distance phone calls and charge them to his number.

One man stayed on our list for six months after pulling a gun on Gary—this time I wasn't with him. He had his windows rattled on numerous occasions by exploding cherry bombs, watched a steady stream of unordered taxis pull up to his front door, turned away dozens of pepperoni pizzas, had rotten fish thrown in his front yard, and in the final coup de grace of juvenile vengeance, walked out to answer his doorbell one hot summer evening only to discover a burning bag of cow manure on his front stoop. He screamed, slammed the door, came running back a few seconds later with the kitchen broom, and swatted helplessly at the burning bag in a futile attempt to extinguish the flames. The smell must have lingered for weeks.

Given that history, I was stunned when I first heard that those same people are now fighting to preserve Cortez. Self-interest certainly makes strange bedfellows. Their anti-netting legislation would have destroyed Cortez, but now that new development projects are threatening their water supplies, overloading their sewage treatment plants, and backing up traffic on Cortez Road for miles, they have come to the realization that the preservation of Cortez will protect their own way of life.

Well, in a war you take your allies wherever you can find them, and converts are better than nothing. Unfortunately, that lesson has yet to sink in for many Cortez residents. To them, a "damn Yankee" is a "damn Yankee," and they make no distinctions between veterans and rookies. They're all Yankees, and they're all damned.

But Wyman Coarsey doesn't see it that way: "These people are not the enemy! These people from Coral Shores and San Remo and Sunny Shores have fought their hearts out against the high-rises. I don't mean to down anybody here, but I got more help from those people than I did from the people in Cortez. They filled the county courthouse so full that there weren't seats for all of them. I've seen those people sit up late and plan and work and plan and work, preparing to go up to the county commission and really unload on them. These people in San Remo and Paradise Bay don't feel helpless; they realize that you've got to fight to win. I just can't understand why the people in Cortez won't fight."

The focal point of the high-rise battle so far has been the Marker 50 Yacht and Racquet Club, a 126-unit project with two 11-story towers, which was slated for construction right down the road from Wyman Coarsey's house.

The Marker 50 story is a good illustration of how big developers circumvent the law and manipulate local politicians to get their way. In 1978, Bruce McCabe, the owner of an existing marina, went to the Manatee County Commission asking for commercial zoning on a small piece of property adjacent to the marina so he could expand his business. After the zoning change was approved, McCabe turned around and sold the property to Playa Investments, Inc., of Holmes Beach, which immediately announced plans for Marker 50. At that time, county ordinances allowed multi-family units on commercially zoned property.

Public meetings were held in which Wyman and others argued that Marker 50 would aggravate an already hazardous traffic problem on Cortez Road, that the Cortez Volunteer Fire Department could not provide adequate fire protection, and that residents could not be safely evacuated in the event of a hurricane.

Despite the protests, Marker 50 was approved. Pat Glass, chairwoman of the Manatee County Commission, told the *Bradenton Herald* that commissioners were never told the truth about Marker 50 until "it was too late," and their hands were tied by the zoning ordinances. This controversy did prompt the Manatee County Planning Division to revise county zoning ordinances in 1980, making it illegal to build multi-family units on commercially zoned property without special permits. "If Marker 50 were proposed today it would never be approved," said Bruce Hosfield of the planning division.

Cortez lost the Marker 50 battle in the political arena, but ultimately won it at the bank. The project never got off the ground because of financial problems, and in 1982 the bank foreclosed on the developer.[1]

Cortez also got lucky on the next proposed project: Colony Cove Condominiums, which was going to be built in 1982 behind the Cortez school. It was supposed to include 412 units in two- and four-story high-rises. "We fought that one for almost two years and we got the high-rises stopped," said Wyman. The developers backed down from the concept and announced their intent to build duplexes, but due to financial problems, nothing has happened so far.

The only condominium project to have actually been built in Cortez is Mariner's Cove, which was built on Wyman Coarsey's old family homestead in 1983. The new zoning ordinances restricted it to two stories, with parking underneath.

As far back as 1978, the County Planning Division recognized that zoning loopholes would endanger Cortez and other small communities in

[1]"Marker 50 high-rise condominium plan leveled," Bradenton *Herald*, 3 June 1982, B:1.

the county. It proposed that four traditional communities—Cortez, Parrish, Myakka City, and Rubonia—be granted village zoning, which was intended to "preserve the existing character of established neighborhoods." "The village zoning concept would allow residents to determine what kind of structures they wanted in the community, what kind they wanted outlawed, and what kind could only be built with a special permit," said Hosfield.

After public meetings in all four communities, three agreed to the village-zoning concept, but Cortez refused to go along. "The people in Cortez just wouldn't believe us," said Hosfield. "They thought we were trying to screw them, and that any kind of zoning change would open the doors to let the high-rises in. So we had to do away with the village concept for Cortez. But I can't really blame the people for not trusting the planning division."

On that last point, Wyman Coarsey agrees. "He's right! That's a hundred percent right! There ain't but one thing he said that I can agree with, and that is that we don't trust them! They held a couple of meetings down here and they were trying to convince the folks here that village zoning was going to be perfect—that it would protect us because the local people themselves would help draw up the zoning ordinances. So I held my hand up and asked: 'Now under this new village zoning, when a question arises about whether to have a special exception to build a high-rise project, who is going to have the final authority to say yes or no?' They said, 'Well, we'd have a public hearing about it.' I said, 'I'm gonna repeat my question, but first I'm gonna tell you that we have that now—we have public hearings and the people tell you what they want and don't want and then you go the opposite way and do regardless of the people. Now is this still gonna be in effect under village zoning?' He said, 'Well, now you're going too far out,' and he started talking it off. I let him go awhile and then I held up my hand and said, 'I want to ask the same question again. If the people here vote 51 percent against an exception, is that going to hold or is the county commission and the planning board still going to have the power to overrule it?' And he said, 'Well, when you get down to it, the county commission will still have the power to overrule.' I said, 'Then what are we going to have that we don't already have? You people are in charge of it and you take the money under the table and then the county commission votes to let those projects through.' And that's when we said to hell with village zoning. We weren't getting a damn thing with village zoning. They've already proven we can't trust them."

Wyman Coarsey still doesn't trust the county commission, even after it approved a new Cortez Area Plan in August 1983, which set zoning standards for the entire Cortez peninsula. The plan limits construction in the village to ten units per acre, with a height limitation of three stories over parking.

"It's difficult to apply standard land-use principles in Cortez because there's such a mixed use of land there," said Carol Clarke, chief of Comprehensive Planning for Manatee County. "It's unlike any other place in the county because there is industrial and residential zoning—fish houses and family homes—right next to each other. But it works in Cortez because those uses evolved naturally."

Because of that mixture, the county commission put almost no restrictions on the types of structures allowed in the village. "Virtually any kind of residential, commercial, or marine industrial development is allowed," said Clarke. In exchange for such unrestricted zoning, a Cortez Use Permit is required for all proposed commercial, industrial, or multi-family developments, and such permits can only be granted after a public hearing and the approval of the county commission.

"The main criteria for granting a use permit will be whether the proposed construction preserves and enhances the vitality of Cortez," said Clarke, "although other factors will be considered, such as: noise, potential traffic problems, compatibility with existing structures, and visual impact. For instance, an arts and crafts shop is a commercial development that might work fine in Cortez, whereas a Shop and Go market probably wouldn't. It's going to come down to a judgment on a case-by-case basis."

That's what scares Wyman Coarsey. Rather than establishing more restrictive zoning, the new plan gives the county commission greater authority to determine what is and is not allowed. He is afraid that politics, not the preservation of the village, will be the deciding factor. "The county commission is an instrument of the rich people and the developers," he said. "Those people haven't done a thing to protect us in the past, and I don't think it's any better now."

It's a sad fact that the best hope for the survival of Cortez may be a hurricane. To say that a village may have to be saved by the whims of Mother Nature is evidence of how weak and politically unorganized the people are. There is still time for them to get mobilized to protect their homes, but the fact remains that at this point their best bet is a monster hurricane.

Cortez was destroyed by the 1921 hurricane, when 10-foot seas and 85-mile-an-hour winds roared out of the southwest and obliterated the shoreline. There have been other storms since then, but none have made a direct hit, and none brought the high winds and tides of the '21 storm.

When such a storm returns, Cortez will once again be destroyed. After the winds and waves die down, the locals will return to the village, unravel the debris from the waterfront, rebuild the docks and the houses again, and continue their lives as before. They have too many roots and ties to do otherwise.

But what about the barrier islands of Anna Maria and Longboat Key? What would a major hurricane do to the towering condos and sprawling developments that now dot their shorelines? Twenty-five years ago we would cruise all day along the beaches of Anna Maria and Longboat Key in my grandpa's launch looking for mullet. The only things on the islands then were scrub pines and mangroves and a few small beach cottages that Yankees rented in the winter. But during the 1960s and 1970s, the Arvida Corporation and other development giants covered the islands from one end to the other with hotels, condos, tennis courts, and golf courses.

In 1979, I was driving down Longboat Key at four in the morning with Wayne and Gary, delivering their nightly catch of shrimp to bait stands on the island and in Sarasota. As we passed a huge condo, sitting dark and tomb-like against the night sky, Wayne pointed at it and said, "I bet Daddy is turning over in his grave about what they've done to this island."

As the condos rolled by, one after the other, I felt a knot of hatred and disgust winding itself ever tighter in my stomach. The spirits of men like my grandfather, who have roamed these shores for a hundred years, were alive in the air that night. I felt the truth and anguish of Wayne's words in my gut.

Money, power, and prestige have conquered the dunes of Anna Maria and Longboat Key, and carved their triumph in concrete and asphalt across the face of the islands. But all of that glittering display will come tumbling down in one night from a good-sized hurricane.

"The Gulf Coast and southeast Florida are the most vulnerable areas in the United States," says Dr. Neil Frank, director of the National Hurricane Center in Coral Gables. "Yet we have hundreds of thousands of people living on islands and on coastal tidal lands who don't know that their homes will literally go underwater someday. Part of the problem is that there has been no big bad hurricane in Florida since the enormous population increase on the coast."

Fears of hurricane damage were heightened in 1980 when the federal government announced that it will cease to underwrite flood insurance, as it has done since 1968. That decision will force homeowners to buy flood insurance from private companies at much higher rates.

There are people in Florida who await the coming of hurricane season with great anticipation. They watch the weather reports on TV each night, waiting anxiously for each new tropical depression to reach hurricane strength in the Caribbean, make its slow trek across the latitude lines of the tracking charts, and bear down on the Florida peninsula.

With tight-lipped grins, they follow the storm as it veers towards the warm waters of the Gulf or the Atlantic's Gold Coast and slowly approaches. As the hourly reports come in from the national tracking service, their hopes grow stronger that the storm surge will thunder ashore with full fury and cleave away the foundations of the condo towers, washing away all traces in the outgoing tide.

I don't know how many people think like that. I only know that I am one of them and, though I hope for no loss of human life, I would glory in the wholesale destruction of Florida's coastline. I suspect that Cortez residents, Wyman Coarsey among them, and many native Floridians would join me in that celebration.

I wish that there was another way to save Cortez. I wish that the Manatee County commissioners would heed the efforts of their counterparts in Sarasota, who are trying to limit growth by restricting the number of building permits and establishing tougher coastal construction setback lines. I wish that the members of the Florida legislature were as enthusiastic and committed to passing a growth management law as they are about making Florida a haven for high-tech industries and international banking.

I wish, most of all, that the residents of Cortez would develop a plan for saving their village and then go out and build alliances with their old adversaries in Sunny Shores and San Remo to make it work.

I wish all of that would come true. But if it doesn't, then I hope that one day soon a storm will roll in from the southwest, once again bringing those 10-foot waves and 85-mile-an-hour winds, and that it will roar ashore on Longboat Key at midnight and sweep the island clean by morning. I know, of course, that such thoughts are naive, simplistic, and possibly insane, but even now I thrill to hear the news of an approaching gale, and I spend my days pleading and praying for the coming of a mighty, cleansing storm.

"Just Say
You Read the Book"

WHOOEE! I TELL YOU WHAT'S SO," said Charlie Guthrie, as his high, whining voice went up half an octave to make the point, "the Lord give us the warm climate—and then the Yankees come!" Amen, brother. Charlie Guthrie was making the closing arguments of a rambling, hour-long monologue on life, death, and the future of Cortez. His bushy eyebrows were twitching furiously, reminding me of former Senator Sam Ervin, whose eyebrows put the finishing touches on Richard Nixon during the 1974 Senate Watergate hearings.

At 91, Charlie Guthrie is the oldest fisherman in Cortez and the last of the old captains. He also has a reputation of being an ornery old cuss, which made me steer clear of him until the end of my stay in Cortez. But when I finally walked over to his tiny cabin on the edge of the bay, I found a wiry little man hunched up in a wheelchair, with a thick shock of white hair and wonderfully expressive eyes. The walls of his cabin were covered with beautiful seashell designs—diamonds, stars, geometric patterns—that Charlie had made himself.

When I arrived, he was on the rampage because of a recent stay in the county hospital, where he was confined for three weeks because of a broken hip. He won't be going back anytime soon. "I'd hate to carry a dog up to that hospital—that's the most bloodless place for a human being I've ever seen. They can carry me out to the stockyard in Wauchula or to the cemetery first, but I ain't ever going there again."

Charlie Guthrie is one of the last surviving links between Cortez and its North Carolina ancestry. He came here in 1910, at age 16, because North Carolina was too cold. "I grew up on Bogue Sound, and boy oh boy, it was full of clams and oysters! And flounder! Them creeks up there is the home for flounders. I tell you though, it got cold up there on the Neuse River, and I fished all that winter just to make enough money to buy me a suit of clothes and a train ticket to Florida."

For me, Charlie Guthrie was a symbol of Cortez's heritage, and, after talking to him, I drove to Carteret County with my six-year-old nephew Ryan Green to uncover those early roots. I spent two days poring through the county archives and the public library and discovered the original land grant from the King of England to Joseph Fulford in 1709. I also found the missing link in the Fulford family tree, my great-great-great-grandfather, Thomas Fulford.

The next day, Ryan and I braved the winds and rains of a passing hurricane to roam the back roads between Straits and Gloucester, tiny fishing communities on Bogue Sound, looking for the old Fulford homeplace and the family cemetery. We never found the cemetery, but we did find the old homestead; it was on the edge of a cornfield. I left Ryan sleeping in the van and bulled and burrowed my way through a 20-foot wall of brambles and thorns, finally emerging in a little clearing on the banks of Bogue Sound. There in front of me stood the old house, rotting and decayed.

This was where Capt. Billy Fulford was born, and where he and his brothers began their long journey to Cortez. The historical significance of the moment was rudely interrupted by swarms of mosquitoes that threatened to carry me away, so after a few quick photographs, I left. Alex Haley found fame and fortune tracking down his family roots; all I got were skeeter bites and scratches.

The most striking irony about the trip, more than the genealogical discoveries, was learning that Beaufort and Morehead City, the county's major towns, are tourist attractions—because of their history and traditions. Tourists come to roam the quaint streets of old Beaufort, visit the nautical museum, chuckle over the fishing tales printed on paper place mats, and talk to the old salts who wander along the waterfront on Saturday afternoons.

Just the opposite is true in Cortez. Tourists couldn't care less about its history and traditions, its quaint streets and houses, or the old salts who come out every day to sit on the front of the docks and tell stories. No, tourists come to Florida not to praise the local culture, but to bury it—literally.

I don't really blame the Northern tourists and retirees anymore, although I used to. I have a better understanding of why they're leaving the North. As more and more factory owners close their plants and run away to pay starvation wages in Korea, Taiwan, or South Carolina, Northern neighborhoods and communities are slowly withering and dying. Given a chance to escape the emotional and financial hopelessness—and the miserable weather—their decision to leave is understandable.

Years ago, I heard folksinger Pete Seeger make the statement: "You know, Americans have always had the luxury to pull up stakes and move somewhere else if they didn't like what was happening where they were, but someday I think people are going to have to stay and fight for their homes." I think there's a lesson in that for both Florida and the communities up north. People are going to have to stay and fight—for plant-closing legislation to stop the runaway shops, for control of the $200 billion in worker-pension funds, which is the largest source of investment capital in the country, and is currently financing the flight of American corporations overseas. Let's use those funds to rebuild Northern cities and neighborhoods, to purchase abandoned factories and retool them to produce products this country needs, and, most of all, to fight to maintain the family traditions and ethnic roots that have made those communities home.

If that happens, I think the stampede to Florida will end. Given a choice between living in their own revitalized hometowns with friends and families, or moving to an egg-box apartment on the tenth floor of an ugly condominium, surrounded by 500 lonely strangers, I think people will choose to stay at home.

I simply don't buy the idea that retirees move to Florida because they want to sit in the sun and play shuffleboard. The warm weather is nice, sure, but I think they're really coming here to escape the emptiness of their own communities. If this society didn't throw its senior citizens on the junk heap once they retired, but helped them find new meaning in their lives, I don't think they'd be leaving their homes—no matter how cold it is—just to come down here and push a shuffleboard stick all day.

No, I don't blame the retirees—I've even seen some positive effects of their coming. The influx of wealthy, middle-class suburbanites who moved to Miami and the Gold Coast in the 1960s is pretty much a thing of the past. Many of those arriving today are retired workers—autoworkers, steelworkers, electricians—who can afford to move here because of union-won pension plans. There are an estimated 300,000 retired union members in the state, and I've seen them working tirelessly in organizations like the Florida Consumers Federation and the National Council of Senior Citizens to fight exorbitant utility hikes, skyrocketing medical costs, and the irresponsible dumping of toxic wastes.

But their attitudes about the communities that were here before they arrived still need some adjustments. Until there is respect for native people and their communities, the migration to Florida will continue to resemble the Oklahoma land rush in the 1880s. It is a land grab, pure and simple, and heaven help the native Floridians who stand in the way.

The real responsibility of managing Florida's growth must be placed on the shoulders of the state's politicians, at both the state and county levels. If they don't come to grips quickly with the reality of what is happening to this beautiful land, it will be too late to save it at all.

The central question for Florida's future is whether its inevitable growth will be governed by thoughtful planning and design, or by the greed, profits, and mindless boosterism that has dominated Florida politics for so long. Will state and local politicians—so many of whom are developers and real estate agents—have the integrity to transcend their own profit margins and protect the interests of the people, wildlife, and natural resources of this state? And if they don't have the integrity to do it on their own, will the people force them?

Long-range planning has not been Florida's strong suit. As best-selling novelist John D. MacDonald, a Sarasota resident, has written: "And we are where we are today, because in 1958 our leaders were not looking 25 years down the road, to say nothing of 50. On some days looking 20 minutes ahead seems standard practice. . . . We are leagues ahead of the rest of the nation in the fine art of hiding our heads in our own sand."

In closing, one thought has troubled me throughout the writing of this book: What if the book received enough attention to turn Cortez into a tourist attraction? God, no! The thought of carloads of tourists creeping past the fish houses, gawking and squealing at Charlie Guthrie and the other residents, would be almost as bad as turning Cortez into a parking lot for a condo project.

So, if the book has touched your heart in any way and given you an appreciation for the people of Cortez and the life they want to preserve, then please, don't go sightseeing in Cortez. If you want to stop in and buy some mullet, that's another story. But otherwise, just say you read the book.